BLACK STUDIES IN THE UNIVERSITY

A Symposium

BLACK STUDIES
IN THE UNIVERSITY

A SYMPOSIUM

edited by

ARMSTEAD L. ROBINSON

CRAIG C. FOSTER

DONALD H. OGILVIE

Yale University Press, New Haven and London, 1969

102414

Library of Congress catalog card number: 77-89827

Designed by Karl Rueckert,
set in IBM Press Roman type,
and printed in the United States of America by
The Carl Purington Rollins Printing-Office
of the Yale University Press, New Haven, Connecticut.

Distributed in Great Britain, Europe, Asia, and
Africa by Yale University Press Ltd., London; in
Canada by McGill-Queen's University Press, Montreal;
and in Mexico by Centro Interamericano de Libros
Académicos, Mexico City.

CONTENTS

PREFACE

Armstead L. Robinson

By November 1967, the Black Student Alliance at Yale had formally recognized the urgent necessity for including the study of Afro-American societies and cultures in the curriculum of Yale College. This recognition was based on a growing awareness of the glaring inadequacies which then typified the intellectual treatment of the Afro-American experience. We began working toward correcting those inadequacies, but after several months of determined effort, we discovered that little progress was being made in the struggle to convince the faculty at large of the validity and importance of our concerns. Early in the spring of 1968, therefore, we decided to sponsor what we called "an educational experience for professional educators." Realizing that the problems we had encountered were not confined to Yale, we sought to bring together key faculty and administrative personnel from a number of schools with a group of respected and recognized black and white intellectuals who were vitally concerned with various aspects of the Afro-American experience. We viewed this symposium as an opportunity to create an atmosphere in which those persons who were in pivotal positions in a number of educational institutions could engage in active and open intellectual exchanges on questions related to Afro-American studies.

This volume is the edited record of those proceedings—a living record of one of the first comprehensive attempts to thrash out the intellectual and political issues connected with implementing a program of Afro-American studies. These papers constitute no definitive solution to the vast array of problems pertaining to Afro-American studies, but they stand rather as an indispensable pioneering inquiry into these questions. We hope to capture the flavor of that extraordinary give-and-take conference, whose major purpose was to raise serious issues, though not necessarily to answer them. There are, of course, significant omissions; for instance, little attention is paid to the Caribbean or to Latin America. Yet, these omissions result not from ignorance of the obvious importance of the experiences of Afro-Latins but rather from a decision about what might be dealt with adequately, when limited to a two-day conference.

Our symposium originated as a response to the resistance in educational circles to pressures for Afro-American studies; this resistance, in turn, flows from two major concerns. First, many educators question the moral responsibility involved in complying with public pressures for curriculum reforms; they worry lest they might be deserting their obligation to maintain high standards of excellence in curricular offerings by responding favorably to insistent protest from local groups. Second, many educators seriously question the assertion that the experience of black people in Africa and in the New World is a subject of sufficient amplitude and depth to justify general study and instruction on all education levels. Undoubtedly, much of the hesitancy with which educators have met demands for inclusion of such materials in their curricular offerings arises from a perfectly understandable ignorance of the Afro-American experience. Yet, the rhetoric of almost all such reservations is phrased in intellectual terms—questions about matters of "academic responsibility," and the "intellectual defensibility" of using black issues and themes as a basis for instruction—rather than granting the possibility that there are things worth teaching of which even most academicians may be unaware.

This unwillingness to admit that even educators may be woefully ill-informed about vitally important issues is symptomatic of the malaise of educational institutions in contemporary America. Too often, what passes for education actually only succeeds in ignoring the relationship between what education deals with and what the real world is like. Most amazing of all, some educators argue that their refusal to "contaminate" the purity of intellectualism is a "guarantee" of the sanctity of academic endeavors. If this is true, then academic endeavors are in for a very rough time, since such ivory-towerism deprives the educational process of its most vital function: to prepare students for the society in which they must live.

Academic unwillingness to confront reality—especially an unpleasant and threatening reality—must change, if for no other reason
than that students will not allow it to continue. Many educators
suffer from the delusion that agitation for acceptance of racial issues
and themes as valid subjects for general instruction and study is a
new phenomenon. W. E. B. DuBois, writing in 1903, said: "The
problem of the twentieth century is the problem of the color line—
of the relation of the darker to the lighter races of men." Though
this and other eloquent voices have been raised for many years,
general acceptance of its message and of the importance of implementing its suggestions has not been achieved; the Afro-American
experience is still not considered a valid object for instruction on all
educational levels.

American educators have been woefully negligent toward their
responsibilities in this crucial area. Their negligence has been, at least
partially, a function of this society's pervading mystique that conflict and rivalry are individual concerns and do not involve racial and
ethnic groups as groups. When combined with an even more pervasive racist view of black people as collectively incapable of doing
anything worth studying, one can see why blacks have remained
invisible for so long; the "troublesome presence" of black people
raises fundamental questions about the "rugged individualism"
which supposedly typifies America's past and present. Rather than
confront this incongruity, American educators chose to ignore it.

This country's educational institutions can no longer afford to
participate in what amounts to societal myth-building, while ignoring one of the central objectives of education; to describe and interpret reality as cogently and impartially as possible. Students can no
longer be given a myopic vision of America as a homogeneous, placid
and idyllic land of the free and home of the brave. From this archaic
educational perspective, America is a paradise, devoid of the "un-
pleasantness" associated with internal ethnic and racial rivalries and
conflicts or with the brutal abuse of weaker peoples in maintaining
an inequitable distribution of power. With this social background,
American students cannot avoid being left with the implicit assumption that this country has never done any wrong, fought any unjust
wars, or exploited any of its neighbors or citizens.

This naive and fallacious view, however, no longer serves to conceal reality. Students are demanding more "relevance" precisely because they are recognizing that most of what they have learned has no *revealing* relationship to the way the world functions. It is the rude shock that comes as a result of being made forcefully aware of the incongruity between life as it is described in school and *life* as it is in the streets that lies at the heart of most contemporary student unrest and ferment.

America's educational institutions are faced with a choice that will soon confront the society as a whole. Fundamental inequities and incongruities infest the structure of the educational establishment. These tensions will be relieved. It is still not too late for educators to choose to assist the process of reforming their institutions; how long that option will remain theirs is any man's guess.

Because of the current debate concerning the proper descriptive terms for people of African ancestry in the Americas, be it black, Afro-American, or Negro, considerable uncertainty exists over correct usage and capitalization. In an arbitrary effort to create uniformity in this volume, the following editorial decisions were made: use of *Negro* conforms to present convention, and *Afro-American* complies with the same rule. *Black* is capitalized only when it appears as part of a proper name.

A number of persons contributed a great deal of time and effort to the series of events which produced this book. Robert Dahl, William Kessen, Edwin Redkey, Charles Taylor, Craig Foster, Raymond Nunn, and Donald Ogilvie, members of the Yale African-American Study Group, worked long and hard on the symposium; we are grateful also to the Black Student Alliance at Yale, particularly its Moderator, Glen DeChabert. Mrs. Josephine Broude's determination and will to work were important factors in making the symposium the success it was.

Howard Lamar, William Kessen, Sidney Mintz, and Paul B. Jones read and criticized the manuscript; their suggestions are appreciated. Thanks go too to Miss Jane Olson of the Yale Press, who helped in so many ways to turn a rough manuscript into what hopefully is an exciting book.

The editors wish to express their gratitude to the participants in the conference for contributing so largely to its success. They are listed here with their affiliations.

McGeorge Bundy
President
Ford Foundation

Lawrence W. Chisolm
History Department
State University of New York
at Buffalo

Harold Cruse
Writer in residence
University of Michigan

David Brion Davis
History Department
Cornell University

Nathan Hare
Director of Black Studies
San Francisco State College

Maulana Ron Karenga
Founder-Chairman of US
Watts, California

Martin Kilson, Jr.
Department of Government
Harvard University

Gerald A. McWorter
Sociology Department
Spelman College

Sidney W. Mintz
Anthropology Department
Yale University

Boniface Obichere
History Department
University of California
at Los Angeles

Donald H. Ogilvie
Student
Yale University

Dr. Alvin Poussaint
Department of Psychiatry
School of Medicine
Tufts University

Edwin S. Redkey
History Department
University of Tennessee

Armstead L. Robinson
Student
Yale University

Charles H. Taylor, Jr.
Provost
Yale University

Robert Farris Thompson
Department of History of Art
Yale University

INTRODUCTION

Charles H. Taylor, Jr.

This meeting is the result of student initiative and interest here. In the middle of the winter, our Black Student Alliance arranged a thoughtful evening's conversation with an invited group of faculty, administrative officers, and deans of the University. We were deeply impressed with the extraordinarily careful preparations they had made, both for that meeting and for the presentation of their case. One of the things that has pleased me the most in my encounters with the members of the Alliance has been their genuine and deeply felt concern for what *happens*. We know well that such is not always the focus of contemporary protest; but these students really care about results, and that is why we are here. In fact, without their extraordinary energy and their great determination this symposium could not possibly have taken place.

I think we are all aware that much black student unrest exists on our campuses today. I need hardly tell you that at colleges—both predominantly black and predominantly white—there have been various kinds of protests, sit-ins, and other demonstrations, expressing concern about conditions on the campus and the nature of the curriculum: at Morgan State, Howard, Bowie State, as well as at Harvard, Princeton, Columbia, here on our own campus, Vassar, Rutgers, NYU—the list is substantial. The demands, although they vary in specifics from place to place, almost always include a desire for more relevant curricular offerings than we have had. This concern echoes also protests in many of our public school systems, not long ago in New York, especially in relation to I.S. 201, in Boston, Washington, Philadelphia, and here in New Haven, particularly at Hillhouse High School this winter.

The fact is that our society, our schools, our education, suffer from white racism. This racism is both conscious and unconscious—much of it unconscious, but nevertheless real, as the Kerner report emphasizes. It shows up in a variety of ways in American life. The system seems in many respects to be loaded, often quite without that intent, against the black student and the black person, in the tracking of our schools, in the way promotions are allowed to go through when the supposedly required level of education has not been attained, and indeed in the universities in the intellectual traditions of the study of our own subjects. For example, in history it is all too great a temptation for the white man to study the history of the events that are visible to him, and that study often fails to include the events that are today, in the racial crisis in which we find ourselves, terribly important for a proper understanding of our condition. Our indifference, intended or not, has left us ignorant of what it is and has been like to be a black American.

The truth is that black America knows very much more of white America than white America knows of black America. This is understandable in some respects, for we have been a dominantly white society—television, the press, the educational system, not to mention the tax base and majority politics, have all been run by whites for whites. Take television as just one example—consider how much of white society and white values are seen clearly every day in almost every black home in America. Ask yourself how much of the black world we see on television each day. I remember one cartoon, not many weeks old, where one sees from a distance a couple on an elegant penthouse roof and, beyond it, the ghetto smoking in the background. One penthouse dweller says to the other over a cocktail, "How can I be responsible for the ghetto? I've never even been there." Such is the condition of American life, and the need for greater understanding is abundantly clear.

What we are faced with then in our black students' protest is not simply, in some respects not even chiefly, their proper demand to know more about themselves, about *their* heritage and *their* tradition, but rather their consciousness of how important it is for American society, for us, the white majority, to know a lot more about them. We need this knowledge to attack not only conscious prejudice, which is easy to identify, but to overcome unconscious discrimination, that simple lack of awareness, the ignorance from which we all suffer in white America.

Only with much deeper understanding can we counter the tendency to projection which is common among whites, that kind of projection which imagines a minority—the most visible minority is the black minority—as harboring what we don't like or reject in ourselves: violence, hatred, instinctual drive, or whatever it may be. How often white violence is excused, for example, by imagining it as either actual or potential self-defense. To understand such projection is a part of growing up—recognizing that you cannot blame on the other fellow what is really an aspect of yourself. For white society as for the individuals who compose it, coming to have a really felt awareness of the black man as an individual, a real human being, and to know more about his heritage and experience, is a challenge to our maturity. Either we will meet this challenge successfully, both as a society and as individuals, and be the better for it, or we will fail to meet it, and suffer the consequences.

How, then, are we to respond? Our educational institutions, as that part of society's structure which is responsible for the development and transmission of the knowledge on which understanding depends, must do justice, as we have not, to the black man's share of American history, American politics, economics, and art. I think that's not so hard for us to see. But the focus of this symposium is really to ask the question, Should we do more than that? It hopes to inquire, What is the intellectual significance of focusing a part of our curriculum consciously and directly on the black experience? or, as President Brewster put it in one early discussion, Is race a proper organizing principle for the curriculum? We do use geographical, national, religious, and ethnic distinctions in our organization of the curriculum and our attack upon intellectual problems, but we have shied away from race—and shied away from race for reasons which I think among the liberal white intellectual community are understandable, reasons which have to do with the history of the 1930s, World War II, and Nazi Germany. It is understandable but not sufficient that many of us would rather not talk about race. And so the symposium asks this set of questions: Is the special study of the black experience intellectually valid? Is it educationally responsible? And, is it socially constructive for both blacks and whites?

THE INTEGRATIONIST ETHIC AS A BASIS FOR SCHOLARLY ENDEAVORS

Harold Cruse

On behalf of the Black Student Alliance of Yale, I am pleased to be called before you to discuss this very unique and very important problem: the significance of the black experience to intellectual pursuits and scholarly studies. I have been asked to concentrate on one theme, namely the failure of the integrationist ethic as a basis for scholarly studies. And from that point of departure, I will attempt to deal with this problem in a way which will be in consonance with what you call the "framework," or method of attack on this problem.

It is my belief that the integrationist ethic has subverted and blocked America's underlying tendency toward what I would call a democratic ethnic pluralism in our society. This ethic has been a historical tendency stimulated both by Anglo-Saxon political ideology, rampant industrialism, racism, and an Americanism whose implied goal has been the nullification of all competing subcultures indigenous to North America. It is my belief that both black and white scholarly rationalizations have historically supported the integrationist ethic in pursuit of the ideal of the American creed. This approach was obviously predicated on an intellectual consensus which held that the political, economic, and cultural values of the Anglo-American tradition were sufficiently creative and viable enough to sustain the American progression to realization of its ultimate potential. But the present internal social and racial crisis we are experiencing proves beyond a doubt the failure of this integrationist ethic. As a result of this failure, at this present moment we have no viable black philosophy on which to base much-needed black studies programs.

Upon examining the black and white reactions to this failure, we find different reactions on both sides of the racial fence. You have separatist reactions coming from the black side of the equation, and you have white intellectual resistance toward acceptance and ratification of another ethic in scholarly endeavors. In response to pressures for black studies, whites often attempt to speed up piecemeal integrative processes in favor of black integrationists. Another response to demands for black studies involves questioning the validity of separatist doctrines; whites question the nihilist, irrational, or anarchistic tendencies they note in separatist doctrines and, by extension, question whether the whole approach, including a trend toward black studies, is valid. Thus, black intellectual critics of the integrationist ethic—students, writers, scholars, critics, historians and so on—must assume an obligation to establish black studies in the curricula whose subject matter, critical thrust, and social objectives fully answer those who would question curriculum reform in the direction of black studies.

Such black studies programs must achieve or establish certain critical and/or creative criteria which would make manifest their validity in the face of white intellectual criticisms. Needless to say, this is a big question and a complex one. I don't know how far we can go into the analysis of it today. However, from my own point of view, having thought about these perplexing questions for many years, having based my whole creative life on the examination of, and the response to, these pressures, I have something which I think is of value in lending understanding to the problem.

I believe that if it were left to the black students themselves, the black scholars, the undergraduate students, the graduate students, the writers and the critics, to create this black studies curriculum, they would employ a historical approach. I think one of the main points of departure in an approach to the content and the thrust of a black studies program can begin with an analysis of black middle-class formation from generation to generation, beginning possibly after the Civil War and proceeding down to our day; this would involve a minute analysis of the class ideology noted in middle-class formation from era to era. I think an investigation into plantation life should begin to verify whether there were sharp class divisions on slave plantations between field hands and so-called "house Negroes," and to see whether the social carry-over into Reconstruction and twentieth-century developments really reflects a sharp class division, evolving out of plantation origins. All this I think could be verified as a historical basis for the beginning of a black studies curriculum.

I think an examination should be made of the extent to which the white Protestant ethic has achieved the American creed's stated aims of democratic inclusion of the Negro in American society. To what extent has the Protestant ethic aided, abetted, or checked what we would call normal middle-class development on the black side of the racial fence in American life? Was the intention of the Protestant ethic to aid and abet the development of a black middle class? Or was the racism inherent in the approach meant to deny the democratic inclusion of this black middle-class development into the American mainstream? Carrying this analysis further, how has the retardation of the black bourgeoisie historically affected the outlook of the "intellectual class" in black life? For example, how did this retardation of normal development affect W. E. B. DuBois' contention that the black race in America required the development of a kind of talented-tenth leadership stratum which would deliver the Negro mass from its degradation? I believe that a black studies curriculum should investigate DuBois' thesis of the talented-tenth and ascertain to what degree this expectation was rooted in our historical development. These questions are some important points of departure toward laying the basis of a black studies program.

I make these assertions mainly to answer certain questions about intellectual procedure in the approach to the establishment of a black studies program. From the standpoint of these historical considerations I think that by looking at the problem of developing intellectually valid black studies curricula, one can see a legitimate point of departure.

To get deeper into this problem, I think that the whole question of the demand for a black studies program falls under the heading of what we would call a movement, a tendency, an ideology of "black cultural nationalism." This phenomenon is emerging today among the young black intelligentsia, the young black students, and the young black activists. This tendency is emerging in response to the feeling that at present there is no viable intellectual approach to the problems facing both blacks and whites in American society. Though these activists have espoused cultural nationalism, it is understandable that at this moment the historical roots and implications of cultural nationalism in our society are quite unclear to some members of the younger generation.

It is my belief that cultural nationalism as an ideology, nurturing the whole desire and thrust toward a black studies program, can only be understood if it is approached, first, historically, and then, by analyzing many of the deep problems which enmesh the Negro intelligentsia today. All over the country, in different aspects of the black movement we can see a general thrashing about, a frenetic search for method, and a search for both internal and external criticisms. We see splits and factions; we see movements running into dead ends and, we see the assassination of Martin Luther King and the outpouring of people's anguish, both black and white. We see all this and we have to ask, as King asked before he was assassinated, "Where do we go from here?" And how?

I have cited several historical antecedents to make it easier to understand how to deal with the current manifestations of these historical problems in the black world. These problems must be confronted; the effort to resolve them should be reflected in affirmative actions in relation to the demand for black studies. Black studies must be geared to the question of black institutional development on all levels—political, economic, cultural, and social. I believe that the black studies program, using the thrust of cultural nationalism, might for example base one of its approaches upon the study of the development of the black church, especially from the class aspect, from the Episcopal and other "higher" denominations down to the store-front church. It might deal with institutions such as the theater. It should deal with black business trends and it must investigate, on an economic level, how the black movement is going to adjust its aims within the context of American society.

How best to respond to demands for black studies is a very complicated problem because we have two distinct trends in the black movement, even though these trends are seldom verbalized. We have implied here what is often called a "radical" or "revolutionary" thrust, and we also have what can be described as a "slow reformist" thrust. Even though this conflict is not verbally expressed in all instances, we can see, if we look closely enough, a clash of aims and methods involved in these underlying trends. We can describe this problem in terms of a conflict between "radical-revolutionary" and "reform" or "gradualist" thrusts toward the achievement of stated goals.

This conflict presents a peculiar problem in America for the simple reason that at any moment it cannot be determined precisely whether American society, as now constituted, is conducive to a revolutionary rate of social change for any kind of adjustment, be it for the black man or for the white man or for any other kind of man or class. Moreover, the implied rate of social change, as it is effected in the reactions of certain strata in our society, may lead one to accept slow reformist methods for social change. This presents a very complicated problem for all concerned, particularly for the spokesmen, the activists, and the leaders of the black movement. It also presents a difficult problem for those who want to institute black studies programs, because in either case we have to deal with a method of study which is related to the realities of the society around us; this throws everyone into a quandary—"everyone," black and white—but particularly the blacks, because the young generation today is very impatient. They do not desire slow change; they demand rapid change.

Whether we are going to have rapid change or slow change is important. Aside from that, we must determine the quality, the thrust, and the approach of any black studies program. Will its content accept—or be based on—slow gradualism? Or will the studies thrust the gears, hopefully, toward radical change? This is a problem. Those who want to institute a black studies program must take into consideration all of these realities, because hopefully the black studies program will be used to speed positive social changes in our society; I think the program has to begin with careful consideration of the necessities of the present situation and with the ultimate possibilities for change in this society.

Leaving that question for the moment and getting back to the content of the program in general, I want to reiterate that the question of deciding upon the content of the program is very difficult to resolve. But we have to begin to pinpoint this in order to give some immediate direction to these efforts.

Black cultural nationalism has to be seen as an attempt, a necessarily historical attempt, to deal with another kind of cultural nationalism that is implied in our society, namely, the cultural nationalism of the dominant white group. You might call it a kind of cultural "particularism" which is found when you examine the cultural particularism of the Anglo-Saxon group or the WASP or whatever name you want to give to this stratum. I think we find that an ideology exists which *has* to deny the validity of other kinds of cultural values that might compete with its own standards—whether in the social sciences, the arts, literature, or economic activity. We find this particularism of the Anglo-American implicit in all that is done in our society, whether it is done unconsciously or consciously.

I think that this particularism provides a clue to the problem of the acceptance of the validity of the concept of black studies. It has been assumed in history that all that was required to make America attain its ideals was the confirmation and the extension of an Anglo-American political and economic creed. Today we see that this creed, unfortunately, has reached the point where it is seemingly unable to deal with the crises that beset the nation.

This failure demands that *another* set of cultural and political values be extended into our society to fill the void. Black studies must make the dominant particularism, the dominant racial creed, more capable of dealing with the internal crises facing us all. I think that this awareness is something that has to be cultivated meticulously by any black student movement. There must be a quality of intellectual clarity and intellectual patience in dealing with those tendencies in the intellectual world which would resist both the institution and the thrust of such a black studies program. I think that those who would institute the black studies program must not only understand their own particular black history but must also grapple with, and understand, the dual tradition that has been nurtured in this society and that has given our society its unique character. I think the question of a black studies program is intrinsically a two-way street: a black studies program—even if it expresses black particularism—is a kind of particularism which understands its own limits and its social function. Its social function is not to replace one particularism with another particularism but to counterbalance the historical effects and exaggeration of particularism toward a more racially balanced society, a society which would include expectations regarding the democratic creed.

Previously I mentioned certain particular aspects or approaches that I feel black studies must begin with. I mentioned the church, I mentioned economic activities, I mentioned institutions such as the theater, I mentioned criticism, literature, and the allied arts, and so forth. I believe this is an adequate starting point. I have also dealt with the overall ideology and with black cultural nationalism as the main intellectual spirit behind the increasing demands for the institution of black studies programs. However, I want to extend that concept into a discussion of how the academic thrust of black studies might begin to impinge upon and to modify the broader social structure.

Such considerations are necessary because, after all, we are not going to study black history in a vacuum. We are going to study black history with an eye toward its being socially functional. We are going to have black social studies with the understanding that this is a new social method of dealing with the infirmities of our society. I believe that a black studies program must at all times keep its eye on the broader manifestations of what I would call—and I mentioned this in my book—the functioning of America's "cultural apparatus" in all of its aspects. I believe that in terms of the society at large, whatever long-range effect black studies will have on the broader realities of America must first begin in the general area of our cultural apparatus.

For example, the university is part of our cultural apparatus. These are institutions of a special kind engaged in socially useful activities. But beyond that, in the broader society, we have other impactful and meaningful manifestations and functionings of the cultural apparatus. It is in this general area that black studies must direct its initial interest and attention. Black studies must begin to deal with the effects of the communications media on the society as a whole as well as with the effects of the communications media on the black community. It must also begin to examine the role of the film and the role of the theater in black society. It must begin to deal with the impact of the music world on the cultural life of the black community. In short, black studies must initiate a critical examination of, and a critical approach into, the manifestations of these aspects of the cultural apparatus.

To take one example, consider the Negro in the theater—one of my pet subjects. The theater, if one studies it very closely, reflects in many ways all of the successes, the failures, the ups and downs, the defaults, the want of criticism, and the adaptation of the black intellectual class and the black creative class to the larger society. If one examines the position of the Negro in the theater today, he will have an example, set apart from all other institutions, of the plight of the black intellectual, the black creator, in all aspects of American culture. The theater should become one of the prime laboratories of those who are going to use cultural nationalism as a basis for the creation of a black studies program.

As an institution, the theater reflects the failure of the integrationist ethic most uniquely and most glaringly, perhaps more clearly than any other institution that we can name in the cultural sphere. A historical examination of the black experience in the American theater will show that it is a good barometer of the rise and fall, the successes and failures, of all other black institutions. At one time Negroes had a thriving theater, particularly in New York. It was an autonomous institution. It was crowded with talent, creativity, and pioneering. This happened at the same historical moment that the American or white theater was beginning to make its debut in American society as a unique American institution.

There was a time when there was almost "democratic" collaboration between black and white in the development of American theater. Somewhere down the line, around World War I and thereafter, the manifestations of what I call the white cultural particularism began to assert itself in the American theater; and mind you, this trend has reference also to the plight or the status of the white theater today. From that point on, black creativity began to wane and the black performer and creator was, little by little, pushed out toward the fringes of the theater.

This development paralleled developments in other areas of black-white relations—this is why I claim that the theater should become a prime laboratory for a cultural approach to a black studies curriculum. In recent years, the Negro performer has raised the question of exclusion and discrimination in the American theater. These complaints continue unabated. Black complaints about discrimination come at a time when the American theater is in a crisis to the same degree that the nation itself is in a crisis. Therefore, at this moment, the Negro performer calling for integration echoes the contention of the black students who are questioning the integrationist ethic. Paradoxically, the Negro in the theater must—at this moment—maintain that the solution to his plight is more integration. However, he is losing sight of the fact that the theater is a sick institution and cannot accommodate the aims and desires and potentialities of the black presence in America.

This indicates, as far as I am concerned, why the black theater can and must become one of the prime exhibits here in dealing with the failure of the integrationist ethic. The Negro in the theater, as in all areas of American life, can only begin to regain or to win his rightful place within the American set-up through a retrenchment into self, a retrenchment into history. The creation of black studies must reflect his black history and an investigation into his past. These are the only ways in which the black student, the black intellectual, or the Negro of any calling or class can begin to re-examine his position in society as a whole, and then to begin to work from there toward a more equitable and democratic inclusion within American society.

THE INTELLECTUAL VALIDITY OF STUDYING THE BLACK EXPERIENCE

Martin Kilson, Jr.

Mary McCarthy, the novelist and superb and eloquent critic of the grotesque Vietnam war, remarked in the *New York Review of Books* not long ago that, whatever intellectuals do with their skills and their cleverness, they should never shirk doing what they do best—namely, to "smell a rat" and to dissect its nature and character, letting the chips fall where they may. Now, to some extent in my brief remarks on the intellectual validity of the black experience this is what I shall attempt to do: to smell a rat. I think the best approach in addressing this topic is to assess conceptually what the black experience has been and has meant. Such assessment, I think, is not easy at all. For one thing, what contemporaneous yardstick does one use to define the historical limits, the starting point, and the context of the black experience? How do we decide what is meaningful and valuable in the social, cultural, and political realities of the black experience? Furthermore, what community or segment of that vast group of people known as black people should be used as typifying whatever the black experience is and has been? For example, should we use as typical the Republic of Haiti where black men have ruled a sovereign state since the nineteenth century? But where, also, such black rule—or, if you prefer, black power—has been oppressive and dysfunctional for the black masses or lower classes? Or, perhaps, should we take the present-day state of Nigeria, where the polity is rent asunder by fratricidal warfare that was sparked by a grotesque genocidal act committed by one segment against another in this largest of all black communities in the world? Or, perhaps, should we take as typical of this thing, "the black experience," the Afro-American community which was subjected to chattel slavery for over two hundred years and in the past century has been denied the elemental attributes of modern citizenship and humanity by devious, grotesque, and brutal forms of white racism? For some Negroes, particularly those imbued with an intense black racialist outlook, the answer to these perplexing questions is, unfortunately, rather easy and self-evident. From this vantage point, white police brutality against blacks in Harlem or Mississippi or South Africa or Rhodesia should constitute the contemporaneous yardstick for the historical delimitation of the black experience. With this yardstick, therefore, it would be unthinkable, if not treasonable, to use the Haitian political experience as a historical example of something relevant and meaningful to the overall black experience. Instead, one would have to select a historical event like the slave trade to the Western Hemisphere in order to find the ideological, emotional, and therapeutic sustenance for what I call the black racialist or black nationalist view of the black experience. In this view of the black experience, the slave trade is seen as the beastly act of beastly white men, or, in Malcolm X's memorable phrase, "white devils," who without pity or remorse wrenched millions of Negro Africans from their ancestral homeland for enforced and dehumanizing labor in the plantations of the Western Hemisphere. Moreover, this horrendous historical act by "white devils" has, in the black racialist view of the black experience, endowed the black man with a special aura of righteousness—indeed, that same righteousness that has been applied to the oppressed and wretched of the earth ever since the birth of Christianity.

Now, of course, the typical black nationalist would not today attribute to Christian doctrine his view of the special aura of righteousness accruing to the oppressed and despised black man. Yet, it is certainly one of the striking ironies of the black nationalist approach to the black experience that the Christian doctrine, now considered a historical agent of the black man's degradation, actually informs the notion of righteousness now considered a special preserve of the black man and the black experience. In this connection, it can be remarked that all men, black and white, yellow and red, choose those historical paradoxes or ironies found suitable or useful for a given occasion and reject those lacking such utility. In this respect, therefore, the black experience is, I dare say, little more than an offshoot of the human experience—no better and no worse.

Perhaps I could put this point in sharper relief by reference to other features of the slave trade to the Western Hemisphere that seldom appear in the black nationalist's view of this horrifying historical event. To those who take the historiography of the slave trade seriously, as I do myself, it is commonplace knowledge that leading and entrepreneurial groups in traditional Negro African societies were voluntarily privy to the slave trade. These groups saw the trade in slaves as an economic relationship from which enormous wealth, profit, and political and military advantage could be derived. When such gain is available, men, I submit, will seek it. They are not likely to let cultural or racial or other bonds stand in the way. What is more, the African brokers in the slave trade—of whom there were literally tens of thousands—were not restrained by knowledge that perhaps 40 percent of the human cargo in Middle Passage perished before reaching the plantations of the Western Hemisphere. In short, I would suggest most firmly that the black experience is truly nothing more than a variant of the human experience. Put another way, and rather cynically, power is what power does.

I trust that what I have been trying to say illuminates some aspects of the intellectual validity of the black experience. I have purposely refrained from defining specifically what I mean by "the intellectual validity of the black experience." I happen to hate definitions. I have also consciously refrained from attempting to deduce a conception of the validity of the black experience by emphasizing the oppressive aspects of this experience as exemplified in the past three centuries of black-white relationships.

I am, I think, reasonably knowledgeable about the bloody and dehumanizing record of this relationship; but I consider it neither unique nor a startling event. All men are capable of it and, indeed, all men, black and white, yellow and red, have been privy to such. Moreover, I cannot quite accept the viewpoint that the black man's experience with white oppression has endowed black men with a special insight into oppression and thus a special capacity to rid human affairs of oppression. I would argue, in fact, that this viewpoint is largely a political one which certain groups find serviceable in the contemporary conflict between Negro and white in American society. Indeed, it is a common fallacy to believe that what is momentarily politically serviceable is *ipso facto* intellectually virtuous. I personally understand this viewpoint as held by black nationalists. Indeed, I am compassionate toward it. But my intellect rejects it. Like Mary McCarthy, I begin to smell a rat and feel compelled to dissect it for all to see.

QUESTION PERIOD

Question

I am prepared to recommend the inclusion of black studies for the relevance of the educational experience of our students, both white and black. In the nature of the case, the revision and expansion of our program is a continuing thing. Over the years different topics received different emphases, and it is undoubtedly true that the curriculum of studies in very many subjects hasn't kept up with developments. A great many of the concrete suggestions in both talks today would be, I think, valuable and accepted by my colleagues.

But, now, what troubles me is a certain ambiguity in the presentations. From one point of view, the justification was education in advocating the inclusion of these studies. But from the other point of view, the justification of these studies was ideological and practical, in the sense that it was suggested that these studies of black nationalism would serve as a focus for reform, revolution, and transformation of the society in which the black has been exploited.

This introduces a difficulty; those of us who have devoted our lives to scholarship are puzzled by the statement that the failure of the integrationist ethic can be a basis for scholarship. I don't see that that's been made out at all. From our point of view, the truth is one whether we discuss the phenomenon of black nationalism or the phenomenon of Aryan nationalism. We don't recognize a "black truth" or a "white truth" any more than we recognize "Aryan physics" or "Bolshevik biology." And I am sure that I would have great difficulty persuading my colleagues to introduce a subject matter which was devised for purposes of political transformation. They would smell that rat that Professor Kilson so well called attention to. But on the other hand, I think I could make a very good case for the fact that our anthropology courses, our sociology courses, our courses in economics and history have not tapped material that they should.

The statement by Professor Kilson that the black experience is part of the human experience seems to me to be the premise on which we can accept anything which is educationally valid—and not only about blacks but about other groups in our community. But if you were to insist that this educational point of view should be coupled with an ideology and a program, I would be bewildered. First, because I'm not sure that the ideology of the black nationalists represents the beliefs of the Negro people. For example, in this morning's *Times* there is a remarkable letter by Roy Wilkins referring to James Reston. Now, Roy Wilkins takes a position with which many whites agree—presumably James Reston was describing a position with which some Negroes agree. Therefore, my colleagues would have to determine what political point of view should determine the inclusion of studies. We don't do this in other studies; why should we do this in black studies? And so, to conclude my overlong "speech"—I'm really asking questions rather than criticizing what has been said—I'd like to have a clarification of what appears to me to be an ambiguity, a very fateful ambiguity because the future of black studies depends on its resolution.

The question is whether we can incorporate the legitimate subject matter with what we are already doing and trying to do, and I think with good will, or whether we are confronted with a political ultimatum that we adopt certain points of view independent of the processes of inquiry on pain of encountering—to put it mildly—"difficulties" on our campuses.

Cruse

I see what you mean. There is always a readiness, indeed over-readiness, to equate certain unequatable factors in life. You can't equate the inclusion of black studies in the university at this juncture with the status of other studies, because if that were true there would be no special need to *have* black studies. In the absence of black studies, the demand for black studies is unavoidably a radical innovation from the outset. The inspiration behind the introduction of black studies is a radical imperative in society at large. That is unavoidable. Therefore, I don't see how we can mince words or escape the conclusion that ultimately the inclusion of black studies must of necessity reflect the world *outside* the university in political movements, both black and white—and in response to what radical changes are taking place on the campus.

As far as I can see, this has always been the case in American society. I think we have to face these questions squarely. The black movement, of which black studies is a reflection, seeks certain social changes which will include the realities of the black presence in America more equitably. I think I tried to deal with the question of radical changes versus reform changes in a way which would preclude a definite answer to the rate of social change in which these studies will result. That is not for me to say. However, the urgency with which black students are demanding the inclusion of these studies seems to imply that all of us concerned have to accept whatever political results manifest themselves outside of, beyond, and as a result of the introduction of these studies.

I don't believe that at this juncture of our development we can mince words or shirk facing up to the implications of what we are doing or what we are instituting. I would hazard a guess that America as a society is doomed for some rather radical shock from the left or the right of the center, *irrespective* of whether black studies are introduced in our universities or not. It is my contention that whatever radical shocks we are to experience in the future, we will be better able to deal positively with these crises if we look toward a sensible, intelligent, and positive inclusion of things in the university curricula which have been historically missing. Their absence has helped to create the undemocratic climate in which we live; this climate spurs the social dislocations which, when they come, shock all of us.

Question

My question is directed to Dr. Kilson.

I gather from your remarks that you are saying that the victims of oppression, be they black or white, have no insight into the consequences of oppression that the oppressors cannot share. My inference is, then, that oppression is a kind of "morally neutral" type of thing, and that the victims and the oppressor have no particular difference in their insights in terms of this phenomenon—that therefore there is no place for a kind of moral self-righteousness which—as

I see history—seems to have been a potent force in relieving the oppressor of the oppression.

Kilson

No. I wouldn't argue, and I didn't mean to argue, that the oppressed have no insight into the nature of oppression. Surely they have an insight into the nature of oppression, into the mechanisms that mediate oppression. They surely must have an insight into what it means, how it feels, to be oppressed, what it means to have whatever talent one possesses limited, restricted, hemmed in. My point is that, whatever particular understanding oppressed groups have, in and of itself it does not represent an intrinsically superior position—in the sense that most ideologies of the oppressed would lead us to believe. That is to say, if the tables are turned, would the oppressed automatically find the system of values which would inform the new status with something that was not there before? There is certainly no empirical evidence which would suggest this kind of intrinsic, almost built-in, automatic ability of the oppressed, once removed from oppression and launched to the status of the dominant group, fundamentally to alter the historical pattern that has been known to us. Now, this is kind of cynical in its view of men and their institutions and their capabilities, but it is my view and I haven't quite yet been persuaded from it. I don't know how else to answer your question, because it is ultimately a theoretical or ideological question: you, to a large extent, must stand on one side or the other—and I happen to stand on one side of the matter.

Question

I felt burdened by Mr. Cruse's talk and I felt teased by Martin Kilson's. Burdened by the first because I don't think that black people in America today ought to be asked to take on the responsibility for making their experiences and their aspirations relevant for institutional change—or better, and more specifically, to take on the responsibility for inducement of institutional change, *or* social-structural change, in a way that is going to be "adaptive," as I think you suggest. I think that the responsibility now rests upon white academicians and white Americans and those of us who are black academicians to make that bridge wherever we think we can make it. But as far as black students are concerned, if they think that the only way in which their society is going to see them in a different perspective is that they are going to have to exaggerate, if you will, presentations that they are going to have to make within the university community and outside, I suspect that maybe this transitional kind of step is exceedingly necessary.

I felt as Martin Kilson talked that, certainly, one of the things that needs to be said to revolutionary black students is that there is a human dimension that too often is ignored. There is evidence of an extreme sense of selfishness as they insist upon introducing change at a pace so rapid that even those who most strongly support them aren't quite able to keep up with them. But there *is* a human dimension and one has to consider the legitimacy of the complaint, even though we may not always have at our fingertips the mechanisms of the change. I do not think that the black experience has nothing new or relevant to introduce into the educational structure or framework. I once asked W. E. B. DuBois what he thought was the role of the black professor at the predominantly white college, and he said, "He doesn't have any role because he's not there." I suggest to you that black studies is at this moment neither programmatic nor of intellectual content or significance, because neither of them are there. And underneath what I see as the plea of the generation of this moment is that the university take cognizance of the fact that I am *here,* and that I am here *not* to be lost in the predominant culture—even on the grounds of the university campus. The significance of black students asking for black dormitories at Northwestern lies not in radical separatism but rather in that they are saying, in effect, why should we as black students, if we elect to live in a dormitory, always have to live in a dormitory that has shared predominant white values? And I would hope that should such a dormitory be built on Northwestern's campus it not be the burden of the black students to apply the integrationist ethic, but that white students would have to come forth and say, "I think that I am able to think within the relevant framework of black students and if they will invite me in to live, I want to live in *that* dormitory."

I think finally that there is a kind of contribution that black student militants can make to the larger society, and that contribution, it seems to me, is the insistent, unremitting demand of people who have been left out to say, "I want a share in the decisions that are being made about me." And I think that black students may in this sense be making a contribution to white students as well, to Puerto Ricans as well as to black people in the ghetto. In a word, I would like to take some of the burden off the black student to correct some of the maladjustments in our society and permit him to have his face seen and to be considered as displaying the kind of integrity and sense of worth which I think the black movement represents.

Cruse

It is not my intention to attempt to say at what speed or at what rate racial equalization is going to proceed in American society. I tried to say that the inclusion of black studies should facilitate equalization of the black man in American society. This can come about as a result of added emphasis given to the black presence on the campus. I am not a student. All I can do is attempt to reflect the feelings and the motives of the black student body as they make their demands and try to determine what inspires them. I can also try to see what connection there is, if any, between student demands for black studies and general black demands for equality.

Yesterday I had a talk with some community workers in Harlem who are involved in a lot of efforts, one of which is the Poor People's Campaign. They were also involved in discussing, on a community level, the impact and meaning of the Columbia University situation for the black community as a whole, particularly for nonstudents. Some of these community activists told me yesterday that the black students at Columbia cannot begin to have any impact or meaning at all until they connect their campus work with community work.

As far as I am concerned, the aspirations of the black students and the aspirations of black community activists are in consonance on this level. It is inescapable that whatever is included and implied in the inclusion of a black studies curriculum has to reflect and be connected in some way with what is happening *beyond* the campus.

For if it is the function of the university to prepare all students, black and white, for a more meaningful role in society at large, then we have to ask ourselves what meaningful role black studies will effect for the black student upon leaving the university campus. It follows that we are preparing the black student—and he is assisting in being prepared—in a much more effective way for all kinds of expected social changes and social transformations that seem to be on the horizon for us all in American society. Therefore, neither I nor the black student nor anyone here can avoid these ultimate implications of black studies.

Question

My question is for Mr. Cruse. As I listened to you, I gathered that you were making the plea that in order to make the black experience relevant, using the historical approach and so on, the major endeavor ought to be in the hands of black scholars, black students. If this is true, then one thing bothers me, and I wish you would help me resolve it. When I have worked in black and white universities or colleges, the main attitude I detected is the indifference or reluctance of black scholars, including black students and professors, to learn about the black experience. If it is true, as recent studies indicate, what, then, are we to expect in putting this very practical challenge to these people? Can you help me resolve this dilemma?

Cruse

What you have observed is quite true about the average black university in America. However, I have tried, in my brief exposition, to point out some of the historical reasons for the type of scholarly dereliction that is typical in many black schools. Traditionally, the emphasis on education in black schools has not been to understand or enhance the quality of the black presence as you are now discussing it. Their emphasis has been to educate for social status. This tendency has been one of the dominant characteristics of Negro institutions. There are many historical reasons for this, but we can't go into all of them here. It is obvious that some of today's black students recognize this flaw; it is *always* a minority that recognizes these faults in our way of doing things. A minority of students are now demanding a change in the functioning, the outlook, and the whole quality of education, not only in so-called white universities but in black universities as well. They are attempting to revolutionize the whole approach toward black education, and in so doing they are hoping to rectify these general deficiencies in black education and change the picture to the point that education is for social use rather than for social status.

Question

Mr. Cruse alluded to the importance of the communications media and the significance of their influence on the American people. Now, the book *The Confessions of Nat Turner* by William Styron has been at the top of the best-seller list for many many weeks. I have heard the book highly praised in some quarters and thoroughly condemned in others. I am wondering whether either Mr. Cruse or Professor Kilson might have some comments or reactions to this book?

Cruse

Well, I haven't read the book, but I have read the criticisms. I don't know whether that disqualifies me from speaking about it, but I have certain reactions to the criticisms I have read. From a literary point of view, after reading the basis of the criticisms, I'm for Styron. This is not the first time there has been a controversy over the depiction of Nat Turner, and I maintain that in dealing with a work of art the writer does have a certain licence in depicting historical events. I don't happen to believe that in writing historical novels one is bound by every aspect and every fact of the character's life. The author chooses certain highlights of this character and molds them into a work of art.

I don't particularly like the political direction from which a lot of the criticism is coming; that is, from certain sectors of the white literary establishment. I don't agree with that criticism. As far as the black nationalists' criticism of it is concerned, I suspect that we are dealing here with a question of authorship. A lot of black nationalists do not believe that a white author can deal adequately with this character. But I notice that some of the same black nationalists who have criticized Styron *also* uphold certain historical analyses of slave revolts written by a white author, namely, Herbert Aptheker, who criticized Styron's Nat Turner. I don't know exactly how to pinpoint the locus of the inspiration for the criticism in *either* case. We do have a phenomenon in black nationalist thought which questions the ability or the validity of any white author tackling black themes, particularly themes of a historical nature. Not having read the whole book, I have to confess that I am not aware of what the black nationalist objections are to this book other than that the author is white.

Question

I would like to ask a question of Professor Cruse. As I understand it, you are asking the university to be hospitable to two aspects of what you call the Negro thrust. One of these would be to include in its curriculum studies of the Negro experience; another would be, also, preparation for some kind of public service work once a student left the university and went back into society. I think one of the arguments that was posed here has to be faced: Are you asking that the university accept these courses *despite* the fact that they contain a certain ideological bias? I think your argument that they ought to be and have to be thought of as taught by black people carries that implication. If that is what you mean, how do you justify it? Do you insist that these courses must be taught by black people? And why?

Cruse

At this moment I couldn't possibly answer that question with any degree of finality because it's understood that at this initial phase during which demands are being made for the inclusion of a black studies curriculum, you use what staff resources you have, black or white. However, as this new course of studies proceeds, it follows necessarily that one primary aim has to be the development of more qualified black instructors; an additional number of qualified *white* instructors are going to emerge regardless of the circumstances. If black studies is to be continued and enlarged, it follows that a major emphasis has to be on developing more and more qualified black scholars and black teachers. One of the fundamental problems now hindering the initiation of black studies is the lack of black instructors. One of the results of this course of study naturally will be the production of more black instructors—I think the emphasis should tend in that direction.

Question
And these courses ought to be taught with an eye to the cultural nationalism of the blacks? Could you say more about that?

Cruse
Perhaps I didn't explain my point clearly enough. The ideological inspiration in the black world today with regard to black studies, or to any other kind of emphasis on the black experience, is a reflection of what is generally called "cultural nationalism." What is cultural nationalism? Simply this: in a society such as America, in which you have the ideas and achievements and aspirations of black people constantly de-emphasized, "overlooked," unrecorded, or excluded in the general realm of ideas, any attempt to re-emphasize these ideas must take the form of cultural nationalism. Cultural nationalism is nothing but the attempt of a group or nation or minority to express what is indigenous to its own historical background in order to enhance its public image—social image—in the eyes of the world. Unless there is a spirit of cultural nationalism, you would not have any national or ethnic group resurgence on any level, in any sphere. In America, where it is difficult for the white outlook, and often the black outlook, to accept the fact that the black group exists in many ways in a world *separate* from the whites, it is difficult to accept the validity of cultural nationalism on the part of the Negro as a group in American society because this is not the way we have been conditioned, educated, or trained to see this particular aspect of social reality. Cultural nationalism is nothing but an attempt to prevent the cultural particularism of the dominant white group from continuing to overshadow and submerge the essence of the black experience in America. If you examine this society as a whole, you will notice that *all* American groupings and sub-groupings have resorted in the past to the cultivation of their cultural nationalism in their attempt to adjust and gain recognition in Ameri-

can society. Without this impetus, there cannot be a concerted drive or thrust toward the creation and perpetuation of a course of black studies in the university. You have to have this as a motivation, or else the whole idea of the institution of a black studies program becomes very meaningless.

Question

I wonder if I may address a question or present an opposing point of view to both of you gentlemen which I think will be unsatisfactory. Let me say by way of preface that I am by profession a lawyer and therefore "have no views or principles of my own—my business is only to facilitate those of others."

Mr. Kilson, you wound up your presentation by saying that you smelled a rat. I found myself wondering whether you weren't in your concern about the rat threatening to throw the bath out with the rat. Conversely, Mr. Cruse, it seemed to me in your statement and also in your answers to questions that it has been an indispensable part of your view that the case for black studies of black experiences intimately depends on the fact that the request comes to the university on the initiative of black students. Now, I wonder if we can go back to the question which was the agenda item: Is there intellectual validity in the black experience as an organizing principle of curricula? Is that question, Mr. Cruse, separable in your mind from whether the request is made by black students or not? I would hope that the question whether there is intellectual validity in such a curriculum is a question which would receive the same answer whether it came from black students or white students or a mixed bag of students. I would hope, in short, that if there is a large range of material which has been heavily ignored in our colleges and universities and, even more important, in our primary and secondary schools (and I agree with you, there is), I would suggest that the ignorance is an ignorance which is at least as detrimental to whites as to blacks and therefore that there is as much intellectual integrity in remedying that ignorance for all segments of academic society and the society at large *regardless* of where the request comes from.

This university has produced extraordinary alumni, some men of great distinction, who have gone out to do a great deal of evil in the world—men like John Calhoun. We have had extraordinary men on the Yale faculty who have uttered the most appalling nonsense in the particular areas that we are now considering—I think of William Graham Sumner. Now, I wonder if both of you gentlemen wouldn't agree that men like that might have done more good in the world if their intellectual diets had been a great deal broader? By the same token, wouldn't our college students, black or white, wouldn't we ourselves be a great deal better if our intellectual diets were considerably more nutritious than they are? Can I get agreement from the two of you on that much?

Cruse

I agree.

Kilson

Your point is very well taken. In my case there was the danger, which I was aware of, of tossing the baby out with the rat, and I accepted that in order to impose my point more impressively on the issues that we are considering here. I would obviously agree that questions of cultural nationalism have their role, even in their most intellectually bizarre and distorted form: they have the role of simply putting men and groups in motion around new possibilities and new goals. I would obviously not disagree with this at all.

Now, on this question of whether or not a more varied intellectual diet for William Graham Sumner and John Calhoun would have produced different men, I don't really know. We *presume* this as part of the intellectual, liberal, educational tradition of which we are part, but I don't really know. We have a lot of really important people of evil in our own country and in other parts of the world who, I should suspect, have received a very rich and healthy intellectual diet—I know one such man. My point is, I don't know what the intrinsic connection is which you suggest. We hold out a hope, I hold out a hope; I think there is some connection. We almost hope in despair that it will some day impress itself on the institutions and structures and mechanisms which govern our lives, but I can't quite get myself to believe that there is such an automatic connection, that if we have black studies for the next twenty years somehow there will be a fundamentally different kind of ruling, influential, strategically important group in society. I hope this, but I just don't quite understand the link-up. I wish I did. I am a pessimistic sort: I hold out tremendous hope and prospect for all of us, yet I am so diminished by the inability to realize those prospects. I can't respond in any other way to your obviously profound and searching formulation.

Question Continued

I just want to make it clear that I wasn't insisting that that piece of salesmanship would establish the intellectual case I wanted to make. I think I could match your pessimism, but it seems to me that the question before this university is whether there is some intellectual integrity in widening further and further the range of inquiry and the range of discussion in looking at new problems and also those problems which we've never explored before. If I can win your assent to that [*Kilson:* Quite obviously.] then I suggest that we've created a viable basis for expanding the curriculum and inquiry without acquiescing in the notion that tied to such expanded inquiry has to be any particular programmatic notion of how our society should be changed.

Question

I was going to ask Mr. Kilson what "intrinsic intellectual validity" might be. It strikes me that there is something very convenient about pessimism—it saves a lot of energy—whereas the real problem may not be one of applying some abstract criterion of "intrinsic intellectual validity" under which *many* aspects of the curriculum might suffer, but rather to avoid adopting the ideologically fashionable just because it's fashion. It is true that universities as institutions develop blind spots. The history of the university would show that at one time they were religiously dominated and certain subjects couldn't be brought up; I taught once in a Baptist school in which there was some difficulty in teaching about evolution. I think we may be in danger of a fundamentally white, middle-class university simply developing blind spots. There are certain things going on which *have* a literature and which *can* be taught that ought to be put in the curriculum, making a special effort if necessary. As for pessimism and its convenient lack of action, we can say in justification that we *are* often blind to new possibilities and it takes something special to call our attention to it.

Kilson

My · pessimism might have suggested a certain serviceability—I think all stances are best seen as serviceable. I'm basically a kind of pragmatic sort, and if you ask me the very difficult question of how educational institutions arrive at this notion of the intellectual validity of whatever they're about, I would say the test is always best put in terms of problems. Universities therefore study the social structure of the lower-class Negro family ultimately because it constitutes and represents certain kinds of problems that the society as a society can no longer ignore, and when somehow and in some way there is a relative consensus that the bloody thing *is* a problem, it automatically gets intellectual validity. I don't know of any way of responding to what is, after all, a very difficult question except to reduce it to, in effect, a kind of pragmatic problem-formulation.

Question

It seems to me that many of the queries are not keeping in mind the service of this gathering. As I understand it, this gathering grew out of a firm belief on the part of the Yale Black Student Alliance that for various reasons the value system and the culture which seems to support it, together with its institutions, is somehow not very meaningful to them and that therefore they set out to persuade or at least to precipitate a dialogue among people of various intellectual traditions and institutions of higher learning. I think in that sense we're sort of presented with a *fait accompli;* that is, there *are* individuals in *many* states *here* who are very, very concerned with the extent to which the black experience has been neglected; they are petitioning politely in some cases, not so politely in others, to their institutions to seriously consider incorporating the black experience into the regular curriculum. Now, I'm afraid that what I've witnessed here today, with a few exceptions, is an attempt to intellectualize out of existence and significance the very important ques-

tion that the young Yale black students are posing; that is, I think
we are trying to intellectualize ourselves out of common sense.

Another point I'd like to make is that we should try not to burden
ourselves with solving administrative tasks that are better left to
deans and curriculum committees as to how to stimulate scholars
along these lines. Let's instead come to some agreement as to whether or not there is a case to be made for the inclusion of the black
experience into the regular college curriculum. I would like very
much to ask Mr. Kilson if he believes—as he has already implied, that
given his personal researches into the area, there is not that much to
be gained by putting the black experience into the curriculum?

Kilson

You put the issue wrongly: your tone is anti-intellectual and I
don't like anti-intellectuals. I was not trying to intellectualize the
issue out of existence. Quite the contrary: I was trying to give the
issue a wider setting in meaning, in value, in what experiences have
been with respect to black men so as not to make awful mistakes
and awful errors and not to track along silly, bizarre, and essentially
therapeutic lines. I was not trying to intellectualize out of existence
this problem, trying to run away from the problem, with respect to
actual curriculum. I'm not a curriculum man—there are people here
who are; I can hardly work up my three lectures a week in Harvard
College—it's hard work, for me it is, let alone to work up a curriculum which would cover all the things that some people would like to
see done in the field of black studies in the university. It's not fair to
ask me that question.

Obviously, I consider the black experience one that is reducible to
serious intellectual endeavor. I was not questioning it. Do you want
me to tell you what courses should be in it? I can't do that. I have an
idea, but one must be modest about these things. I have an idea what
courses should be put in for the study of modern African politics,
which is what I spend 90 percent of my time doing, and I also
dabble in the study of contemporary Negro political leadership. I'm
about to undertake the study of leadership in the ghetto in Philadelphia, where my brother happens to be a politician, and when I get
the monograph underway another year or so from now I shall be

able to make some suggestions from my own experience as to what American Negro politics ought to look like as a course—but I think it's unfair to say that I was trying to run from the issue.

Question

At the risk of belaboring an issue, I want to return to what I still regard as the crucial question, a question which I am not satisfied that Mr. Cruse answered. In order to be clear in my own mind, I want to say a few things about that. What I want to say is based, I think, upon the principle of education as common sense, which I don't believe has any racial parameters. The literature which brought me here said that we were going to discuss the relevance of the study and teaching of the black experience in relation to issues that have been presented and questions that have been developed for the inclusion of these issues in *general curriculum offerings.* Now, I'm here not to examine the curriculum as developed for the black students; I'm interested in the curriculum for *all* students at Yale University, black and white. On the basis of my own experience in philosophy, I think a very good case can be made for including more black history, more reference to black art, than there has been in the past in terms of historical conditions. But I'm puzzled about the expectation of that phrase "the black experience," because there are two moments here in the black experience—one was the moment of knowledge, the other was the moment of commitment. Not to put too fine a phrase on it, it was really a *revolutionary* commitment which was implied in Mr. Cruse's position.

Now, when I try to formulate an educational basis for expanding the curriculum to do justice to materials that are not included—not only *black* experience, but Mexican and other experience—I pitch my argument to my colleagues on the basis of educational validity and on the grounds of educational common sense. I appeal to my black friends to realize that it would be a little futile to try to convince my colleagues of the validity of such a commitment, which is a precondition for their accepting something which is educationally viable. There are all sorts of differences among white teachers, just as there are differences among blacks—as was stressed by these first speakers. The least common denominator in the university is our activity as members of the community of scholars, and it's on *that* basis that I think a strong case can be made. I am confident, on the basis of my educational political experience, that if this is confused with the notion of revolutionary commitment, then we may end with a sort of educational disaster.

Let me present to you, Mr. Cruse, a rather bizarre historical analogy. I spent a few years in the Weimar Republic and observed the rise and growth of Nazi sentiment. Now, the experience of the Jews in Germany turned out to be worse than what has been experienced by Negroes in the United States, and the great key to Nazi propaganda was a racial myth. Now, I am convinced if there had been a scientific study of anthropology in the German university, or if there had been some reference to the Jewish experience which didn't merely identify it with the activity in retail trade, which the Nazis expressed, but had also given it some historical perspective—if that had been done, I think it would have been very difficult for the Nazi mythology to succeed. But now, suppose that someone had said, "Let's study the Jewish experience, but to study the Jewish experience you must also commit yourself to Jewish nationalism, to Zionism—and make that a prerequisite to the study." Well, it almost sounds like a *reductio ad absurdum* of the view, as if the validity of studying the truth about race is not important enough to justify it educationally without any other further justification. I am prepared to maintain that the educational validity of studying the black experience, when it is divorced from any specific black nationalist standpoint, is a study which might include an analysis of both the black nationalist standpoint and the *critics* of that standpoint. Such a point of view would do much more, I think, to further the educational maturity of our students than what you have proposed. And so I submit that unless we resolve this very clearly, we have not yet understood the impact, even the content, of your view.

Cruse

You present a difficult challenge; I would relent and agree with you that one satisfactory basis for proposing the initiation of black studies is to affirm that it is of educational value as an intellectual pursuit, as in the case of *all* social studies in the university curriculum. If we further included in that approach the possibility, as you suggest, that one could discuss the black nationalist ideology and the pros and cons of that ideology, I would accept this approach as a premise for the inclusion of black studies in the university.

I would, however, have to differ with you on your attempt to equate the black situation in America with regard to black studies and the situation in Germany with regard to the Jewish question—or any other European minority question. I don't think these two facts of social life are equatable in Western intellectual terms. I would argue that this confusion is one of the main intellectual rationales that has been used for many decades to serve to obscure an already obscure question in America, namely, the relationship between a white race coming from the Western tradition and a black race which historically does not derive from that tradition.

I would maintain that, in the case of Germany and the Jews, we were dealing with a historical problem, a social problem, involving two peoples *both* of whom derive from the same tradition. The struggle—the ideological struggle, the social, class struggle—between them was one in which both factors were themselves products of the same tradition. The roots of this struggle in Germany had other different roots from the sources of the black and white crisis in America. The question of the Jewish minority in Europe was one where the fortunes of Jews in different countries varied considerably. Jews had their "ups and downs" depending on the age, depending on the society, depending on the cultural development of the respective countries in which they resided. In Germany, the Jews had reached the pinnacle of social acceptance; they had reached the pinnacle of economic, cultural, and political equality within German society. The arguments and the conflicts between the Nazi ideology and the Jewish presence did not derive from the consensus that Jews as such were racially or intellectually, economically, or socially inferior. That ideology came from a Nazi party, to be sure; but it came *after the fact* of Jewish acceptance into the social and cultural body politic.

In America the point of departure, from the standpoint of the black experience vis-a-vis the white reality, is one in which the thrust is for a greater degree of social equality. It is impossible for me to say at this moment whether or not this is going to succeed. It is impossible for me to say whether the black experience, once it (hopefully) achieves absolute social equality, might not suffer the same reaction that the Jews suffered in Germany after having attained a certain status. I can only speak from the perspective of the contemporary situation in terms of what the demands of the hour are, irrespective of how any intellectual approach might view this. At this moment I don't think that anyone, black or white, can counsel intellectual evasion of a clear and present problem in race relations by introducing all kinds of considerations which might have related to other instances in other societies at other times and use them in such a way as to lessen the importance or the meaningfulness of what we are trying to achieve. I don't believe that attributing ideological or political ramifications to the acceptance of black studies detracts from the importance of the inclusion of such studies in any way. I don't believe that mere consideration of these ramifications as possible deterrents to acceptance of the idea should, or does, lessen the importance or urgent necessity for inclusion of black studies.

For too many years the intellectual world in America has been hemmed in and delimited by a persistent form of what people are pleased to call "the pragmatic method"—of teaching, of philosophy, of instruction. This pragmatic approach has had widespread ramifications to American life, to university curricula, to the role of the university in society, and to whether or not the university should play a purely scholarly role or social role. I think the present situation at Columbia University is a direct result of the insistence among members of that intellectual community on hemming themselves in with this traditional pragmatic approach to scholarly responsibilities. I don't think that anyone at Columbia University—student body or faculty—wanted this sort of breakdown of the university administration to occur. But, it came. And it did not come because someone deliberately planted or attempted to include a course of studies which led to this sort of dislocation in the university's function. Columbia's problems resulted from the chosen role of the university itself. This role is now open to question, and has been open to question for many years. Columbia is suffering the effects of its lack of social responsibility; it is suffering because it has maintained a traditionally pragmatic approach to scholarship and the role of the university in social life.

I am sorry to say that in the resistance to implementing black studies, we are seeing the same kind of attitude presented toward this new problem as has been expressed traditionally at Columbia on other, broader social issues. The major thrust for black studies comes from a part of the student body; I think that the university should consider this fact as well as what is happening at other universities due to a dereliction of responsibility on scholarly levels before any decision is made to reject black studies on traditional pragmatic grounds.

THE BLACK COMMUNITY AND THE UNIVERSITY:
A COMMUNITY ORGANIZER'S PERSPECTIVE

Maulana Ron Karenga

I would like to start off by saying something that is not as academic as it is relevant, and that is: *All praise is due to black people.*

I came here in the dark, in a sense, because I didn't know who I was going to be talking to. But whether I talk to blacks or whites, somehow whites always tend to get the message. Now, when I say that all praise is due to black people, that suggests the scope and content of what I'm going to say tonight. I'm not as impressed with academic distinctions as I am with concrete programs that might better the lives of black people in this country. My first commitment emotionally is to black people; everything that I do, think, or say is intended for their benefit; and I would sacrifice the discussion of philosophy for the satisfaction of any concrete need.

Now, my title is a bit long—I've almost forgotten what it was—but I suppose the question really is whether or not white universities have anything to offer black communities. That's a good question. If they do have something to offer, what is their role? That is also a good question. I see no difference between white universities and white people; and we have three roles for white people as well as for white universities. For the sake of academic courtesy I suppose I should offer them as a "syndrome." There are three things: nonintervention, foreign aid, and civilizing committees.

What is nonintervention? What you have to understand is that you cannot intervene in the black community. You don't really have any role in the community; your basic role is outside the community, external to it. And you also have to understand that the university is not basically an educational institution—it's a *political* institution. Everything moves in terms of political power, because without that power nothing is accomplished. The educational institution has traditionally been, and is now, one of the institutions that the power structure maintains, in order to reinforce its own position. One learns to be a "better American," I assume, by going to an American university; where else could one learn to be a better American than in a university? What you have to understand is that you should not fool yourselves by thinking that education is an academic thing; it is basically a political thing, and it provides identity, purpose, and direction within an American context.

If you are a white institution, for example, and blacks come in here, then the blacks come out "white," too, unless they have some different identity, purpose, and direction to shield them from all of this. The only relevance I see for a white institution in terms of blacks is for learning technical skills; there is little else that whites can teach them. As far as the humanities and the social sciences are concerned, white people have little or nothing to offer.

I suppose I should like to be challenged—I prefer a debate to assertions in situations like this, if for no other reason than the convenience of conversation—so let me briefly recapitulate what I was saying. It can be summed up in a sentence: the white university is not primarily an educational institution but a political one, and it seeks to maintain the power base of American society. All those people who go to work for the CIA, for the government at large, for big industry (which is government, in a sense) come from the universities. What you are doing here, really, is trying to find out how you can stop intervening in black people's affairs.

The experiment of Columbia University in terms of black people's affairs is very relevant here. That was an intervention in the community. We say that we are another country—you have to accept that. We are a colony ruled by a mother country—that's the outside world—we live in another world. What we have to do, then, is to try desperately to keep the outside world from imposing its authority and its value system upon us. Its values are communicated best through its university system. And again, the first thing I would propose for a university is nonintervention—nonintervention in terms of political intervention, that is—not taking over things in the black community, tearing down buildings and putting up your things.

Now, of course, when I say these things I am not petitioning you and asking you. I am doing this simply for the sake of conversation—because I suppose I owe it. I don't believe we should ask you not to do this; I believe that we should build enough power to *stop* you from doing this. But I am just identifying your actions now; I am not dealing with the matter of how we should *curtail* them.

Nonintervention also means that you should not try to control those bodies in the black communities that would create for black people what similar bodies in white communities create for white people. You have to realize that you cannot make decisions for us any more. If we are going to be a free people and gain the identity, purpose, and direction which will let us be black people, we cannot be under external influences from white people.

The second thing that you could do—and I suppose must do—is to provide "foreign aid." If we are "another country," then certainly you are "foreigners." Now, that aid should be broken down into two parts: financial aid, which is self-explanatory; and technical aid, which might need some explanation. Financial aid has to do with the money that you have collected. The university is a financial institution of sorts; it has access to money that other people don't have. Now, if one is really going to do something for his country—not for us, but for his community, for the community around him, which is closing in on him, he thinks—then it would seem politically expedient, not out of love of humanity or black people, *not* to take a tape recorder, put on tennis shoes, grow a beard, and go into a community to "investigate," and produce another study that only bores you by its length, and does not inform you by its content. *Stop* things like that, and *make* those financial contributions—contributions that are really reparations. Such a relationship would involve our having the financial institutions to receive that money—and there's that first point again, of nonintervention. What white universities usually do is "set up projects." By controlling the finances of such projects they control at the same time the political allegiances of the people in that institution. Again, I repeat, universities are political institutions. They would not *exist* unless they went along with the political climate in the country or in the region where they are functioning. So the first thing under "foreign aid" is financial aid, without strings.

The second thing is technical aid—technical aid in terms of research. White people have an affinity for research. Research bores me—statistics and collecting. I don't have the "pack rat mentality" that I've noticed in others. Yet the university has always been a framework in which people could do this type of thing, do research. Do your research and produce your research—so that black people can take it and use it to their own advantage. But the research should be done without interpretation. Data should be collected and turned over. It should not be interpreted, for when it is interpreted, it becomes of use to you only. But it could be technical aid, in terms of the ways and means that black people might better themselves, if they had certain data not available to them now.

The last thing—and this is really the most important thing, because white people are not going to give up anything that is not to their own advantage—is a civilizing committee. Perhaps that's a harsh word, but I didn't come here to please people; I came to inform them. We have witnessed the phenomenal way in which white people have tried to civilize us for 450 years when it was they, I suppose—and the "I suppose" is for social courtesy—who were uncivilized. To civilize is the university's first real duty, and the strength of your duty would depend on how you communicated a *new* ideology to the people outside of the university, or perhaps even to some instructors and administrators within the university.

Actually, I was trying to keep you university people out of this, so that you could just do the "humanitarian" thing that I suppose you believe you would like to do. Universities always like to think of themselves as liberal institutions, humanitarian institutions; they even teach subjects under what they call "humanities," which I suppose has something to do with "liberalism" and "humanitarianism." So I would say that those universities that have the money, personnel, equipment, and technical know-how ought to figure out some way to inform those white people in this country who don't have the views that they're supposed to have—that is, humanitarian views.

I see that as a major project, and I think that if white universities would spearhead this effort, it would be much more successful than it is now. Not that it's going to meet with overwhelming success, I assure you, because there are political considerations, and there is going to be political pressure on you to stop this nonsense. Nonetheless, you owe it to your tradition, at least your avowed tradition, to make some effort in this direction. It is needed, and I think that perhaps you would provide the best source of it.

Let me recapitulate—and I was brief intentionally so that you could argue with me. There are three things I see the university as needing to do. First, nonintervention with regard to the black community: stop imposing yourself through projects that only benefit you and the white community, or the business community. Stop trying to make political decisions about what we do. Do not pass value judgments on what we do. Second, afford us foreign aid— financial and technical. As I said before, the university is one of the largest financial institutions in the country, and as a matter of reparations perhaps some kind of transaction could be made so that we could be repaid for some of the efforts that our forefathers made. Technical aid should be given in terms of universities having the facilities and personnel to collect data that we can interpret and use to our own benefit. Third, and the most important thing, create a civilizing movement in this country among whites. I think that if you don't have any social content in this educational thing, then the academic institution is of no importance at all. That is why we concluded long ago that we use reason too well to be overly impressed by other people's use of it. We are more interested in living life than in discussing it. I would suggest that the civilizing movement start from the university—this on the very basis that the university has always had an avowed tradition of liberalism, humanitarianism, and a few other "isms" that are related, but should not be mentioned, lest you be bored by the long list of complimentary adjectives, and forget what else I have said.

QUESTION PERIOD

Question

Mr. Karenga, given the fact that there are black people in predominantly white institutions, and following up your line of thought that one of the things that happens very often to black people who attend such institutions is that they come out so white that they are of very little value to the black community, do you feel that there is anything these predominantly white institutions could do to provide a kind of *positive* nonintervention, to provide a countervailing force to the conditioning of black people which takes place in such institutions, given the value system under which they operate and their political nature? What specific things might they do to prevent that?

Karenga

That's a very good question. I suppose I should answer that in terms of the foreign aid thing—that would be on the educational level, which I didn't discuss because I was sure that it would come up. Something very profound has happened; whites really don't understand it, and some blacks have a very difficult time understanding it too. Black people want three basic things, identity, purpose, and direction, and unless black people can be provided with this they will not be able to function as black people but will end up always as servants to white people. In the end they will bore you, even at your "conversation parties," because they will have nothing to say except a poorly selected quotation from one of your writers, not from their own. The black studies curricula that universities have should be supervised by blacks; you should import black teachers. I know there is a shortage of black teachers, but then perhaps you could even provide a separate institution where we could learn. If the salaries were right, I'm sure even some of us would come and provide you with the beginning knowledge of what should be taught. Most people really don't know what to teach; they are still interpreting things as whites have written them. For example, if someone argued that we should put Negro history into every high school and university in this country, I would say that to teach "Negro" history—with that word—is really to do us a disservice. Operating under an old historiography, we are really only concentrating black inferiority and giving complexes. We would propose that a *new* historiography be developed, and that it be developed along three lines: change of frame of reference, change of definition, and change of interpretation.

In terms of frame of reference we can apply this demand to any subject, and social science let us say, because like in mathematics there is racism, but we don't want to belabor this point. For example, Jane and John, one and two white people make three white people, that type of thing. In terms of frame of reference, let's take history as an example. If I am going to refer to someone as great as Marcus Garvey as a "Black Moses," what am I saying? I'm saying that Garvey was tough, but Moses is really what's happening and Garvey at best is second. And if I want to call King Shaka a "Black Napoleon," I'm again saying that Napoleon is really what's happening and Shaka, well, he's black. Now, I'm saying that without a change of frame of reference we need not even teach black subjects. I don't even want to hear any "Negro literature." A peanut is really no symbol of racial pride, and Jiffy and the rest of these comics have done more than George Washington Carver ever did. If I communicate this information, using the same frame of reference as the whites who wrote my history before, then I cannot even develop myself; I have no appreciation of myself. All I am doing is getting inferiority in a concentrated structure. I'm against that.

I'm for changing the frame of reference, because psycho-linguistically I could deal with definitions and interpretations in which "white" becomes that which is not really happening and "black" becomes something beautiful. You see, it is not enough to say "black, black, black." One must define black, and if one is in an academic situation, one must move not only to *feel* it but to *define* it so that one can communicate it to others.

For example, if I say, "What is 'black'?" and somebody says, "It's a feeling," well, I say hate is a feeling, too—and they say, well, man, what do you want me to define this for? It is because—if we have any academic appreciation for things, we must have definitions.

Psycho-linguistically the lack of positive definitions of blackness is what *destroyed* us. One need but look at the white man's use of his language in which everything associated with black was inferior—"black market," "blackmail," "black nigger," etc., to understand what I mean. I'm saying that in terms of curriculum, unless you change those three things—frame of reference, definition, and interpretation—I would not even like to see black studies taught. What the university must do is to change the curriculum, and change it in terms of those three things.

I am sick of white people "communicating" things to me. There's something about them when they do it. Either they're overzealous in their attempt to prove the nonexistence of racism within them, or they're "new liberals" who don't care and are uninfluential and uninformed; the moment they don't care about who they are talking to, they don't care about the subject matter that they are gathering. The result is that their work is poorly put together, but they think they have a right to say it because they're white. And then there is the paternalist, who is boring and who is really behind the real world.

I feel that *black* people should communicate black things. Why? We teach that methodology is very important in instruction, but unless one understands that education is more than just the communication of ideas for political effect, we'll never see that education is basically two things: the provision of inspiration and the provision of information. Now, we put inspiration first, because black people are an emotional people and our first commitment is an emotional one. Quite a few times myself I have been extremely rational, and blacks have no counter to it, but they disagree—either out of a false sense of Socratic tradition, which says that it is intelligent to disagree even if someone is right, or because he has been emotionally estranged from me. We teach that the first commitment is an emotional one. I cannot become emotionally committed to a white person, no matter what he says: I can laugh at what he does if it's ridiculous enough, but I cannot become emotionally committed to him. I must have an image to identify with and that image must be personified in the man who's communicating that thing to me or the images that he projects. I'm saying that education is basically an inspirational thing and that methodology should take into consideration inspiration before information.

Think of most black students in high school and even in the university. They come here only because their parents sent them or to escape the draft or for five other reasons that we have developed in a syndrome to communicate to them. They never really understand why they come, and so they ask the question, "Why should I go to school?" If they were inspired, that would never be the question. Sterile data has nothing to do with real life, so change the curricula and change the methodology.

Question

I'm asking what I hope is a methodological question. The bulk of what you said revolves around attitudes, values, what you've classified under "inspiration" as contrasted in your methodological point with "information." One point of "information," as I picked it up, that one might necessarily include as a cover to the black experience—assuming that my attitude is partly right, that I can get to the values—is Marcus Garvey. Now, is there more "information" of a specific sort that you would want to mention as appropriate to a black curriculum? Or is the black attitude, value, etc., the information itself? [*Karenga:* What you're looking for is "subject matter"?] Well, assuming that I can live up to your expectations of the understanding of attitude, value, etc., let me go on to the question whether there is any specific "information" that I ought to add to the curriculum?

Karenga

Of course. The first thing that we think of is black history. That's the most accessible subject and that's really the place where one is "inspired" and "informed." One is inspired by the images that are projected and one is informed by the processes that these images went through, whether they succeeded or didn't in the real world. Now, we have developed another type of interpretation in which we say that none of our black heroes fail. We believe in progressive perfection: they did as much as they could given the time and circumstance. I would never expect Garvey to do as much as I am doing, if for no other reason than that he didn't have this mike or tape. So, let's say black history.

Another thing is sociology. Sociology is what, really? The study of groups? There are many, many black people in sociology; in fact, there is an overabundance of black people in sociology, it is no doubt the easiest course. What I would suggest, since it overlaps with political science so much in terms of its theoretical content, we ought to dismiss it. I would think that "political change" and "social change" could be combined; there is no difference big enough for that distinction. I never really understood why sociology became a separate discipline from political science.

As for political science as an academic thing, I think it's of no use either. I remember when I was at UCLA in graduate school and we were studying international relations. The professor asked the students to evaluate his course—and I suppose he needed that: he probably felt very bad about what he had done the whole semester—so he came to me and said, "What did you think of it?" I said, "Well, I think it's a bit too theoretical and I have an ethnic aversion to theory." He said, "What do you mean by 'ethnic aversion'?" I said, "Because of the theoretical influence of Christianity on black people, they've been more concerned with swings over Jordan than shoes on earth, and I had hoped that this class could give me some political mottoes that I could concretely apply in my dealings with larger groups." I think we should learn how groups can deal with each other, how they can increase their power. I think that if social change is not taught in terms of how to increase power, it's meaningless.

Those courses should be dealing with concrete issues, and the examples they use should *not* be examples that Marx gave, *not* examples that Lenin gave, but they should be examples that black people are familiar with in terms of reference even if not in terms of reality. There is enough data and "subject matter" right in this country. If you're going to make a study, collect data that you can communicate so that people can learn how to deal on the political level with the community, the state, and the nation. Those are the things, *practical* things, that should be taught.

In literature, take LeRoi Jones as an example. Why should somebody be teaching Shakespeare today, with his "thee" and "thou"? People don't talk that way any more. I don't want to hear it. White people can. I'm not saying white people can't learn it—they like that sort of stuff. But it's not the real world to *us,* tight pants and funny hats. LeRoi Jones' work deals with the reality black people know. His work communicates with blacks and is therefore useful in an educational context.

I have never been a chauvinist in terms of *our* culture: I say what we have is good for us, not for you. And likewise I would like to impress upon you that what is good for you is not good for me. There should be a *division* in America. You try to impress everyone that we're all one country. Let me speak absolutely: America is *divided*—and therefore your curriculum must be divided. And it must be divided in terms of how *black* people see it, not in terms of how white people would like it to be. After all, Uncle Sam doesn't look like me—for obvious reasons: I'm younger!

Question

By way of preface, I am not a sociologist. [*Karenga:* That helps!] My first question is this: Aren't you compromising the purity of your apartheid doctrine by speaking in English, which is, of course a "white" and "racist" language? But if you find the use of English helpful to you, isn't it possible that there might be other aspects of what you call "white culture" which might be helpful to blacks in America? That's my first question—I've forgotten my second question.

Karenga

Well, if you can forget your second question, I'm going to forget your first! I mean, don't produce unnecessary hostility.

First of all, you must have gathered by now that it is a bit presumptuous to identify my philosophy as apartheid. You could have saved time by asking me, since I speak too well for myself to be spoken for. I think that's an Afrikaner word which really escapes me in terms of relevance. So, why English? I could speak in Swahili, but how many people here know it? I thought I came to talk to white people. When one goes to China, one speaks in Chinese; I thought that was understood. English is not a part of white culture that I've assumed; I've only adjusted to my audience—that's a *double entendre*. I don't like people to tell me what I'm saying. I like people to *ask* me what I'm saying. The English language is a convenience; it's a technical thing that I'm doing in terms of the people that I'm talking to. I just don't see the relevance of your "point." Perhaps you should have another chance so that you can rephrase what you've said—I would concede that.

Question Continued

The reason I characterized your position as one of apartheid is because of your emphasis on separateness. You have stressed the importance of separating Negro or "black" culture from white culture. You yourself talked about the fact that the English language was, so to speak, "drenched" with race-consciousness, and you pointed to the significance and connotations of the word "black." Therefore, I think it was a legitimate inference on my part that you regard the English language as part of the white culture which you reject. That's the background of my first question. May I ask my second question? [*Karenga:* Of course.]

My second question is this: On the assumption that you speak for the black people of this country—[*Karenga:* Now, please. No, no, I *don't* "speak for" the black people of this country.] —on the assumption that your goals might represent what the black people of this country would want, I would be in favor of helping you. But my problem is that you don't seem to make it possible for those who are not black to help "put the shoes" on black people, to help black people get jobs, food, and power. You can't always do it on a local level—you have to do it on a national and federal level. Therefore, all my life, through the NAACP and other organizations, I've been in favor of a coalition of action with Negroes, with Labor, and other groups, in order to make more "shoes" available, more jobs available, more vacation available for blacks who may have your point of view. But according to *you*, all we can do is "not interfere," give "technical aid," and become "civilized." I would like to know where is the place and function of cooperation or coalition in order to achieve some of what I think are desirable objectives of the black people in this country.

Karenga

Well, it's very difficult to respond to that. You said so much—I was wondering whether I should add anything to it. Any addition would take from it. I would just say that really you didn't understand what I was saying. First of all, you refused to let me stop you when you were assuming that I was speaking for black people: I'm only speaking for those people who believe what I believe. Those are the only people I speak for, and that should be obvious.

As for the second thing: you belong to the NAACP, right? Well, the NAACP is a black group so I have nothing bad to say about that. That's good. Somebody should send you a letter for that. I have nothing else to say about that. And as far as its program is concerned, Roy Wilkins could explain it better than I, since he's in it. As far as your wanting to help to give us shoes—no doubt you have some knowledge of Christianity: Jesus said "Man does not live by bread alone"—that's an African phrase: Jesus went to school in Africa (you remember that he was absent for some time)—what I am saying to you, Sir, is that your helping *me* is not the point. What you should be helping is your society—that's what is in need of help. And I'm saying that *not* in terms of a scare phrase. You were so interested in labeling me that even when I showed you that I wasn't the person that you thought you were talking to, you refused to stop talking. Because you had so conceived of what you *should* say that even though I said something totally different, you refused to hear it. In an academic community—I thought this was understood, that's why I didn't mention it earlier—one should always try to avoid labels. Labels relieve one of the responsibility of thinking: one could call a man a "communist" and dismiss everything he said after that; even if he said, "America should survive," you'd say, "No, that's a Communist statement." I would say that you really can't help me.

You've got to get out of that brand of paternalism. You can help your society, though. Help this great country of yours, because this country is in trouble. I don't want to be as mundane as to talk about things that are happening in the street at such a university as this, but I should refer to it briefly: things are not as they were when the

NAACP was formed. So, I would urge you not to develop programs to help black people, because *black* people must do that. That's why I talked about nonintervention.

You end your statement by saying what *I* think. Of course, this is an academic community, so I'm welcoming ideas, but no one would welcome them in the street. The whole cry is for self-determination—that is the reality you have to face. You have to face the political reality of the black community just like you face the political reality of the national community, the white community. I'm saying that it is good that you want to help, but help *yourself.* If you've got a humanitarian urge, then help America—and then if you help America, you will save this society.

What is America's biggest problem? I suppose we should forget about "the credibility gap" with regard to the President and accept the report. And it said something about "racism," among other things that were really too tiringly listed to be read, so you should understand that the problem of racism should be solved. Not for me, but for America: Why do I have to say you should love me? I never felt I needed that. Do you want me to send you a book?

Someone else should ask something, because I don't want to keep going on this man: someone's going to feel that I'm going overboard.

Question

I only venture to speak as a result of your comment on sociology, since I am a sociologist!

I happen to agree with nearly all you've said. My question is to press you a little further. Let us assume that the white community in this country heeds your advice: does not intervene, provides foreign aid, and performs a civilizing function among some groups, as it should. What then do you see for the future? What is it that we're going to? What kind of society will we then achieve? What is the result?

Karenga

One could have two visions, but as I'm not a prophet, I shall deal with only one. I could see a balance of power. The whole question is a question of power. Simply stated, power is the ability to realize one's will. I think that the reason why whites are having this discussion and why we have to meet and organize is because we like power—and because if we had power, these questions would become irrelevant and we would realize our will as we saw it. I can see a balance of power. I don't see us co-existing until that power balance is achieved. I can say that now, but the intensity and quality of the struggle will really determine the relationship: you've got to understand that. That is why the civilizing or—let's change it, let me use a euphemism—the "humanizing" movement is so important. If it works, the intensity and quality of the struggle will be different than if it falls. The make-up of the future depends upon the struggle itself. For example, me: I am really only interested in love and study; I'm not really interested in violence and stuff like that, but here we are. This is a violent world, and I can't pretend I don't live in it. That should be considered.

Let me recapitulate and sum up all this by saying that I have no answer as to how things will come out. As for me, I am only interested in the balance of power—that no one have the power to determine my destiny except me, that I live in a place where I can realize and fulfill all my desires and needs according to my own determination. I have no real desire to enforce my will on anybody: we make a distinction between nationalism, which we practice, and racism, which others practice. Racism says, What I have is not only good for me, it's good for you and I'm going to enforce it on you. Nationalism says, What I have is good for me, it is not necessarily good for others. So, I would like to see just a balance of power. The struggle, however, will answer your question.

Question

Some of us really aren't much of anything, but we're on curriculum committees who are hard-pressed by students asking for the inclusion of black studies in the curriculum. Do you have any friendly advice to us? That is, to those of us who have to go back and talk to these students? Should we go back and try to turn them off, or should we go back and try to turn them on?

Karenga

For black studies? Definitely, you should encourage them. I think it's very interesting that you should say "friendly advice." I don't mean to seem hostile—I've always been mild-mannered. I read an article in the *Post* where the man said I was deceptively mild-mannered—he was angry with me. But I think you should encourage the development of black studies as much as you can. Better than encouragement, though, I think you should do it. I tried to tell you to stay away from pushing for anything for blacks, except in terms of the technical things. Now, if you're on a curriculum committee, then you have access to that and you can do that. So, then, just do it. Black people tell you what they want emotionally. White people used to say, "Wait a minute now, that's too emotional, how can that be done." White people have computers: what we tell you emotionally, you devise it technically. That would solve the problem.

Even if you do initiate black studies your work should be evaluated. It would be good if you brought in black consultants, who are much more informed on these things than some other people. I think you should have one—I didn't mean to communicate that you shouldn't have one; I was just saying that the quality of it should be determined by those people who are more informed about it, and those people are the black people.

Question

Let me push you a little bit further, if I may. You've played academic games, you've got a feel and an ear for the street people, you know what's happening. What in the way of courses would you recommend? You talked about history, you talked about some other things; but if you were in charge of the Yale curriculum committee, how would you handle it? In terms of developing specific courses or sets of studies, not in terms of rhetoric.

Karenga

One should not dismiss the word; in the beginning was the word. And even if I discuss the curriculum, I shall have to use words. So, don't discourage me.

I didn't bring a list of courses with me. I suppose I could be creative on the spot—we're impulsive anyhow. Let's go down it again. One, I would have black history; black history in two things: Afro-American history and African history. Second, I would have Swahili, because I am interested in psycho-linguistically moving black people to a language which can communicate collective values. We're against individualism. We're for personality, not individuality. We say that personality is that which is me in relation to everyone else—individuality is me in *spite* of everyone else. What white people have developed in terms of individualism is good for them; I would not attack it—it's an "American" thing, and one should not attack "American" things.

If we move from African and Afro-American history to Swahili, then the next thing that I would teach is cultural philosophy. There, I would develop a syndrome of seven basic values black people should have and give substance to all of those. Those are mythology (that's black), a value for history in terms of the frame of reference I gave you earlier, a model for social organization, a model for economic organization (which, of course, would be cooperative economics), a model for political organization (which would give black people a model of how to gain, maintain, and use power), a creative motif (which we've developed also in terms of functional, collective, and committed art, like LeRoi Jones'), and finally, an ethos that would be based on achievement of the other six.

I would move from cultural philosophy in terms of values to political philosophy in terms of the political trends we've gone through—from the early nationalism of David Walker to the abolitionist philosophy of Frederick Douglass to the father of black nationalism, Marcus Garvey, to religious nationalism in the form of Islam under the Honorable Elijah Muhammad to religio-political nationalism under Malcolm X to the politics of Black Power with Carmichael and SNCC and Rap Brown, and move finally to the cultural nationalism that US has produced and developed. These are political trends. I suppose I could go on indefinitely in terms of things I would like to see done, but if you pay me and give me a consulting job I could come back . . .

Question

On the language thing, why particularly Swahili as opposed to other African languages or a combination of other African languages?

Karenga

That's a very good question. We use Swahili for our organization, and we chose it on the basis of two things: (1) Swahili is a pan-African language, that is, it is non-tribal, it is the only language in Africa that is non-tribal; (2) we cannot claim any tribe, we can only claim Africa itself, so we are the first Pan-Africans, of a sort. If we choose Hausa, there's a Hausa tribe. If we choose Zulu, there's a Zulu tribe. So, then, where should we go but to Swahili, which has no tribe? And because, also, linguistically Swahili adjusts better to the conversations of modern day: it has been able to absorb at a more rapid pace those technical terms that are necessary in terms of communicating modern events. I would suppose there are no challenges to that.

DECK THE IVY RACIST HALLS:
THE CASE OF BLACK STUDIES

Gerald A. McWorter

Following Brother Karenga and the previous discussion, I feel it best to make two introductory comments. First, like many black intellectuals, I recently faced a crisis in my own life; and so, though I have to admit the fact that by training I'm a sociologist (and occupy an academic position), I speak really as an extension of the black community. The other comment is simply that I think the symposium that's being held here is very impressive, but—as many people feel—I think there are many false issues being raised. I don't know whether or not these are consciously being raised as false issues, but I think the question whether or not the black experience is one worthy of intellectual inquiry is indeed, beyond a question of a doubt—and everybody here, it seems to me, as intelligent human beings ought to recognize that if *any* human experience is relevant for intellectual consideration—the black experience has to be included. And the notion that it would be questioned in such an audience is too grotesque to be amusing. This morning I was thinking, what would be the reaction at Fisk University if someone stood up and asked the question, "Is it intellectually relevant, significant, or can one defend being concerned about the black experience?" Apparently, there are some people here who are having difficulty with that question. I also wondered what would happen if you were in China and you raised the question about the Chinese experience—or you were talking to a group of American Jews and you raised the question, whether or not it was relevant to be concerned intellectually with the Jewish experience. I don't know what the other brothers and sisters in the audience felt as some of you debated it, but then it was merely another typically sick American experience.

In beginning, it is important to understand that as black intellectuals think on these issues more and more, things are becoming very clear. Basically this clarity has to do with a set of assumptions that black people have made for a long period of time. We rationalize our various positions on the basis of those assumptions. I find here that people have different sets of assumptions and are asking black intellectuals rather than to rationalize positions on basic assumptions *black* people hold, you're asking that black people make rationalizations of positions based on the assumptions that *white* people hold. I could also make the same point when we raised the whole question of science and ideology: the "race relations" debate that white people carry on about "science" and "ideology" is something that we feel, basically, is a closed question. Whatever you do, the *fact* is that this is a racist country and that the scientists who have operated in this country, by and large, have been racists. Intentionally or unintentionally, the fact is that they have functioned as such and so have their theories. This is something that we have reacted to on the basis of survival needs. So, when black social scientists speak, if white people are confused as to whether or not they are speaking ideologically or as "detached scientists," that's not something that black people are concerned with. Rather, we are concerned with survival, we're concerned with prospering, we're concerned with living the life I would assume all human beings in human communities want to live.

As part of my opening statement, I would like to refer you to an essay by the late Dr. DuBois (in *What the Negro Wants,* edited by Rayford Logan) where he reflects on his own experiences, where he talks about the way in which he really believed white people in institutions of higher learning. He basically says that, up until the point that he really came to terms with Marx and Freud, he thought that "truth wins." But when he came to reflect on the set of lived experiences that he had, and the notions of these two men, he saw that if one was concerned about surviving, if one was concerned about progress, if one was concerned about "the good life" and moving any society toward that, then you had to include a little something *other* than an interesting appeal to "Truth" in some abstract, universal sense.

I would like to reflect briefly on five statements. The first statement is that the university has functioned as an agent of racism in these United States. The second statement is that the university can be conceptualized as a manifestation of focused powers, a set of powers. The third statement is that, if the university is to live up to its highest aims, it must be committed to creative change in *whatever* society it finds itself—and become *involved* in that change. The fourth statement is that the black community in this country has matured in an unanticipated way necessitating a re-examination of the peculiar historical dynamics of the black community. And the last statement that I want to reflect on is that if the university is to be relevant for the black community, it must be honest—not only within itself, but within society—and it must use the powers that it has for the kind of positive change that it must become involved in.

Now, the first point about the university functioning as an agent of racism is quite clear. I think that many things that have been said conclude this (often implicitly), not only by speakers but in questions. For example, to raise the question of alternatives between universalism and particularism is really a false kind of issue: the university has functioned in this country like a table with one leg—that is to say, its leg represents an extension of the dominant community, white America, the WASP. In essence, it represents a leg that is grounded in some community other than the black community, while the top of the table is identified as being "universal principles that apply to all human behavior" without the additional legs. So, indeed, that's fantasy, because I don't know of many tables of any size and scope that stand on one leg.

It seems to me that there are any number of ways that we can talk about the university as being an agent of racism. Simply reflect on the change that's occurred in colleges like Yale University and Harvard in the admissions policy, in the standards of evaluation, and in the body of knowledge contained not only in the libraries but in the people walking around it. The dramatic change in the last few years represents, it seems to me, an admission that the university has systematically excluded black people—systematically excluded them in admissions, systematically excluded them in devising standards of evaluation that have nothing to do with the styles of life and the indigenous culture of the black community. And, moreover, when the admissions policy is changed, which indeed must reflect a change in their standards of evaluation, black people are exposed to a body of knowledge which in effect excludes them—not only excludes them, but defines them as being evil, illiterate, and not capable of taking over in this society. It seems to me that the important standards have to do not with the minimum acceptance in any society but rather have to do with the maximum: that is to say, any black person who wants to live as a man must think of himself as being a possible leader among men, and to admit black people into an institution like a university with the notion that we are going to send you out basically to be a minor person in society is *racistic*. It has to do with saying that you have limited opportunities in this society and that you indeed are not as equal as somebody else.

Let's move on to the second statement, which is, it seems to me, more open to question: the university should be conceptualized or re-conceptualized in terms of a set of powers. I would like to mention three such powers. One is the power of knowledge: the university is a reservoir of knowledge. The second is that the university is indeed a social and political institution. The third one is that the university maintains certain powers of socialization, that is, to make people certain kinds of people. In terms of the university being a reservoir of knowledge, there are at least two ways in which this is true. One way is that the university maintains a tradition—that is, the accumulated body of knowledge of a community of people that it can transmit back to that community and maintain over time. The second way in which it is a reservoir of knowledge is in terms of research: the university is committed to innovation and concerned with revealing new knowledge about the world and the people who live in it.

Now, in terms of tradition—and this goes back to the whole question of racism—it seems to me that the black people have been excluded and/or defined as being evil. Black people have, until very recently, in effect gone through a process in the university where they have faced *ahistorical* images; that is to say, black people had no meaningful history but simply a reflection of white people who've had them under their control. I think the second important point about this traditional body of knowledge is that white people who have performed as scientists and as academicians and scholars have indeed been apologists for whatever racist practices exist in society today. The one appropriate example I need mention is the renowned sociologist of Yale University, William Graham Sumner, whose work was used to support the belief that what white people believed had to be changed by the goodness of their hearts and that the government (and other agencies of change) could not produce any significant change, that white people had to sort of naturally agree that everything would be cool so *then* black people might be admitted to the society. Now, we find that at no point in time did the black community accept this.

There are many other examples, a more recent one being the U.S. Department of Labor report by Daniel Moynihan on the black family. Just as a lot of people operate within the framework of the status quo, by and large, social science has been a normative science operating with implicit equilibrium models. What that means is that basically it doesn't have anything to do with *me*—anybody who's concerned with equilibrium, anybody who's concerned with the status quo, has basically defined me *out,* because up until this point (and I suspect it will have to do with the rest of tonight and tomorrow) this is a racist country defined as being totally against me.

The third point, in terms of the traditional body of knowledge, has to do with defining the black community in pathological terms. This again goes back to the whole question of ideology and science, and it relates to the question of whether or not social science is normative or not. It seems to me that, beyond a question, the traditional approach is to define a community of black people on the basis of standards of the white community—and not only the white community in general, but specific white people in particular. Rather than an intelligent approach, that black people are different so one must understand the way in which *they* live and try to determine *their* values and standards, other values and standards— white values and standards—have been imposed on black people.

Now, it seems to me all that's clear, and most of you, I assume, would accept these points. But also take the question of research, that is, innovation, creating new bodies of knowledge: it wasn't until approximately the 1930s in Chicago that black people represented a group of folks that warranted any kind of *empirical* research. Robert Park, Charles Cooley, Louis Worth, and others started moving to create an atmosphere that black students found possible to survive in, so that we had the first really serious generation of black social scientists coming from Chicago. But, if you read the works of these men closely, you find that it reflects the racist American norms of the day: Robert Park thought of black people as "the lady of the races" and wrote about our emotional make-up and what we liked and didn't like as if he was writing some kind of romantic racist novel. This should suggest that, while empirical research started then, it falls far short of what the black community today would accept as being respectable.

One must also mention in this concern with "race relations" the book by Gunnar Myrdal, *An American Dilemma,* which to black people contains the white Myrdalian dilemma, not the dilemma of black people. Here I want specifically to note the whole question of "race relations," because in the beginning period of empirical inquiry it was race *relations* that was a concern—that is, people were concerned about the relationship of black people and white people and not, *not,* the life within the black community. I suppose that's natural, since these people were concerned about the survival of the society which was white. Now, the Myrdalian dilemma essentially is that, even though he had tremendous contact with a significant number of black scholars, he saw black people basically the same way as William Faulkner, the white racist novelist of the South. That is, he said that white people presented all of the alternatives available to black people, and if one ever wanted to understand black people, you merely had to look at white people who were around them, calculate the obverse of what you saw and you'd come up with what black people are about. There was no inkling in his mind that over a period of time black people could create a community, a culture, that would be functionally autonomous from the white oppressors who raped them from Africa. Again, it seems to me that this should be clear to anyone with knowledge of recent research who is listening to voices coming from the black community.

The last point under research is the fact that there has been a beginning of basic research done by black people. Here, one needs to mention four people who have been very significant: E. Franklin Frazier, Dr. W. E. B. DuBois, Charles Johnson, and Carter G. Woodson. These are people who were trained at the University of Chicago and Harvard University who decided to hell with white academic life—and, I might add, in part this was because white society was saying very dramatically to them, to hell with you. They decided to create a body of knowledge. Carter G. Woodson: without his work much would be lost; he collected many documents and indeed set up an organization and participated in setting up a press in order to *present* this material. But, for the most part this material has not been included in any significant way in social science curricula that have been used in universities or public school systems. I can only reflect, very personally, on an experience at the University of Chicago—which has the reputation of being a "great liberal institution" and of being the kind of institution that includes a "very strong" emphasis on race relations, and yet I know conditions in Chicago and they leave much to be desired.

The last point I want to raise about research is merely to make a few comments reflecting on the recent research on riots. (Again, I have a very personal relationship with the University of Chicago, so I have to reflect on it; I'm sure that if I were a graduate of Yale, I could probably do the same.) Morris Janowitz, chairman of the Department of Sociology, is part of a group called the Center of Policy Studies, a very prestigious group of scholars at the University of Chicago, who meet to discuss relevant questions of the day. They had a long series dealing with the problem of China—and I don't mean Formosa, I mean China—and recently became concerned with "urban problems." The first paper published by this Center of Policy Studies dealing with urban problems had to do with "The Social Control of Escalated Riots." When I read that title, immediately certain things happened in my mind so I decided to read it. And when I did read it, I discovered that Morris Janowitz was following one of his major professional interests (which has to do with police and military concerns): he mentions *in passing* the interest of the black community, but mainly his focus is how in the hell can police departments stop these niggers from raising hell? *Basically,* that's his concern. Now, he talks about how to civilize police departments, the possible benefits of having constables to walk around with billy clubs and not guns because people do weird things when you put guns on them, how the symbolic meaning of a bayonet causes people to do weird things. He contends that what is really needed is efficient police action during the initial stages of a riot to prevent the escalation of snipers. The National Guard and police departments aren't used to snipers, and, consequently, they do weird things when confronted with them. Basically, the riot escalates and that must be stopped.

The second point about riot research has to do with the Kerner Commission on Civil Disorders (and there are a lot of other government reports that also fit this kind of criticism). While the Kerner Report comes to the conclusion that this is a racist society that is racially *divided*, the alternative it opts for is still one of integration. It does not significantly accept the fact that the black community— whether or not it is *now* a viable community is beside the point—is saying that we are going to *be* a viable community or we are going to destroy America. Or America will have to destroy us. Now, it seems to me that the "liberals" on that commission who seem to want to be relevant could have raised the whole question of how to invest resources in the black community as opposed to how we can invest the black community in the white community. But this was not done. I mention these things to indicate the shortcomings of the university as a reservoir of knowledge.

Viewing the university as a social institution, one can raise the question of social dysfunction about most American institutions. That is to say, the university is concerned with organizational maintenance over community service. Those of you who are students of social change know that frequently an organization will become very static and concerned with maintaining itself as opposed to achieving those goals it originally set out to achieve. Indeed, this is the case with the American university. In Chicago it was widely rumored that a man who was involved in the urban renewal department actually suggested separating the university community from the black community with a retaining wall four feet high. I'm really sorry that didn't happen, making the position of the university crystal clear. He then was appointed to an urban studies program at the University of Chicago which, I understand, has several million dollars. In urban studies they initially started out discussing issues like land use, because of the relocation of the packing industries in the stockyards—that was the most relevant urban problem they could identify in Chicago.

Now, it's not even a question of community service, because the university *is* concerned with community service—*before* it's concerned with cooperating with communities that are near it and that it must relate to. Here people feel basically that while scholars generally are a pretty impotent bunch—except when they go to Washington and make that consulting money, and then there's a sort of psychological thing about power—basically it's, We have something that people need, so we're going to take it and put it on them. Much the same, I agree very much with what Brother Karenga said about projects, that there's a real problem in determining what "expertise" means: involving not only faculty members but administration and students in the community is a very risky business. But by and large the university uses the model of, We've got something and we're going to put it in there, as opposed to dealing with some kind of cooperative arrangement.

The last point on the university as a social institution is that regardless of how it identifies itself in public it is indeed an institution which functions for the establishment. You only need to look at where university faculty get consultant checks from, who funds research, the secretive research that goes on in Defense Department relationships, etc. The real question is, how can the university go on defining itself as being *apolitical* or *nonpolitical* when indeed it functions in relationship to these institutions which have in mind maintaining the status quo over and against various communities which exist in this country that are committed to radical change.

The last point concerns the university as an agent of socialization, and here the whole question becomes what does it mean to be a man or a woman? It seems to me, regardless of whether or not the university has intended this (though, again, in the history of higher education universities have intended various things, none of which have been black), inevitably it comes out that what it means to be a man is basically what it means to be white and successful. Though a lot of white people are discouraged because they're white but not successful, there is greater clarity in the exclusion of blacks. The campus reality of role models, admissions policies, peer groups on campus, and other aspects of student experiences have been completely white-oriented. And here, again, most of these comments I'm making also refer to predominantly "Negro" colleges, though they're not as successful in being as evil as most white schools because they don't have the money or the staff—but they're just as sick, since one must add the additional "Negro" colonial pathologies to this.

The third major statement is that the university must be committed to change and become involved. That is to say, I think the university has to be a place not only committed to what *is* in society, but indeed to what *ought to be*. There are three principles, among many, that can be mentioned here. One is that the university must "go to the thing itself," that is, make a radical turn to the experience that one talks about, free of assumptions, facing it, confronting it. The second point is that, in this going-to-the-thing-itself, the university must be concerned not only with knowledge, but with the *utility* of knowledge. As someone mentioned recently, "art for art's sake" is incest: the point is that we have to be concerned with the utility of knowledge—what does it mean to *know* what we find out? It seems to me that anyone who has followed the student movements since the sit-in through Berkeley till now (and certainly anybody who's been concerned with the black community) has to be aware that the utility of the knowledge the university possesses is an important and relevant question. The third guideline I would mention is that the university, in being committed to change and becoming involved, must conceive of itself as a *servant* of the community. This servant relationship to the community must be defined cooperatively, for only in that way can the university maintain a balance between relating to what is and relating to what ought to be.

Now, the fourth statement is that the black community has matured in an unanticipated way, necessitating a re-examination of its historical dynamics. Again, this seems to be a fairly self-evident statement. One need only think, for example, of the terms and definitions that people have used to identify black people to know the limitations of what America's relationship to black people is at the moment: as Brother Karenga has said, the word "Negro" is something which in many quarters has taken on a very special negative meaning. Many of you might have noticed that black people have chosen to call themselves by different terms during different historical periods. At one point in our history Dr. DuBois—and in this he was joined by Booker T. Washington—was concerned about using the word "Negro" as opposed to using other words that white people chose to use. Well, maybe this hasn't changed as a result of the peculiar character of American history, but the fact is that today people want to be called "African Americans," "Afro-Americans," or "blacks." All that means is that people don't want to be called "Negroes." And it seems to me that this and other terms like Black Power represent a problem that white people face and that this country faces. The problem runs much deeper than simply the expedient use of language or the practical use of a term to communicate an idea; it represents the crying demands of an experience, a communal and historical experience, that white America has to come to grips with, has to listen to—and has to listen to with open ears and closed mouth.

The second point I want to make about the black community changing is the fantastic move toward new unity. Many black people, particularly young black people, have come to understand that Malcolm X and Martin Luther King met the same fate, that any ideological differences these people had, or seemed to have had in the white press, somehow were reduced to a common denominator. The movement in Washington, D.C., with the Black United Front and similar moves throughout the entire country should indeed strike the bell of alarm in white institutions, agencies, and communities around the country, because black people are getting together and they're getting together with ideologies that are more inclusive than perhaps ever before. Indeed, you *seldom* find a young black brother who will stand and seriously criticize any other black man—for the simple reason that to make appeals to "truth" as a value makes little difference, makes absolutely *no* difference, when you're dead. If you take a man, lock him in a cage, and keep food and water from him, he'll turn into an animal and do almost anything in order to survive. Black people have, in one sense, been reduced to that kind of unity, because we *know* that both Brother Malcolm and Brother Martin died—and we suspect that they died at the hand of the same kind of assassin. This, again, is a fact that has to be recognized. I might just mention this: I don't know how many white people here looked around in the audience as Brother Karenga was speaking, but I'm sure that a lot of people here laughed and responded in funny ways because they didn't really take what he said seriously; but if, instead of indulging yourself that way, you had looked around the audience at the *black* people, you would have gotten a whole different vibration. (Think on it!!)

The third thing I want to say about the black community is in terms of the set of alternatives being presented to America. (It seems to me they're very clear.) The terms of one alternative put forward by white people along with supporting social scientists are, "Well, you're only ten percent of the population and what can you do, you're located in these ghetto areas, etc., etc." There are two responses to that relevant to the concerns of this symposium. One is the census—which to secular America is like the Bible—it's something you have to believe in because it's the only thing like it, every ten years and there it is, it's got all the data in it. Black people have said a lot of different figures because we knew the census wasn't true, but we didn't know what was true, so we just said what we wanted to say. The census finally agreed with us and admitted that they were wrong. We all have to accept the fact that we don't know how many black people there are in this country, nor do we know what kind of black people they are, nor do we know where they are. I suspect it's much like Nigeria where the black people used to go into the bush and hide when the agents of the colonial regime would come around and count heads; then when the first *Nigerian* census came out, they were convinced that maybe census was a good thing. In any case, the whole point about the census being a basis of truth needs to be seriously questioned, if for no other reason than the white people who run it said that it was messed up.

The second response is that I remember being at an international conference in Geneva, and white people from the West stood up and were very concerned about nuclear holocaust. But *I* was listening to the brothers from the Third World who basically said that as far as they were concerned, in the bush (be it in Zimbabwe or be it in Vietnam) the whole business about a nuclear holocaust was a Western myth, that basically white people want to use the whole notion that they have bombs that they're threatening each other with to prevent people from participating in movements toward national liberation. Basically, they're saying, watch out or we'll blow the world up, so you have to be cool; and basically *we're* saying, in the jungle of Vietnam or in the guerrilla groups invading Mozambique and Zimbabwe, we say, to hell with your bombs. All we know about are Molotov cocktails and bullets, so if you have a bomb you'll have to drop it because we're moving toward national liberation anyway. It seems to me that this is what the black community is saying; once again, it's saying that we're going to do it and if you want to exterminate us, then you'll just have to do that because we're moving toward liberation.

Now, the last point I want to make is perhaps most focused on the point of this symposium, or the needs of the people concerned with black studies. That is, how can the university, in the light of all this stuff, be relevant and use its powers for change? I want to mention a couple of ways in which I feel the university might be relevant. Take the whole problem of knowledge—I would mention two things. In terms of courses, the most relevant way to deal with the black experience is to first try to come to grips with the set of questions being raised by black people. Let me give you an example: in economics, it seems to me that one could have a year course dealing with two questions: Why don't black people have any money? and, How can black people get some money? It seems to me that in my talking with students at Fisk University that's what they're interested in: Why *don't* we have any money? Well, obviously you would have to talk about the "forty acres and a mule" kind of myth, as part of that myth you would have to talk about the Freedman's Bank and how Southern racists and their Northern kin got to stealing money and checking each other, then tricked Frederick Douglass into taking the leadership position in it before it folded. You have to talk about those kinds of things in order to talk about the failure of an entrepreneurial spirit or delayed gratification becoming a factor in the values and life-styles of black people. To talk about how black people can get some money, you have to raise the question, how have black insurance companies survived?—I'm talking about North Carolina Mutual, Atlanta Life, Metropolitan. And how has Johnson Publications survived in such a vicious industry where great firms die every day? This is something that's immediately relevant to black people.

It's also relevant to white people: I assume that the body of knowledge relating to the experiences of white oppression have not been handed down, so that the sons and daughters of captains of industry in business school don't, in fact, hear lectures about how people have systematically excluded black people from the economy, or excluded black people from having access to resources to develop economic institutions. These are the kinds of basic concerns that are most relevant, and to try to move from the point of abstract, theoretical considerations that appear in other departments and immediately try to do the same thing with the black experience would be perpetuating either the same kind of educational system that *white* students are rejecting around the country, or at most would include the very, very poor literature that exists.

This leads me to my second point about what can be done. Take research: I believe that the black curriculum cannot be created today—not the black curriculum and the black university that I'm interested in being a part of. The simple fact is research does not exist, the findings do not exist, when it comes down to the black community. I notice that there are many social scientists concerned and involved in black studies: What do they know? What has been written about the black community? Politics: the James Q. Wilson study of Chicago, Gosnell's study of Chicago, and a few very scant studies in the tradition of community decision-making. On the whole question of what's happening in the South, there's one book, by Matthews and Prothro, which is an interesting exercise in methodological whatever, but in terms of coming to grips with what's happening politically in the black community it simply doesn't exist—it doesn't exist enough to build a curriculum on, certainly.

Take the whole question of the cultural experience of the black community. White America was gassed by Keil's study, *The Urban Blues,* but the fact is that Keil merely attempted to develop a set of concepts or articulate the way in which black people assign these concepts to white America. The significant kind of research that has to go on in terms of just exactly what's happening here, whether or not it's the experience of the Harlem renaissance, the experience of the WPA project, or the current cultural revolution going on today, is simply not *known.* Moreover, the "Negroes" that white people have created perpetuate what they do, and not in the interest of black people. So, the simple fact is that the literature doesn't exist; it just doesn't exist. I remember sitting and talking with some blues musicians and they told me some things that just completely blew my mind. Otis Span, the pianist with "Muddy Waters," told me that in 1940 they were writing protest songs—blues wasn't always singing about resignation and disaster, this cat was writing some protest music. And he said, we never used to sing them in the Delta of Mississippi, but everybody knew the songs. Now, I didn't get a chance to follow that up, but I'm interested in what he was talking about—he was talking about human experience and translating it into melody, and *that's* something Leonard Bernstein hasn't dealt with in discussing jazz. It seems to me that this is the kind of black knowledge, the knowledge about the black experience, that is important and relevant. And frankly, I'm speaking out of an extension of communal respect and love for the brothers and sisters at Yale who sponsored this symposium. I couldn't really give a damn whether white people are concerned with that body of knowledge or not, and to talk about "the intellectual validity" of this seems to me to be absurd and grotesque and very much a reflection of the *white* experience in America.

In any case, the whole point about research is very, very important. It's just *now,* with books like *Tally's Corner,* with books like *The Urban Blues,* that certain kinds of psycho-linguistic studies talk about the fact that black people speak a different language from white folks. If a man doesn't speak French, and you put a French book in his face and he can't read it, you don't say he can't read, what you say is that he can't read *that* language. It seems to me that people concerned with black studies are talking about the curriculum and how we want to rush and do this or that, but not with new knowledge in mind. I know why it's being done. There are pressures, the country's burning down. If the country wasn't burning down, the people controlling higher education wouldn't be a damned bit concerned. Secondly, there's the whole business about black students. White people made the mistake of letting them in and now they're raising hell; black studies wouldn't be here if that wasn't going on. So, let's don't mince business and act as if we can afford to raise all kinds of theoretical questions: America is catching hell and that's why white folks are interested in black studies. Don't talk about "the intellectual validity of the black experience." Go to Yeshiva University and you talk to them about the validity of the Jewish experience and see what they tell you—you can just take that as an answer, whatever they give you.

Now, viewing the university as a social institution, again, let me raise the question that Brother Karenga raised about providing funds and facilities. I understand that there are some foundation people interested, and also Yale and other similar universities. All are sources of wealth (I know university people think they're not wealthy, but I come from one I *know* is poor, so I'm in a good position to say). When major problems come up in this society, the way people handle them, first, is to amass a certain amount of resources. The University of Chicago wants to concern itself with urban studies, and several million dollars is made available. Other people come up with problems?—big corporations are established. In fact, at one point when white people were concerned about the race problem, the Carnegie Corporation got enough dust together (I don't have any idea how much it was) to support Myrdal's thing. (And, incidentally, some black people got a little mileage out of it, Charles Johnson among others.) The same is true for one of the most gigantic studies of all time, the Coleman study dealing with the educational experiences of blacks and whites.

The question I raise is really a challenge. The challenge is simply this: there are a number of black people in this country who have taken the time and suffered whatever they had to to be licensed by institutions of higher learning, and some of these have kept their minds on the needs of the community that they represent and are linked to, both out of a positive affirmation of self-identity and because they are forced to by this society. The question is this: Is it possible in this great country that a few million dollars—which is *not* a lot of money—could be made available to black social scientists to investigate the whole question of the black experience and the body of knowledge that must be amassed, knowledge that is authentically an extension and reflection of the black experience? Is it possible that these great American institutions and agencies, with all of these resources, could see their way to do this?

Let me give you my rationale for this kind of request. There are a lot of colleges concerned about black studies programs, and everybody is in search for a black person to be associated with that program—whether one admits it or not, everyone realizes that somebody at each school has raised that question. Now, from the interests of the national black community I see this as eventually producing diminishing returns. If we spread ourselves thin all over the country, and each school has their black man who can be sent to deal with those unruly students and who can deal with the white liberals both professionally and at white (non-Molotov) cocktail parties, this merely means that we're not getting the job done. Again, it's a matter of incentives: you have the jobs and the money so that you can make some of us do things that we might not feel comfortable doing. But if you're the good guys, as much of your PR says you are, I put the challenge to you: Can you postpone the personal, individual, institutional needs you have right in through here as major institutions? Can you group up and encourage foundations to facilitate the kind of black group and black host institution to spend two years, three years, however many years are necessary, to at least *try* to seriously investigate the black experience?

I understood very much when Professor Kilson said, look, I have enough trouble preparing three lectures a week without trying to draw up a curriculum dealing with the black experience. And I also understood it very much when Brother Karenga said, well, if each of you are interested, then hire me as a consultant and I'll come and talk to you individually. The fact is that if you think of the national community, it seems to me crystal clear that we can't *afford* to have the brothers and sisters who can do the job spread out on the basis of a distribution *you* create, as opposed to a distribution that's in the interests of our community. Here again I repeat the plea: it seems to me that there are a lot of young black social scientists who are capable of doing the job. A *minimum* descriptive statement would be that they're licensed at the best schools in the country— they have degrees and their reputations are secure, so it's not strictly a risky business; I can't emphasize this point enough. As a black social scientist I read the life of DuBois and I wondered about this whole country, I think about the fantastic innovations of the conferences that he held at Atlanta University, and those he planned to have. But Dr. DuBois couldn't get funded for that, and at least part of the motivation for going back home to Mother Africa was that he couldn't get anybody to fund his work. Now, here, suddenly everybody is interested in doing this and doing that; and I say to you that if you want to continue the racism that you've been accused of, then go ahead and set up your black studies program, get yourself a black man or black woman, maybe two or three. But the few black students that you're going to put your hands on aren't going to handle it, because there's not enough time. And that's going to remain a fact no matter *what* you do. But I would suggest that a much better risk for you is to group up and say yea, we've *all* been guilty, so let's create something really new in higher education by cooperatively setting up some kind of a program where black intellectuals can come together to really do the work that's needed. There's *no literature* to build a black studies program on. Do it if you want to—but do it with these criticisms in mind, because the black community is going to be thinking about them, as will black students.

Now, the last point I want to mention is about socialization, the "is" and the "ought." This is something that has to do not only with the inside of the university, but with the relationship that it has with the community. The "is" function requires that the university create within itself a microcosm of the society. That is to say, if there are all kinds of people in this society, you've got to have all kinds of people in the university. If there are black people in this society that live in segregated situations, that's exactly what you have to create on the university campus. So, I would fully support the demand by black students at Northwestern University to have their own living quarters, to have cultural events that speak to their needs, etc. Also, related to this notion is the question of who you consider an expert. Now, we all know the joke in that—that we're called upon to do all kinds of things, and that while our conscience prevents us from doing some things, we do other things that are questionable for expedient reasons—money, time, prestige, what have you—and that few of us ever really transcend that expediency.

Speaking from the context of the black community, it seems to me that expertise is *not* something that's defined on the basis of diplomas or on the basis of the traditional kind of curriculum vitae that we relate to academic life. For example, if one wants to learn about social welfare, I would suggest that there are people out there representing three generations on welfare and these people might have peculiar kinds of insight into the way in which welfare operates. We must bring these people together with social workers and other people in schools of social work to get a more complete reality. Only by having *all* of these people interact can we come to try to understand this very perplexing phenomenon. So, the point is to create a microcosm on the campus, a microcosm of the society at large.

Now, of course, this runs against much of what some people believe in terms of the exclusiveness of the university, or how important the university is in terms of who's there and who isn't there. But I'm sure the people at various foundations and major business people who suddenly realize they have to sit down with people off the block and listen to all kinds of things, feel all kinds of emotional vibrations that they're not used to feeling, can be helpful here. I'm sure that when the community people leave and these executives sit around and talk to each other, they raise questions about what in the hell was going on and what do these people mean, what did he mean by that or this, or why did he accuse me of that or this? I would suggest that these executives, while in school, would have benefited by coming in contact with these kinds of people, just as people have reflected on the positive experience of the young man who's going on to become important in one government going to the same kind of school as another man who's going on to become important in another government.

The second point about socialization has to do with the "ought." Once the university deals with creating what *is* on the campus, only *then* can it move to the point of seriously being concerned about what ought to be. To think about recruiting some black students and some white students who are special types, getting them together and creating a new model of man that's going to go out and relate to the world, it seems to me, is fantasy. Black people have to relate to the black community. If you develop a physicist who goes off and works with white people, then that's what he is—white. But anybody else who goes out who has to relate to the black community is black. It seems to me you have to create the "is," and *then* the creative challenge of how to mold a man, a universal man.

Let me conclude with this thought. The voice of change in the black community comes in many forms. Some brothers have chosen to make it the crack of rifle or the clash of broken glass. People participating in this forum, as most black students, are choosing to use words, the concepts and ideas based on the *same* communal experience as those brothers who are using guns and other things. The simple fact is that you are among those who might be able to help choose between these two alternatives. But your choice is not one that we're going to wait on, because time is moving on—and so are black people.

SUMMARY AND COMMENTARY

As I was sitting here thinking back about what's been going on here today, it seemed to me that the setting itself was important, that this was an extraordinary gathering—as Mr. McWorter said, we all know why we are here. It's an extraordinary gathering: many men have interrupted their habitual patterns of life in order to come here. I think there is a widespread sense that intellectually we are unprepared to understand what is happening and what has been going on in our own society and in the world; that educationally we are not at all sure that we know what kinds of learning experiences will equip us to understand better what is going on in our society and in the world. And I think that we came here to try to think together in some way about what our priorities might be.

Probably before we came here there were at least two general positions that we came from. Some of us accept the university structure as it is, as fundamentally sound but in need of modification—the question, then, how to incorporate black students and black studies into the curriculum. And in a sense this building, this room, symbolizes that: here we have a nineteenth-century structure which has been modernized partially, acoustically and with lighting, but we still have stained-glass windows; if I were to pull down this map of Asia it might easily be still colored in European colors, I don't know. [It was.] On the other hand, I think some of us came here prepared to re-examine fundamentally the question whether our present educational institutions are in any way adequate for training ourselves, along with our students, to recognize the problems that confront us. Here, again, one thinks symbolically of the hall: after all, we all acquiesce very easily in row seats which cannot move, with the man standing up here as the model of passing on a set body of knowledge as one man sees it, in a symbolically authoritarian setting. We may have become indifferent or habituated to the implications of our environment at the most fundamental levels—our perception of others and our setting.

Mr. McWorter has put it very eloquently in terms of our ignorance of the black community. I think our ignorance of communities all over the world is borne in upon us. There is an ignorance explosion of an extraordinary velocity. As to the question of how to move to remedy this ignorance, I think, again, there is an underlying premise in the remarks of nearly everyone who has spoken from this platform which offers an interesting set of possibilities. The premise was an intellectual one: that culture is integral, and that when one considers the relationship of the university to the culture that surrounds it, one must be aware that the university itself is a subculture and that the surrounding culture includes any number of subcultures which, in Mr. Karenga's metaphors, are really equivalent intellectually and emotionally to foreign lands. The first thing is to admit that this may be the case, to admit that our received categories of social self-understanding may be badly misleading and ill-informed. And certainly if this is the case, if we admit this, it adds weight to the suggestion that Mr. McWorter makes that we concentrate on finding out, on mapping communities of which we're ignorant—and this would surely be a worldwide mapping. Self-critical conceptualization and field work would have a very high priority in any set of programs.

The discussion this morning brings out a difference in attitude which is fundamental. It seems to me that Mr. Cruse assumes that culture is integral and that in any university activity or in any inquiry for that matter, intellectual, educational, and social objectives are inseparable. It was suggested that universities are custodians of a special kind of truth, in contrast to Mr. Cruse's advocacy of programs within universities involving committed men of special persuasion. Mr. Cruse, you will recall, further proposed that commitment was necessary in order, as Mr. McWorter put it, to get people who *cared* about amassing new bodies of knowledge and looking at things from new perspectives *engaged* in this task. But the record of failure is writ large. The question that Mr. Cruse posed this morning as to the relationship of black communities and black studies to the prevailing institutional structure of our society was posed in terms of the rate of change which is possible, or felt to be possible, in our society. Here, again, it seems to me we are profoundly ignorant, that we do not know enough to say how much we can change—and certainly we don't know enough to say how little we can change.

Mr. Cruse's proposals and Mr. McWorter's, when placed together, suggest that the university is essentially a self-critical element in the culture, that in order to be self-critical in relation to the surrounding culture at this historical juncture it must incorporate those elements of passionate and committed criticism which clearly exist. This is, I think, in keeping with the tradition of universities as cultural antennae—or at least, if not a major tradition of universities as currently constituted, a major possibility. To this end suggestions for black studies in terms of black colleges, a black university, a center for black social scientists, propose to introduce into the university and into the culture at large a necessary self-critical factor—assuming that any enterprise has unexamined predispositions, unexamined ideologies, which need the most passionately advocated critiques as a matter of health.

To review Mr. McWorter's proposal once more for the kind of activity that universities might properly carry on, it seems to me that his definition of the university as necessarily a servant of the community echoes the notion of the integrated nature of intellectual activity, education (from a pedagogical point of view), social action, social exploration. And his proposal that black social scientists—when reviewing sociological literature or all the literature of the social sciences—are especially equipped to provide a cultural critique of the methodological assumptions of the practice of social science, it seems to me, is an important point for continuing discussion.

I was struck this morning by the exchange with Mr. Kilson about varied intellectual diet and how essential this was—but what seemed to me really quite extraordinary and moving was the readiness to agree that there was no essential connection that anyone knew of between intellectual training and learning on the one hand, and humaneness and goodness or decency. If this is the case, we are in very bad shape indeed; and I think we need then, as a society, to nurture and—"welcome" is too weak a word—to do whatever we can to discover how, in the process of learning to construe the world, we can also develop a sensitization to the complexities of other human beings in the world at a level of encounter far higher, or at least far more complex, instantaneously complex, than has heretofore been the case. I think at the very least the presence in universities of intellectual nuclei of black social scientists would help—perhaps a center of black social science; it could be a mobile center with economies of concentration as well as mobility. We all need such a center. I would hope that in addition to a traveling or mobile, concentrated community of black investigators of black community and black culture in the United States, that as a matter of course we accept into university life members of other cultures in teams of participant-observers who continually challenge our own unexamined perspectives on what we're about.

The question of how inclusive our ideologies can become is suggested by Mr. McWorter's final remarks, though I'm not sure just how inclusive the ideologies he was speaking of were—but the question of how a series of learning experiences might develop inclusiveness would be one of the major matters on any university agenda.

There is one final speculation that I would like to pose for your reflection, and it is concerned with the world society. It seems to me if one imagines what a university might be like, or what an educational set of experiences might be like, following Mr. McWorter's insistence that universities are concerned with what ought to be and might be: if one starts to imagine what some sort of educational set of experiences might be like in which from early childhood one might develop habitually cross-cultural perceptions of one another—and I think we have the technology for this—then one thinks, for example, of kindergarten and elementary school children literally all over the world and in our own society and in all the schools creating, making filmed diaries of their own lives, of their own subcultures, exchanging these with their counterparts in various countries around the world; again, perhaps video monitors could record how fifth graders in various sections of the world respond to their age-mates' versions of their common experience, and then play these back and forth.

A whole series of culture-learning experiences of an inherently pluralistic sort might be set up, again following along some of the lines of Mr. Cruse's proposals. Whether black studies with its momentum would want to be a part of such a meeting of world cultures, such a re-definition of a world in which children would grow up to feel that the reality of the experiences of children from any number of other cultures and subcultures was available to them on the mean level of bodily motion and dancing, on the acting level of interpreting daily events—this is the kind of thing to which black studies might lead.

It would certainly not be the least of the historical ironies that were suggested this morning if out of the conflict between this powerfully assimilating, dominant, white American culture and black culture, if out of this confrontation came a version of world society or world culture in which, in Mr. Karenga's terms, there was a balance of cultural power such that each man not only would be living in his own culture, but would have a sense of the complexities involved in the encounter of individual to individual, inevitably, anywhere in the world. If such is the case, I think one could take as a prospective motto to place across the first such center of educational experience no better set of words than Malcolm X's remarks when he said, *a propos* of learning Swahili and Chinese and Arabic and everything else: "I would just like to study, I mean *ranging* study, because I have a wide open mind; I'm interested in almost any subject you can mention."

A STUDENT'S REFLECTIONS

Donald H. Ogilvie

During yesterday's proceedings, a number of people responded to the ideas and imperatives presented here by voicing concern over what they believed black student opinion might be. In a number of cases, a misinterpretation of black student priorities and values seemingly relieved certain "concerned" individuals from the responsibility of dealing in an intellectually honest fashion with all that has been said.

It would therefore be constructive to clear the air a bit and to offer you briefly one aspect of black student opinion on "education and the black experience."

Professor McWorter has emphasized the necessity for a center of black social science that would work to create a philosophy of and an analytical framework for a black studies curriculum. Undoubtedly, such a center is the only way to systematize adequately the present body of knowledge and, perhaps more importantly, to provide direction for future scholastic inquiry and interpretation. However, whether this center is established next year or this weekend, it clearly will not be capable of affecting the present generation of college students, and perhaps not even those who are presently juniors and seniors in high school, students who might themselves aspire to be black scholars and academics. Professor McWorter's proposal is necessary; indeed, it is crucial. However, we must also keep our eyes on another perspective: the kind of curriculum changes that students seek *today*.

These changes do not seek merely the inclusion for some undefined interim period of one or two black history courses. Those of you who still think that such token offerings are all this ferment has been about, those who still perceive demands for a black curriculum as a student prank, and who, in response to mounting pressure for an *honest* curriculum, can only facetiously and maliciously refer, as some have in this room, to a "black studies bit," or "b.s."—are bound by an intellectual arrogance of which you have precious little time to rid yourselves.

Black students have thought about what we are missing in our university experience and we see a black curriculum as giving us the opportunity to find direction. Within the present available framework we cannot readily apply the tools of a scholastic discipline to the experience, the problems, the wisdom or the expression of black people. We are saying that this condition must be changed—radically. There is no justification for delay. It is true the bodies of knowledge of which we speak have been criminally ignored by the majority of the intellectual community. Yet no matter how poorly documented *some* of those areas within the social sciences and humanities that touch on the black perspective may be, or how limited in number and scope *some* of the analyses and interpretations are, an initial exposure to this existing material is possible *now.* Universities must furthermore provide through curriculum arrangements a framework wherein the student, under the direction of the faculty, can try to augment this material with research of his own as well as tie in readings, lectures, methods, and insights from existing disciplines that are necessary for both a comprehensive understanding of the total black experience and specialized expertise in any one of the particular aspects of that experience.

This is the type of response we expect. I repeat, not a "black studies bit," not "b.s." We want an opportunity to learn about things that are relevant to our existence and we want to learn in the best possible ways, experiencing the expertise of *all* those who have something to offer. This means exposure in the classroom to men of controversial qualification—on the one hand, eminently qualified to instruct because of *what* they know; yet, on the other hand, grossly underqualified because of *how* they came to know it. Perhaps faculties and administrations will view demands for such men as less of a dilemma if they realize this one central fact: as much as black students repudiate those "academically qualified" purveyors of the traditional white racist perspective, they do not want to see the void which is perpetuated by these "scholars'" existence filled with black charlatans who have little to offer besides their "front." We look for no pedants, either black or white, with magic formulas; instead we look for men who can offer a range of information and insight that effectively provides alternatives from which *we* can choose. Since we are dealing with matters which have been long ignored or abused by whites, while being studied and experienced by blacks, it should be no surprise that most of the experts—though without degrees—whom we find will be black. If knowledge is as important to the university as the "Ph.D. count" of its faculty, then it will work with its black students on this issue rather than raise unreasoned and overemotional objections.

I hope these remarks have helped to clarify a few things. By all means work for the realization of a black social science research center. Yet keep in mind the more *immediate* necessity, in terms of people who are in universities now and will be for the next several freshman classes, people who may not be able to benefit from the analytical framework and philosophy of curriculum the center may someday offer, and who will have to develop, as best they can, this philosophy and provide this framework for themselves.

AFRICAN HISTORY AND WESTERN CIVILIZATION

Boniface Obichere

What I want to do here is to examine the present inadequacies of treatment of African history in Africa and overseas, take a glance at what could be done to eliminate this sad state of affairs, and maybe share a few thoughts with you on African history and the Third World Movement.

Let me begin by narrating a personal experience. When I was living in the then Eastern Nigeria, now Biafra, I was in an English-style boarding school preparing for a London University examination, and of course one of my subjects was the History of the British Empire —and that included North America. In a textbook for this particular examination, which was a set of lectures written up in London at the time, it was very interesting to note that John Hancock was described, and I quote, as "the greatest smuggler in Boston." When I came to the United States a few years later, I was told as a student in a state university, if I wanted an honors degree in history, which I was in the process of getting, I had to do American history. So, I registered for American history for a whole year, and in that particular class I was taught that John Hancock was a very great patriot, and, of course, that his name appears first on the Declaration of Independence. This is a simple fact, but it affected me profoundly later on in my college career, especially when I went back to Oxford. In this example you see the difference in thinking, the difference in attitude, the difference in prejudices and so on and so forth. What I have just said about John Hancock here seems to me to apply to the treatment of African history at the present time. Interpretations are polarized.

Writing in 1960, a Frenchman, Raymond Mauny, called on West African universities, those at Ibadan, Accra, and Dakar, and the American Negro universities to take up the challenge of the new school of African history [1]. I thought this was a good appeal by

Raymond Mauny—whose treatment of African history is resented by many. This was eight years ago and it was a Frenchman speaking. What is significant here is that this Frenchman noticed or detected that Africa and the American universities had to cooperate in bringing out the material and in the interpretation of the new African history. The cause of Professor Mauny's statement was a book on African culture history written by an African, Cheikh Anta Diop, entitled *Nations Nègres et Culture* [2]. Mauny didn't like this book because it didn't follow the traditional interpretation of African history. It made bold claims based on evidence, including one that I think Mauny took issue with in his review of the book: that the bases of Egyptian culture were Negro before the invasion of Egypt by the Semitic-Greco-Roman world.

Taking this controversy a little farther, we see Margery Perham and Professor K. O. Dike, formerly of Ibadan University, entering into a similar controversy. Margery Perham was of the opinion that Africans weren't prepared for independence (she was writing in 1958, of course; she had no crystal ball to see what was going to happen in 1960) and Professor Dike responded very vehemently in a series of articles in *West Africa.* I think that the main theme of all Dike had to say was this (and I paraphrase him, I'm not quoting): that there were people who had a pathological unwillingness to accept evidence about African history and African contributions to world civilization. Professor Dike is a very great moderate, as you know; he is not of the nationalist school, and this coming from him is very strong indeed.

A few years later the battle was joined again, this time at England's premier university—at Oxford. The present Regius Professor of Modern History at Oxford, Hugh Trevor-Roper, expressed the opinion that he didn't think Africa and Asia had any history, except that history which began with European enterprise in these places. This time it was left to English people to do battle with Trevor-Roper. The first person who picked up the gauntlet was Basil Davidson, who countered Trevor-Roper in no uncertain terms. In fact, one of his questions was whether Trevor-Roper considered London a Roman city or an English City. And of course he asked him the origin of Oxford, Winchester, etc. Thomas Hodgkin joined battle also with Trevor-Roper, and we have seen that since then Mr. Trevor-Roper has been very quiet about African history.

These are a few things that will introduce you to the type of controversy that has been going on and is still raging about African history. I think that the basis of this controversy is the inadequacy of the treatment of African history and, secondly, the false interpretation that has hitherto been given to African history. That is, that the whole of African history was, in the words of Professors R. Robinson and J. A. Gallagher in *Africa and the Victorians,* "a gigantic footnote" to something that Britain was doing in Asia or in England, and so on. At the present time we have persons engaged in the study of African history who don't believe in the footnote theory and who think African history is a body of knowledge worth inquiring into in its own right, and for its own sake. Such men as Professors Roland Oliver and John D. Fage come to mind here.

Let us take the question of inadequacies of treatment of African history in the study of Western civilization. The textbook used for this course in History 1 under Professor Wolff at the University of Minnesota is that bible of the history of Western civilization by R. R. Palmer, which, incidentally, has acquired a workbook like Samuelson's in economics—and, of course, Joel Colton has added to the work. In here you are supposed to be studying the history of the "modern world"—but *that* modern world existed only in Europe and, partially, in the United States. I may be right in saying that about 33 1/3 percent of that book deals with German thinking—very little on Africa, and that on Africa deals with Englishmen and Frenchmen and Germans visiting Africa for a very short period of their lives. And I'm saying this very, very seriously. Now how many years did Cecil Rhodes spend in Africa? I think you could even exaggerate, or even be sensational, in saying that he spent more time in Oriel College, Oxford, than he spent in South Africa. Or what of Lugard? How many years of his life did he spend in Africa? Still these textbooks devote almost all of their treatment of Africa to these personalities. MacKinnon for East Africa, and so on and so forth. Take the new text by Stromberg. What do we have on Africa?

I think the only real hope comes in the collectively *Civilization Past and Present* [3], chaired by Professor Wallbank of the University of Southern California. It is in Volume I of *Civilization* that for the first time since I have been looking around I've seen an author devoting more pages to Africa than was devoted to China or India. Probably this kind of lopsided treatment is necessary: in the words of Oginga Odinga, if you've been leaning too much to the right, you have to make up for it by leaning very much to the left so that you'll gain an upright position in the process—because if you don't, you might continue leaning too much to the right.

In the classical world histories, what does one find on Africa? Take the best sellers of the early portion of this century: H. G. Wells' *Outline of History,* Van Loon's *World History,* H. G. Wells' *A Short History of the World.* Or take that American classic of William and Ariel Durant. What do we get on Africa? I would say, nothing, because to them the perspective is very different: African history has no appeal or they didn't want to bother about it. Toynbee's *A Study of History* is also to be included in this long list of inadequacies of treatment.

I'm not saying that Europeans and Americans are responsible, alone, for this type of situation. I think that Africans have contributed to this in a very large way and, with apologies to Harold Cruse [4], the intellectuals especially. We have in West Africa an abundance of historians, more than in any other discipline, except for the recent generation of American-trained graduates who have gone into the sciences and nuclear physics and who have become experts in engineering and technology. Most of the old generation who were trained in London and Cambridge and Oxford were historians and lawyers. This was one thing to do to become a civil servant, get a house in the European section of town with stewards and gardeners and so on (I'm not going into this). The net result of this kind of "unreal" existence is that these gentlemen never bothered with *African* history.

I think this came up yesterday when somebody said that if black people pass through universities and go out and get jobs and buy a home in the hills, these black gentlemen are *white* in their thinking. And I would say that most educated Africans of the older generation, in fact, up to about 1956, were *"Europeans."* There are terms in almost all the African languages calling them "Europeans": the

Yorubas call them "Oyinbo dudu"—that's "black white man"; in Ibo they are called "Beke Ojii"—that is, a "black white man"; and the French-speaking countries have their expression for these people, such as *evolué*. So that it would be too much, taking their circumstances into consideration, to expect them to produce much in the way of African history.

Another reason for this statement that I'm making here is the nature of the curricula in African universities. First of all, feasibility studies had to be done, with grants from the British colonial office, to see if the Africans needed any university, that is, if the colonial power was to establish universities in Africa—forgetting that a very large percentage of the student population in England at that time was African. These study groups, such as the Ashby Commission, went around and looked at all possible factors and decided that commonwealth universities should be established. The Commonwealth Universities Act led to the establishment of Ibadan and Legon (Accra) in 1948. Of course, Fourah Bay College was in existence at this time, but as a college of Durham University. And Makerere College was in existence, but as a college of the University of London. In other words, it was very little different from, say, University College, or Bedford College, or King's College, London, because it had the same syllabus, it had the same examinations, which were given at the same times.

And here, again, I might interject a personal experience. I remember sitting in the examination hall in Owerri (Biafra) and the Education Officer, a rotund Englishman, showed us very clearly the envelope in which our examination questions were sent from England with the seal of the University Senate in London. The regulations were that these examinations had to be opened at a specified time so that they would start at the same time all over. This was to ensure that people wouldn't cable back and forth the questions from Nigeria to Britain. The Officer said, "Here are your examinations," undid the seal of the Senate, and then zip, we started off. It was just as simple as that, because I could have landed on the steps of London University and discussed those questions with the same degree of depth and ability as any honors student in England—because the questions were the same, the people who were going to mark and grade them were the same, living in the suburbs of Essex and Sussex or what have you. So, under these circumstances it would be too much to expect African universities to branch out into the investigation of African history, because only "European History," "English History," and "The History of the British Empire" were on the syllabus. There was no examination in American history as developed as it is today, though some of the British and African universities are changing their position because of pressure from the English-Speaking Union.

The universities in Africa have gained independence in the last few years and some of them have begun fundamental research on African history. But this is still very limited in scope. I take a dim view of this effort, in the light of the way in which it is being conducted. The chairmen of some of these programs and departments are excolonial officials or Europeans whom I wouldn't hesitate to accuse of the colonial administrator's mentality. They see the university as an extension of their secretariat during the colonial period. The universities in French-speaking Africa are notorious for this new role for ex-colonial officials.

For those who have no experience with African universities, the departments are not like the departments in American universities. The chairman of the department is a little despot. He decides what courses have to be taught, what books have to be used. Lecturers don't recommend textbooks, as is the case in America. As a matter of fact, lecturers have very little to say in the formulation of the contents of some of the courses they teach. This illustrates the degree to which the chairman affects the development of the curriculum and research in his department.

In Ibadan University especially we see this predicament in its fullest form. There is an Institute for Islamic Studies—run by a former British administrator, and the material coming out of the Institute reflects this. There was the African History Research Program in the University of Ife, which because of the local political situation became very parochial indeed. It is like the American history section of the History Department of Yale saying that American history was coterminous with the history of Connecticut. I think this would be ridiculous. I'm talking here about the Yoruba History Program initiated by Professor S. O. Biobaku at Ife. I'm not saying that the program is bad, but I am saying that the priorities are not right.

Now, let us go to the scholars on a different level—publications. Do you know that it was an American scholar of African history who told an African, a black African historian, that he should begin to look twice at the documents he reads in the Public Record Office? I'm talking here about the review by Professor Robert I. Rotberg of the book edited by Professor J. C. Anene and G. N. Brown where Rotberg was telling Anene in no uncertain terms to desist from calling Africans pirates simply because Sir John Kirk or Evan Smith writing from Zanzibar in the nineteenth century thought that these Africans were pirates. This goes a long way to illustrate what I'm driving at. Many black historians have not gone through what Dr. Nnamdi Azikiwe described as "mental emancipation," what Jomo Kenyatta talks about in his little volume of collected speeches, *Harambee,* as "dropping the colonial mentality." Of course, Evan Smith described some Zanzibari and Swahili and East African traders as pirates. But when in the 1960s one gets into the Public Record Office and reads these documents, doesn't one have a duty to oneself to question whether these were actually pirates or not?

The reason why I cited this example is that most of the material being published at present by African intellectuals is identical in tone with what was being published by Englishmen in London in the 1930s; in other words, it is a question of the old wine in a new jug. Professor Raymond Mauny's call for "the new school of African history" has not been heeded by some African historians. I think it is a professional thing: these men are tied to fledgling universities that are still subsidiaries of European universities, and therefore have to treat historical questions according to what the European universities require, and demand. In Ibadan University, the University of Ife, and so on, it is still imperative to invite outside examiners from Cambridge or Oxford or London. Even Ahmadu Bello University, located in Northern Nigeria, has outside examiners from Oxford reading the examinations of their students, "to assure acceptable standards." Whose standards? Here, again, I have to knock at an old dead horse (I wouldn't mind flogging it again). It is the unrealistic colonial rule that degrees other than those obtained from England or Commonwealth universities are "worthless."

I think we have seen this colonial balloon punctured and deflated, but still the myth survives. American universities are excluded from the category of the selected, and those who hold degrees from them have a hard time getting jobs in Africa. If any African academics are not mature enough to know who's "fit to be licensed," in the words of Professor McWorter, I don't think they have a business in the university. Such men should end up in a little secretariat signing typed letters or answering phones. But if they think they have a business in the university, I think they should have the intellectual maturity and the honesty of purpose to know who is fit or unfit for university work. I don't think one needs an Englishman to decide that.

Also in this problem of intellectuals is the crisis of publication. Some African writers cannot get publishers because they don't toe the line. I mean this very seriously. Look at the example that I cited at the beginning of this presentation, Raymond Mauny versus Cheik Anta Diop: if it hadn't been for *Présence Africaine,* Diop's book would never have been published. So, those Africans who write, maybe African history or any other type of cultural assessment of Africa, have to toe the line, if they want to be published. I know a few cases and I wouldn't say that these cases are not representative. The question of publication, then, is a very serious one. Africa needs an indigenous press. We fool ourselves, saying we have an Ibadan University Press or we have a Dakar University Press, and so on. Most books are produced in England for Ibadan University: it's like a mother feeding Junior with processed food, because he can't eat on his own. Ibadan University should come of age one way or the other—grants, know-how, foreign aid, I don't care what—so that it could publish its own books just like the Indian universities and the American universities publish their own books.

Another fault of the intellectuals which has contributed to the inadequacy of treatment of African history—and I'm talking about both white and black intellectuals at this juncture—is the question of selection of non-important themes in African history. An Englishman told us in Los Angeles about three weeks ago (I'm talking here, in fact, about Professor Terence Ranger of the University of East Africa in Dar es Salaam) that he visited Ibadan University a few months ago and he said that he was amazed to see Ibadan engrossed in a symposium on "Indirect Rule in Nigeria." For heaven's sake, what is "indirect rule" compared to other themes in Nigerian history? It is this kind of playing-the-ostrich which has led to the crisis in Nigeria. People neglect the issues. "Indirect rule"—so fine, because Lugard described this in his *Dual Mandate?*

During my research at Oxford one of my tasks, and it was an unpleasant task indeed, was reading through all the volumes of the Lugard Papers and discussing them with Dame Margery Perham and others. These papers have been pruned. Those things that people weren't expected to see have been destroyed, with the result the "p. 2" or "p. 6" of certain letters are missing, and so on and so forth. And in there I was privileged to read communications between Professor Reginald Coupland and Lugard when he was writing his *Dual Mandate.* After that I just changed my mind about the book, because Lugard wasn't saying what he did or what he wished to see done. He was trying to become "respectable," since he had retired in England and wanted to become "part of the society." This is my own view of what happened in there. So, for a university in West Africa at this time of the study of African history to spend months on "indirect rule" and to devote, in fact, an issue of the journal of the Nigerian Historical Society to the indirect rule question is, it seems to me, to be irrelevant, or to have the priorities wrong.

Now what has been the result of this concentration on non-important themes? It has been that we are accepting or relying very heavily on the histories of Africa written *outside.* I may say here that no African has produced a solid-type history of Africa up to this morning to my knowledge. The works that are in use are those that have recently come out of Prague, Paris, New York, and London [5]. I'm referring to Andre Sik and his *History of Africa* (1966) in two volumes. This work has been translated into French and into English: then Hureck's two-volume study of *The History of Africa* also is being used, and people are begging for its translation into English and French as well. These studies we know are Marxist and lopsided, because their main theme is imperialism and how it exploited Africa and thwarted African history. It is the responsibility of Africans and "men of culture" in general, as St. Clair Drake said during the Congress of Africanists in Rome (1959), to destroy these myths and to produce the real facts of history.

African history should then be treated as African history and the important themes should be investigated. One would like to see studies of African political structures, structures of states; the functioning of these states should be studied in detail and the personalities should be studied. We were introduced—and I'm talking about my generation who went to school in Africa—to European history through a series of biographies ranging from Moses, Hammurabi, and Socrates down to Winston Churchill. There is nothing wrong with studying African biographies. G. Carter Woodson has a book on this, *African Heroes and Heroines* (1944). It is dated and needs revision.

This brings me to my crucial criticism at this point, and that is the question of *anonymity*. I think it was part of colonial policy to impose anonymity on Africa and Africans. We don't have names. Our countries have no names. They are described by trade names— the Gold Coast, the Ivory Coast—and these stick. If you look at old maps, you'll see that these areas had other names, and some African politicians have revived these historical names. It might have been emotional of these politicians, but the names were worth reviving. Today "Ghana," for instance, is more meaningful than "Ivory Coast," because there are very few elephants left in Houphouet-Boigney's Ivory Coast. So the name itself is anachronistic.

Anonymity can be seen in the treatment of African heroes. Take the example I gave earlier, that Lugard made treaties with the King of Borgu in November 1894. Who was this man? He might have been a more important personality than Lugard, who was a freebooter in 1894. We want his name, Siré Torou, to enter into any historical treatment of that British expedition of 1894 into his kingdom of Borgu. This is one of the psychological problems that the black people in America and Africa have to face together. I think in the extreme version of the Muslim movement we see some people answering "X" because they think that the names they were given coincide with the anonymous treatment of the blacks and so they would rather be *completely* anonymous than go by the name of

"Fine Face," or "Big Ears," or something like that. These names are from the Niger Delta states. We have "Jack Fine Face" and we have "Water-boy," and Bob Manuel. These are names that were foisted on the people of these areas in the seventeenth century by European slave dealers. These names still persist. So, it behooves us today to examine this question of anonymity, and in our writing of African history to make efforts to pinpoint the personalities who acted in Africa before the Europeans and after the Europeans arrived on the scene. In attacking this question of anonymity we should also endeavor to cleanse the historical record of Africa. We shouldn't look at Shaka only as a "bloodthirsty, nasty Zulu" because his European opponents described him that way. We should look at this famous man as a leader of his people; and we should look at him as an innovator in what we see our political scientists wrestling with today, the problem of state modernization. This is a problem which didn't start in the middle of the twentieth century.

To end up I want to look very briefly at African history and the Third World. Since the Bandung Conference (1955) the Afro-Asian world has been feeding on a new mental diet and that diet, whether it is in the extreme form or in the mild form, reminds them that after all is said and done, despite poverty, despite segregation and discrimination, they are the *majority* of human beings, of what we have categorized as *homo sapiens.* I don't know the ramifications of this Bandung statement in the minds of our political leaders, but I think it is a very far-reaching point that was made at the Bandung Conference. Though Afro-Asian solidarity has not been a functional thing in many cases, I think it has been a fact, at least ideologically. Black history or the study of the black experience in America is one extension of this Afro-Asian consciousness. The black revolution in the United States and the political and social revolution going on in Africa and Asia [6] and, in fact, in Latin America cannot be completely segregated in water-tight compartments. George Shepperson of Edinburgh University has published an article showing the early intellectual contacts between the American blacks and Africans. The origins of the African political revolution have been linked to the American universities attended by African leaders. And of course there have been several of such studies [7].

The Brazilians have come out with very many books and scholarly articles on the contributions of Africa to Brazilian life and culture. A Frenchman has come out with a study of Brazil and the West African trade. In the academic field, worthwhile endeavors are being made in the Third World, and the spokesmen of the Third World— "spokesmen" not by popular election, but probably by their arrogating this role to themselves—do drum this into the ears of the inhabitants of the Third World, to give them consolation, yes, but to elevate their spirits, I think, more than anything else. Therefore in the meaningful quest for identity in Africa and for identity in the United States by the blacks, African history has a role to play. People have argued that the blacks in America cannot point to where they came from. Well, this is as it might be; but they can point to Africa and say we originated there *some* time ago. Our forebears came from there. This fulfills an emotional need in the search for identity.

In considering the Third World, I think that certain vocabularies have been built up which are understood easily in Africa and in the black communities in the United States, Latin America, and in Asia. People are reading the same authors. Not only the quotations of Mao Tse-Tung are read, but also Frantz Fanon, Ernesto Che Guevara, and similar authors who think "the hard way" about what the black man has to do to pull himself up by his own bootstraps.

In conclusion, let me say that the inadequacies that I have examined are real. They exist, and I think they call for a remedy. Secondly, the curricula of African universities and black universities in America as well as the predominantly white universities should be brought in line with the needs of the day. If that includes the establishment of the study of the black experience, by all means do it. I would interject here that at UCLA we are now offering a course for credit on "The Black Man in the Changing American Context." This is a beginning and we hope to branch out by the fall quarter into other such courses. Thirdly, it seems to me that the study of the black experience, which includes African history in its broadest interpretation, is a worthwhile academic endeavor. It is enriching. In the words of Ron Karenga, it might "add some zest and some vim and some vigor" to the study of the bland "European experience."

Fourthly, I would like to suggest that those engaged in the field of African history should try to redefine their purposes and their roles and try to tackle meaningful subjects, even though these may seem to be hard on the esophagus. Maybe they wouldn't be that hard when the various tools of research are employed in analyzing and interpreting these subjects.

Fifthly, I would call on those who have influence with publishers or those who can contribute to publications to see that all shades of opinion get exposure. It could be said that Africa is still living through the period of colonial censorship—very subtle, indeed, but very real. Even those Africans who have used all the current tools of the new history are still criticized adversely when their findings lead them to make interpretations different from the old ones. Finally then, I would say that African history has been neglected in the past. This realization has dawned suddenly on many universities, and several of them are trying to give prominence to African history, offering degrees up to the doctorate level in African history. This is really encouraging and I hope that this trend will continue at a faster rate and with broader perspectives and openness of mind.

Notes

1. *Bulletin de l'Institut Français d'Afrique Noire,* Vol. XXII, Series B (1960), p. 551.

2. Cheikh Anta Diop, *Nations Nègres et Culture* (Paris: Présence Africaine, 1955).

3. Walter T. Wallbank, Alastair M. Taylor, Nels M. Bailkey. *Civilization Past and Present,* Vol. I, 5th Edition (Chicago, 1965).

4. Harold Cruse, *The Crisis of the Negro Intellectual* (New York, 1967).

5. R. Oliver and J. D. Fage, *A Short History of Africa* (Penguin Book, 1966). R. I. Rotberg, *A Political History of Tropical Africa* (1964). R. Cornevin, *Histoire de l'Afrique,* 2 vols. (Vol. III in preparation). D. Westermann, *Geschichte Afrikas* (1952).

6. G. H. Jansen, *Non-Alignment and the Afro-Asian States* (New York, 1966). Brian Grozier, *Neo-colonialism* (Philadelphia, 1964).

7. Kwame Nkrumah, *Ghana: The Autobiography of Kwame Nkrumah* (New York, 1957). E. W. Smith, *Aggrey of Africa* (London, 1929). Jones-Quartey, *A Life of Azikiwe* (New York, 1966). A. A. Nwafor Orizu, *Without Bitterness* (New York, 1944). Robert I. Rotberg, *The Rise of Nationalism in Central Africa* (Cambridge, 1965).

QUESTION PERIOD

Question

Professor Obichere, I was wondering if I could ask you three very short questions, possibly answered only "yes" or "no." If we grant that people who have to live in a country and have the experience of growing up in a particular environment may have a certain intrinsic advantage in working on their own society, I would ask, in reference to African history, Can *good* African history be done by non-Africans?

Obichere

The answer is yes.

Question

Do you feel that one must have a particular ideological stance with regard to *contemporary* African problems in order to do good African history, be the person African or not?

Obichere

The answer is no. By my own training—unless you are writing an official history, or unless you are a historian to a political party—I don't think that you could tie yourself down, in all honesty to your own endeavor, to any particular ideology. You're going to produce something that's very tendentious and lopsided. This is my criticism of Andre Sik's book. I've read that book through and through and the more I read it the more disgust I feel for parts of it. It is so lopsided. You can't see through the smoke of the continuous attack on "imperialism," and capitalism and so forth. This is what happens when you get so completely engrossed in an ideology that you want to subordinate everything else to it.

I think, as an African, I wouldn't hesitate to submit to a publisher a manuscript which finds that African history in a particular era is not what the politicians in Africa want it to be. I have to be honest to myself, first of all, before considering the other man. "To thine ownself be true," said Shakespeare.

This brings me to what Professor Kilson said yesterday. In dealing with the slave trade, for instance, you think about the yo-ho-ho type of crewmen with handkerchiefs around their necks, drinking rum all night, who were rounded up in the streets of Bristol or Liverpool and taken to the West Coast. This is fine, it's historically true; one can go to the Public Record Office in England and see the bills of lading. These crewmen are as anonymous as the Africans that I mentioned, and objected to their anonymity. These crewmen were *anonymous,* they're "thirty crewmen, from such-and-such street in Bristol." That's what they *were* in that period in England, but when they got to Cape Coast or Whydah or Lagos, they had to deal with the Fanti chiefs or King Agaja or King Kosoko, who'd sell them the slaves. Even if this is not good for the feelings of those involved in practical politics or in building up ideologies and myths, it's still a historical fact. I prefaced my remarks with the story of John Hancock: as I see it, whether the people in Nantucket Sound believe that John Hancock is the greatest patriot America ever had or not, he still was a smuggler and a tax-evader.

Question

Eric Williams' book called *Capitalism and Slavery* discusses the economic importance of slavery as a revenue-producing institution. In it, he attempts to show that the slave trade may have produced much of the revenue necessary to kick off the industrial revolution in England. I wish you would comment on that.

Obichere

Capitalism and Slavery is a powerful book. To those who have been through graduate work at Oxford in Empire History, the development of that book is still a very lively issue. I don't think in all honesty that you could say that the slave trade alone produced the wealth that touched off the industrial revolution. This would be historically false, economically untrue, and a perversion of English history. There were other sources of revenue in England at that time besides the slave trade. It was a lucrative job, it was a lucrative business; you only need to see the books and diaries of the slave dealers and the companies in London and Liverpool and Bristol who fitted out the ships that went on this business. However, I don't think that if other factors had not been present, the wealth gained from the slave trade alone would have touched off the industrial revolution.

I'm not a one-factor interpreter of history, and this is why I run into problems with ideologues. Eric Williams' position is a valid one. The reason why I said that Williams' experience is still a live issue at Oxford is the fact that his drafts were rejected so many times by his supervisor. Eric Williams' almost didn't make an Oxford D. Phil. because of the rigidity of his supervisor, although he went on to All Souls after that—a great achievement! He ran into trouble and he had to rewrite and recant and revise. Where was that book published? Chapel Hill, North Carolina, wasn't it?—not Oxford University Press! There was an accumulation of capital as a result of the slave trade, but I don't think that one could in all intellectual honesty say that this was the primary and only source of the wealth which led to the industrial revolution.

Question

You chose to discuss the American black man under your section on the Third World and, I think I remember, your argument was that the relationship of Africa to Latin America was in some way similar to the relationship of the black man in America to Africa. I'm wondering, whether you're arguing that there is no special, no intimate, connection between black Americans and Africa, that the thing that's most common that one should look for and emphasize in the black studies view is the experience of colonialism, segregation, and oppression which is common to the Third World?

Obichere

Well, I think what I intended to say, or what I did say, is that there is a relationship, *definitely,* between the black man in America and the black man in Africa, and, of course, the black man in Latin America. There is a special genetic relationship between the black man in America and the black man in Africa. A Senegalese friend of mine analyzed this for me in Paris. He said: "Look, both of you speak English." This is a simple fact, but it hasn't occurred to many of the analysts: the black man in America speaks English and the black man in West Africa, former British colonies, Central Africa, speaks English. Of course, the common experience of oppression is there.

I mentioned George Shepperson's article on the overwhelming influence of black Americans on the nationalist movement in Africa. This was a study done by an Englishman, or shall I say Scotsman, and it's a very valid study. In the African analysis of the Third World, the black American is definitely included. You hear some American militants talking about the situation of the black American as being that of colonialism; this may be very far from the truth—but that is how some African politicians look at it, and this is what is blared out from probably many local radio stations in Africa. It seems to me that this is how we have to look at it. It is a difficult thing, for instance, convincing an African politician whose only contact with Europe was through a cursory visit to London, who has never been a student in a university or, for that matter, a secondary school, that the situation the black Americans are fighting is not analogous or identical with the one that he fought in Africa. This is a very hard task. So, if I've answered your question, I'm saying that the special relationship exists, and in the wider context, of course, the overview is there.

Question

Does the special relationship depend on political issues or on cultural factors?

Obichere

I think maybe not on political issues, not necessarily on cultural factors as I see it, but on race-consciousness. We are black people. I was amazed a month ago, watching Paul Jacobs of San Francisco telling Louis Lomax just as it is. Louis Lomax put it to him this way, "Well, you are a Jew and I'm a black man, but I'm an American; I'm not Jewish, I'm Christian. I am an American first and a Negro second." Jacobs told Louis Lomax that he was living in a false world, that he wasn't facing reality. Jacobs asked him one question: "When the National Guard occupied Watts, if you had dared to leave your home in the hills and gone down to 103rd Street and Century Boulevard, would the Guards have said, "You are Louis Lomax, you are American!"—or would they have gunned you down at sight because you are black?"

This is a fact of life, the black American is *black*. And as long as he realizes that genetic relationship with Africa, I think this is where the ties are. Culturally, he may be different: it took *me* a while to start appreciating Ray Charles! This is culture. About a week ago I was out until 2 AM listening to LeRoi Jones and his theater group perform. But when I was green from Biafra where did I go? The Minneapolis Symphony, because I was taught in the boarding school that this was the ultimate in music. I went to the Guthrie Theater and watched Chekhov's *Three Sisters* and some Shakespeare. But today I can go to a black theater and enjoy it. So, culturally I wouldn't say that there is 100 percent harmony. One has to be acculturated, or "deculturated"—if I may coin that word.

Question

I'm still somewhat bothered by the same things that motivated an earlier question, and although I find your answers quite acceptable, I'm not sure I can rationalize them with some of the things I thought you were saying earlier. You have told us, I think quite well, how the historical record needs to be corrected. I'm reminded that black children in Surinam, the Netherlands Antilles, have a history book that begins telling them about when "the Germanic people came to our country"—not meaning Surinam, of course, but that part of Western Europe where Germanic peoples did come. I'm reminded that the geography texts in Jamaica, I think, have the first six sections on the different parts of England, Scotland, Wales, and Ireland, and finally at the back a very small map of India and the surrounding territories. There's a certain distortion of the world that was being taught to black people there.

I'm reminded of the Rebellion of 1865 in Jamaica where William Gordon was hanged by the neck until dead by Governor Edward J. Eyre at his orders. He was then a traitor, and now the nationalists and intellectuals have rewritten that and while the dates are the same and the names are the same, William Gordon is now a nationalist hero rather than a traitor and they named the new legislature after him. Yale, too, has been involved in rewriting history in Jamaica— over a different map, much to the chagrin of the Italian-American community. You mentioned Diop: in one of his books I think he also makes a claim for the discovery of America, only this time it's the sailors of Senegal who I think he claims also discovered America.

I'm not sure what you're calling for. Is it that we need 130 different versions of history, all viewed from the particular point of view of some particular nation-state? Herodotus wrote the history of the world from the point of view of the small nations, but it turned out that I think he had Greece in mind. That wasn't particularly useful. How can we proceed? Is there a possibility for a universal history on which we can all agree, a human history? Or must we be content with these different versions? I quite agree that the record needs to be corrected. I'm merely asking a question beyond that: Are we going to have to have different versions—national versions, perhaps sexual versions within a country, a black history, a white history, a Communist history, a capitalist history, and 130 nationalist histories? What is the alternative to that?

Obichere

The last portion of your statement brings out your question more clearly, and I'll address myself to that. It seems to me that you can have a universal history in a world history textbook, but I am persuaded to say that you must, of necessity, have 130 national histories and several histories of the same country *in* that particular country, written from different points of view. Empirical evidence proves this, and I'm not persuaded to think that human nature has changed very much. Rather, intellectual activity has diversified greatly, because there are more people involved. Take eighteenth-century England: There were official histories of England, there were handbooks of English history, and of course, with the age of the philosophes, there were things like David Hume's history of England. There is Macauley's *History of England*. It is nothing like Trevelyan's. H. Trevor-Roper is writing: he might come out with a history of England, of the upper classes, probably! A. J. P. Taylor interprets English history to you the way he sees it; his *England since 1914* is an example. That's not the type of history that all the dons in Cambridge and Oxford will produce, but these are histories of England. I think it has been the age-old practice of historians to distill from the wealth of monographs and controversies the facts that seem to be the most salient ones. That seems to be indubitable.

Al Omari has said that the Africans discovered America in the fourteenth century, 180 years before Columbus set out—I cannot dismiss this as false, because it wasn't invented in the twentieth century. It is down there in the Arabic records right from the time of the 1310 Mali expedition sent out by King Bakary II of Mali. It behooves us today to question where that expedition *went*. Sailing in similar vessels out of the Iberian Sea and the Mediterranean, Columbus ended up not over the edge but in the New World; probably these Africans drifted on and those of them who survived landed on some island—which we don't know, but this is my hypothesis; and if historians can't use hypotheses, then they should be honest and say that there is no scientific approach to history. Incidentally, whether it was the Mali sailors or not, Al Omari recorded that the second expedition sailed off and never came back, and there were two attempts. Well, this should be investigated. Why do we have to worry about the fact that the Vikings discovered America and not Columbus, simply because we see some runestones on the banks of the Mississippi in Minnesota? This is healthy inquiry. Once you become complacent, I think you write yourself off. Our knowledge of the past grows with controversy and continued inquiry and investigation.

Now, as for the latter part of the question, I really don't see what I could add to what I have already said—that I don't think history should be constructed around an ideology. It seems to me that this is not what good history ought to be. If a communist in Senegal living in Paris writes a history of Senegal, he will write it as he sees it. If the government of Senegal commissions people in the University of Dakar to write a history of Senegal, of course they are going to say what the Government wants to hear, not what they think. I may refer here to the history of Liverpool and Liverpool commerce—*A Century of Liverpool Commerce*, by Martin W. A. Gibson, which you might have read. Immediately after that book was published, the Manchester Chamber of Commerce commissioned two professors at Manchester University, Arthur Redford and B. W. Clapp, to write *Manchester Merchants and Foreign Trade, 1850-1939,* because they didn't want to be outdone by Liverpool. You can read these books with great profit and learn about Lancashire external trade and how it was organized, but I think it would be very erroneous and dangerous to think that this is the history of Lancashire. On the other hand, if you are writing a history of Lancashire you are going to find valid material in these monographs.

So, what I am calling for here is a continuation of the type of thing you were saying—a universal history that could be used for a universal history course which gives the accepted views and opinions of the development of Africa, Asia, and Europe and America. And where there is controversy, by all means let the students be told that there is controversy over this point. Maybe they will be the ones to find out the answers.

A RADICAL PERSPECTIVE ON
SOCIAL SCIENCE CURRICULA

Nathan Hare

I'm working with the black studies curriculum at San Francisco
State College where we have the same problem we have here this
morning, in that we have already about sixteen courses and expect
to become a department by September,* but we have the problem
of building a black studies program only to find it peopled mainly
by white students. This presents a problem, too, in the way in which
we go about it, because our premise is that education is a part of the
socialization process and, in the old days, before the urbanization
and massification of life, it was very intricately interwoven there.
Now there is a separation of home and community and the educational process to a large degree, with problems accruing consequently for both black students and white students, although we
have no wish to try to take you back to a pre-industrialized society.
As a matter of fact, Dr. Dowdy out there in the audience, from
Howard, where I used to work, will recall that when my employers
began to clamp down on my academic freedom, I told them that I
was once the best cotton-picker in Creek County, Oklahoma, and,
should it ever come to that, I could always burn my doctorate and
go back to picking cotton. They didn't appear to believe it, and I
suppose that some of them now have the impression that I went
back to the cotton patch. We at State College have the impression—
though we haven't bothered to study the history fully—that the kind
of liberal arts education which we have today grew out of the lei-
sure-class mentality described by Thorsten Veblen in his *Theory of
the Leisure Class* and other books, where he pointed out that it was
not enough for a person with wealth to possess it, he had also to

*We subsequently did gain official status in September as a department and
presently offer twenty-six courses.

display it by way of conspicuous consumption. This gave rise to the investment of prestige in nonproductive labor: if you did any work, it had to be of no remunerative benefit to anybody and clearly a useless enterprise. This syndrome spread into their education, which was restricted to wealthy individuals in those days, since others could not afford it, as education had not then been socialized as it is today. So education came to consist of time-consuming procedures and useless endeavors, such as footnoting, with a certain form you couldn't deviate from; in order to document your history or what not, you had to put a little number up there and a little number down here and this seemed somehow to give it more prestige and profundity than it otherwise would merit.

At San Francisco State College recently there arose a contention between the black students and the white administrators because the white department of history wanted a white boy with a Ph.D. from a major university and a string of scholarly publications in "learned journals" (as they kept stressing), whereas the black students wanted a black fellow who hadn't any degrees at all but who knew more about African history than the white historian. This much was admitted by the white professor himself and it was known that the black applicant had spent two years, for example, searching through the Schomburg Collection: So there was a lightweight confrontation, with both sides calling the other's applicant "unqualified." The black students felt that if a white professor of history couldn't understand that it's anachronistic in the present day—just now anyway at this particular point in the black-consciousness movement, though maybe not ten or twenty years from now—for a white professor to teach black militant students black history, then this white professor doesn't quite understand the recent black movement. Consequently he doesn't understand black history, and therefore he's unqualified to teach black history, regardless of how many Ph.D.s and publications he has in the learned journals. In fact, if a black historian is going to publish in one of the learned journals, especially if he's going to publish on the slavery era, he is placed in the very ludicrous and unenviable position of having to footnote white slave masters or the scholarly representatives of that era. The blacks weren't even allowed to learn to read and write, let alone to write history in those days. Even *The Confessions of Nat Turner* as taken by William Gray were not published until fifty years after they had been taken down, obviously biased; this was an era that couldn't bear to see them published until fifty years later; yet this is the era from which we have to get our footnotes and documentation.

So, we don't feel that that history is valid or that any history based on that documentation is valid. We are going to have to declare it all void and to start the writing of that history all over again. This does not mean that we, or the black persons who write history, are going to spend too much time searching around for heroes in history and trying to rewrite everything which the white historians have written; this would cause us to waste time which we could spend on trying to make history. Persons who make history or help to make history in a sense are writing history, because they dictate to some degree what it is that the persons who write history will write.

I was up to a Presbyterian white girls' college about a year or two ago, when I was working at Howard, and at lunchtime they gathered around me slobbering over the fact that the dean of the college had been up there two weeks before with slides to prove that there were colored persons in ancient Greece and Rome. I said, "So what, now they're going to blame us coloreds for the fall of Rome." We're not going to get bogged down in historical trivia, but there needs to be at least some re-examination of the history, as the brother who preceded me has discussed. Looking into sociology, for example—I don't want to spend too much time on that: I want to get into the educational needs, which I think are more vital than social science, even though social science certainly could be used to help solve them—sociologists used to go around and ask people why they did this and that, making polls and such. Finally they discovered that they were aggregating the ignorance of the people because people didn't always know why they did a thing, and if they did, they might not tell the truth about it. So, they began to get very tricky. First of all, the problem might be that you're not measuring the degree of intensity of one's feeling or belief, so you put up "very happy" if you're talking about marital happiness—are you "very happy," "somewhat happy," "somewhat unhappy," or "very unhappy." Then you could compute some formula on that, some statistical analysis, and you would have an index of happiness. But we discovered that the probability of a woman saying she was very happy depended on how far distant her husband was—and I've had them change the response after the husband had left the room. So, sociologists get tricky after that: they say, well, since they don't know, or won't tell the truth, we'll do it by indirection. We'll get an index of happiness—say, kissing (never mind Judas)—and we'll ask the fellow, "How many times do you kiss your wife a day?" and those who kiss their wives five times or less will be regarded as "very unhappy," from six to ten will be regarded as "somewhat unhappy," from eleven to fifteen will be regarded as "somewhat happy," and sixteen or more will be very tired at the end of the day.

This is the kind of thing that they've been doing. I was standing around during the cocktail hour at the American Sociological Association's convention in San Francisco last August, and of course in a convention you know they spend a good deal of time at the bar and in the hallways; more than they do in the sessions. A former professor who was very eminent was talking about his research, and he said that he was very excited about the fact that he had made a survey of Negroes in Chicago and only 7 percent said that they believe in riots. I almost swallowed my Scotch on the rocks whole, and I said, "That's about seventy thousand, isn't it? How many do you think you need to start a riot?" He later found out how many were needed, but I think that he was a victim of the myth of "majority-rule" —which is a part of the myth of American democracy, the utopian ideal of democracy. This leads many persons who are trying to study revolutionary change or to bring it about to get off base.

They tell us, for example, that we can't fight back when attacked because we're outnumbered ten to one, that we're a "minority group." We are eradicating that word, because it doesn't make any difference what our numbers are; the white man rules all over the world. If he's one percent or two percent in South Africa or Rhodesia, he rules. If he's forty percent in Washington, D.C., he rules. If he's forty percent in Mississippi, he rules. Ninety percent in Maine. It doesn't make any difference; it's a mental attitude, and a social organization growing out of that. In Rhodesia the blacks outnumber the whites 23 to 1: each one of the 23 could have taken a finger apiece, gather around a white man, ten a finger apiece, ten a toe apiece, and three any portion that pleased them, and pulled him apart—but instead they grumbled in the dark and tucked their tails because of the mental attitude. So, it doesn't make any difference. Yet—though I could possibly kill twenty white men, cut the throat of one, jump off the roof on another, drop a hand grenade in the whole midst of them—the same persons who tell us that we can't fight back when attacked will turn around and tell me that I can *vote* my way in, when I don't have but one vote and that's between the lesser of two evils. There seems to be a little misunderstanding of arithmetic somewhere in the concept of "minority group."

We're beginning to question these things, and I think this is the major job of both the educators and the social scientists, to begin to question this society; especially if we're going to operate on the premise that the black student is faced with an educational system which is not relevant (as he often says these days) to his own experience, his own community, and indeed is not relevant to white students either. This is because it has strayed away from the community and of course the home. We feel that the only hope in trying to bring about viable educational change and a fuller participation of the black race is through involving the black community, *wedding,* so to speak, the black community and the black student. The issue here is one of motivation—I don't mean in just the psychological sense of the word, because we made studies in Chicago of juvenile gangs and almost to a man they wanted to go to college, but they had a sense of defeatism which they'd assimilated from their circumstances and therefore didn't feel that they could go, or that it wouldn't do any good for them to go. So, in order to bring about the meaningful educational participation of the black race, we're going to have to try to change some of the nature of the society, let alone its education. We have to decide in trying to bring persons to adjust to a society what it is they are adjusting to—and whether they are justified in trying to adjust to a society which is itself maladjusted. It seems that the feeling is, if you're adjusted to a maladjusted society, then you yourself are maladjusted.

The first step, then, is to debunk some of the myths of the Great

White Society—that it is a kind of society which is aiming at or approaching perfection in its institutional systems, including its educational system. Veblen talked about this many decades ago, even though it's still true today: that it's mainly a perfunctory memorization of knowledge, dilly-dallying in fancy, lofty terminology, and assimilating "approved" bodies of knowledge. I used to go into the classroom at Howard and indicate this by making up some concept, preferably with a foreign-sounding name such as "zeigschaft." Then I'd say, that is the concept which describes the predicament in which persons in society are alienated or they have a sense of "nomlessness"—and they'd copy that down, almost slobbering because they were preparing to go back to the dormitory and talk about how much they were learning in the class, and perhaps have their roommates call out the word to them so they could memorize all that and say how "heavy" their professor was. I then say: "but you have to be able to measure this "nomlessness" and alienation in society, and the way you do that is by computing an index, an Index of Racial Response. That is computed by getting a sample of persons and observing them in a given day, observing the number of smiles that occur in that sample as they encounter one another during the day; and divide the number of smiles observed by the number of persons encountering one another, multiply it times 100 and divide the whole thing by the square root of 2—and they'd be copying all of that down. So, I would finally step back and ask them if they could see clearly because I wanted them to get it all down, and then I would explain that I had made it all up and didn't understand it myself, and doubted that they did either. But this is the kind of thing: they think they have an education after they have memorized the professor's gobbledygook and vomited it back up on a test.

One day I walked into a classroom and I noticed the teachers wouldn't erase the board: if they had said something worthwhile (they thought), such as the French teachers and the math teachers, they wouldn't erase the board. The others, sociologists and whatnot, would erase theirs quite readily; but it seems that the language teachers and the math teachers thought that because their stuff was unintelligible, it was profound and nobody could get it if they set their minds to it; so they'd leave it there. After a while, an anthropologist who preceded me in that particular room began to imitate them. One day I saw about forty different tribes listed on the board: you see, the idea is that if you memorize all the tribes, you don't understand any particular tribe. So, I said, "I think these white folks around here are going stone-crazy"—she had them divided into the various institutional forms, divided first by "westernized" and "primitive." Under the "primitive" form, for tracing one's ancestry she had the matrilineal where you trace the ancestry through the mother; on the "westernized" side, she had the patrilineal system where you trace the ancestry through the father—and anybody knows that it's more accurate and superior to trace the ancestry through the mother than it is through the father, because you have to take the mother's word for it and sometimes she doesn't know herself. I told about the young lady in my community named Betty Jo. There was a fellow named Johnny Lee, who had come home to his father happy because he was going to marry Betty Jo; his father said, "I didn't tell you before, son, but you can't marry Betty Jo— that's my daughter, she's your sister; don't tell your mama." He moped around and finally his mother made him break down, and he told what his father had said. His mother said, "That's OK, you can marry Betty Jo—don't tell your daddy, I didn't tell you before, but he ain't your father."

So, certainly we have to begin to question some of these things. We have to question the monogamous system, I think. The Census Bureau tells me that for every 100 males in New York, non-white males in New York, there are 33 extra females. This insures that somebody has got to engage in extracurricular activity, or else some women will be suffering a shortage of the normal processes of life. And this is going to make for family breakdown. (The figures were from 25 years of age to 40 years of age, not for the entire population.) At the same time, they're sending the black males to die in disproportionate numbers in Vietnam: this means that five or ten years from now there'll be even a greater shortage—this, of course, leads to marital breakdown, assuming that we're going to keep the monogamous system we have now, which assumes a one-to-one sex ratio or else it's sort of "unnatural" and "abnormal." Then they're going to send in Moynihan and these other fellows up at Yale and

Harvard to study the black family and to show how disorganized it is and how if we'd just get our family more stabilized, we could do pretty well. Jomo Kenyatta talks about this in his book *From Mount Kenya,* where the Christian missionaries came in and told some of the groups that had polygamy, which apparently was a function of their own demographic, socio-economic needs, that in order to be saved, they had to give up all their wives but one. This led to social disorganization. Then they gave grants to the missionary anthropologists and sent them in to study how disorganized the Africans were.

We have to begin to study these things, to question, perhaps to build a new black morality of our own, at the same time as we develop a new kind of educational system. But I won't spend too much time on sex, because when I told this to one of my classes at Howard I saw the students were pretty shocked, and in order to relieve their shock I assured them that I adhered to their norms of monogamy. And I told them about the year before when I had tried to start an Association of Virgins on Howard's campus, one girl got sick and went home, another one flunked out, and the third one wouldn't march all by herself. I also said that the reason why the clocks don't match at Howard—one says 10:20, another says 1:40, the other says 2:30—is because every time a virgin passes a clock at Howard, the clock stands still. Well, within thirty minutes after that class the chairman of my department was calling me excitedly to say that the dean had said that a student had said that I had said that I was the only virgin on Howard's campus! Which was an honor I wore with great dignity until the day I left.

Certainly, we have got to have a new look at some of these so-called "standards" they set up for us. Once a friend and I made a little test, using our (black) culture. He was teaching at a white junior college.* We exchanged these little "culture tests" containing such things as "hog maws," "black-eyed peas," and so forth, and I don't think a single one of those white students knew what hog maws were. Look at all of them sitting there right now with their

---

*A similar test by a government research analyst recently appeared in *Time* magazine.

mouths open, don't know what hog maws are. So, if we gave a test, too, we'd see that you are "culturally deprived." In fact, I used to tell my white colleagues that they were culturally deprived, because not a single one of them could tell me who Otis Redding was. And he had been on the best-seller list for years, and England had given him the best vocalist prize. We've got to begin to question some of these things.

It seems to me that the educational system as we know it now grew out of the needs—as industrialization developed and some occupations became professions—to shut off the overflow of aspirants to professional niches to balance supply and demand. They set up all kinds of criteria for that purpose; so that you could get through a college course of study making all A's and then flunk a comprehensive exam—I've known persons who did that. Or, you could do all that and pass the written bar exam and flunk the oral bar exam because of your political beliefs—I've known persons who did that. They have all these criteria. Like a French exam: it was a widely known thing at the University of Chicago that nobody finished the French exam in the three hours allotted for it—I'm just pointing this out to show that I'm not bitter, because I had finished it and I was at home and had forgotten about it by the time the three hours were up. But anyway, I passed that French exam, yet it's of no use to me at all now, it was just a waste of time altogether. And so are many of the other things which you have to do to get a degree or certificate of education. Theses, for example, in which professors hold the student's hand and help him write it, are another case in point. The student eventually is brought, not to read a thesis, but to talk about the thesis before a committee of persons who decide on the basis of his talking, not on the basis of his thesis, whether he has written a good enough thesis to justify receiving a degree. These criteria may need to be changed.

An "outstanding young educator" for Washington, D.C., who had been graduated from one of these so-called "inferior" Negro colleges, went recently to California—she has about thirty hours beyond the Masters Degree and had met the demands of boards of education in several places—and they told her she needed fifteen more hours in order to qualify. And then they say we are not qualified. They wanted her to take such courses as California history. This is the kind of thing which we have to question.

I want to round up with what I think is the solution to the problem of education with special reference to blacks. We are working on this at San Francisco State College, where we hope eventually to get incorporated, before the end of the year possibly, a Department of Black Studies. Presently, we have a black studies curriculum. The Department of Black Studies will not consist of a mere blackening of white courses such as persons appear to contemplate as they speak of a black curriculum around the country. True, there is some value in black content alone insofar as it contributes to a sense of identity and involvement: the black student studying his history can get a sense of pastness as a springboard to a sense of collective destiny with his people, and, having this new self-image, may want to convey it to others, and accordingly achieve a higher level of performance.

As a matter of fact, we have proof of that. About forty-five students in our Black Students' Union (who fathered the idea of the black studies curriculum) were on probation before we began the black studies program. Of the forty-five students who were on probation when the courses were instituted last semester, only twenty-three remained by the end of the semester. We also discovered that it wasn't just a case of their getting good grades in their black courses: they also were doing better in their white courses, in almost every case, because, having acquired the new sense of pride and involvement in the education process, they wanted to convey that in their classes. Whereas they used to sit back quietly, feeling inferior and not saying anything in class, now they speak out in class—and they call the white folks down on some of their jive discussions. It's a different kind of thing, and they do better in their classes, whereas in the past they would rather play cards. Many of them would still rather do that until we get the full program instituted. But we feel that it's not just the blackening of the courses which alone will solve the problem, even though we encourage that. As a matter of fact, in order to help solve the problem of the white students flooding the black courses, we are encouraging the existing departments—and they are doing that, for whatever reason—to rush ahead in instituting what one of them calls "dark courses," which will be about ethnic groups, minorities, this, that, or the other, "politics in the Negro society," and all that sort of thing. A sociologist wrote me about that the other day, and she didn't call them "dark courses" any more. I told her about "dark courses"—she called them "color compatible courses." That's the God's truth. If you use "dark" instead of "color compatible," then you're not educated, you see. But that's the kind of thing we're trying to change.

This has to involve a good deal of social organization, because in order to stimulate the black child and give him the push and boost he needs we will have to transform the black community, which has been excluded in the past and has gained a sense of defeatism and has adjusted itself to the conditions which it hasn't been able to change up to this point. Many persons have "escaped"—for want of a better word—the so-called "ghetto" or the black slum, but they are very unique persons. They're like the trees in the forest that survive a forest fire; it doesn't mean that the fire didn't burn down the other trees, just because some trees survive.

In the black community as I experienced it—I happen to have been the third person in eleven years in my community to go to college— there was a disdain for education which had been built up by the history of black exclusion. During slavery it was against the law to teach a black person to read and write. Even when I personally started to read and write I almost stopped, because they gave me those little readers that had some white kids doing strange things I didn't know anything about: "Up, up, Jane," "come, come," "oh, oh," "look, look," "see, see," "my, my"—it had me seeing double by the time I got to the end of the page! And of course I figured that maybe white kids might talk tom-foolery like that; not black kids. They say, "You better come on here, Jane." Then I switched to the Bible, I found a little Bible and I liked it because it was small. I tried to start reading it and there were "nays" and "thous" and "wouldest" and so forth, and I almost stopped reading for a long time: I couldn't bring myself to read much anymore. But this is the kind of thing black kids are given.

Well, in order to involve the black community we feel that the courses ought to be tied there, that theory is useful for its own sake and as a means to application, but it is not enough. The book *The Miseducation of the American Teacher* surveys 7,000 teachers who had taken methods courses where they teach you how to teach but don't teach you anything *to* teach, and found out that the courses had been inadequate, that they had to learn how to teach after they had got out of college. They learned from their colleagues, their co-workers down the hall, because they don't tell you what to do when you get thirty-five students out there looking at you and expecting you to entertain them and inform them for a full day. New teachers have to learn that from the teacher down the hall who tells them how to make out seat work and other paraphernalia to keep the kids busy while they dilly-dally with the others.

So, we feel that if we have a course called "The Social Organization of the Black Community" it will be tied to the black community. Consequently, part of what the student will do in fulfilling the requirement will be, maybe, organizing a social group, say a civic club, or/and maybe become an apprentice of a community organizer. In a black history course they would have to put on panels for younger children in church basements and maybe in elementary and junior high schools—this is endless, any course you think of—so at the same time they are influencing the black community and organizing it and using the resources of the black community.

In a course in black oratory, for example, they would study the themes of the black orators from Frederick Douglass down to Stokely Carmichael: at the same time as they learned speech technique, they would learn what their appeals had been and then they would bring in leaders from the community to "rap," as they call it, before the class, and later analyze what they had done there. Other things being equal, when such students get out into the black community when once they have been graduated, they will be more effective, because first of all, other things being equal again, they would be more committed to the black community, rather than trying to escape it as educational exposure now teaches them to do, where you learn about Shakespeare and Beethoven's Fifth Symphony and so forth.

I tried to get into that one time. They stopped calling it Beethoven's Fifth Symphony and were saying "The Fifth"—I thought they

were talking about a bottle of whiskey. So I ditched it and went
back to listening to the good music, which is Ray Charles and Bo
Diddly and Otis Redding—even though it doesn't mean that I can't
do that other kind, though I never had a course in music. We had a
teacher in junior high school who was playing on a talent show and
she played, I think, looking back, Chopin's "Revolutionary Etude,"
but it was a very vigorous thing and we all thought that she had gone
crazy, because it was known that she had had a nervous breakdown
once before. And everybody started laughing just as you're doing
now. They were laughing at her: she was just going around, falling all
over the piano, falling back, and they were all laughing at her—but I
wasn't laughing, because I thought that somebody who was cracking
up should be pitied and not laughed at. But still, I've written term
papers for music majors, and when a sister wrote me recently to do
two analyses of some pieces she had been assigned, the requirement
was to listen to these recordings. What I did (I didn't have much
time) was rush into the library and read a little smattering on the
selections. Then I used my imagination and wrote up my analysis of
the recordings—haven't heard them to this day—shipped the essays
to my sister, and she got A's on both of them. So, it strikes us as a
lot of jive, these so-called standards.

In this footnoting, for example, I used to have a rule of thumb
that I would have an average of eight footnotes on every page. I used
to go into the library and spend five or ten minutes scanning through
a book to get some footnote or some reference or some quotation.
And then I'd footnote it, and my professor would assume that I had
read each book I quoted in its entirety; and he would say, "I'm very
impressed by your reading." And I would say thank you. And accept
my A. These are the things that we're going to have to start questioning, because even the white student, too, is beginning to grow
dissatisfied with that kind of thing. At the same time as we transform the course content, our new educational process can, so to
speak, help transform the community. Already, now, we have reno-
vated a building for a Black Information Center, where we will put
out a little paper in connection with the black journalism class. We
will try to inform the community about social legislation rights and
health care, put on cultural shows—we brought LeRoi Jones and

Oscar Browne out to a so-called "Black Night" at San Francisco State College recently. We'll put on cultural shows and try to give the kids some sense of their heritage, their culture, some identity, some roots. We will propagandize the children, in effect, tutor them as we are doing now at the lower levels, to seek knowledge and education. Just as there are voter registration campaigns now, we will have campaigns to register drop-outs, having rejuvenated their interest in school, and told them about the new educational things we have in store for them. Many things of this nature which I don't have time to go into now could be instituted, not only to make education relevant to the black community but to make the black community relevant to education. And if this works, then maybe black studies ultimately would be of interest only in the way that a museum is and only white folks would be interested in this sort of thing, maybe twenty or thirty years from now. We are only using it in this crisis period for therapeutic reasons. Most of the persons that lead us—look at SNCC, RAM, the Black Panthers, all of them more or less, except Stokely, who was also a very brilliant person—were A students and above-average students who dropped out. They were making it in business and education, but they didn't like what it was so they dropped out and became revolutionaries—and Stokely himself could be said to have dropped out, because he could have gone on to more schooling, to become an eminent professor, but he dropped out of it. These promising scholars didn't like what it was they were getting. As Rap Brown said, he found out that his professors couldn't teach him anything that was of any use to him.

So, if we can bring this change about, as a course for black students, it will have an impact ultimately on the whites. The white student will use it as a basis for demanding a change in his own curriculum, as he is doing now, and we can bring about an impact, if we're successful, on the entire cemetery of American education as it exists today.

QUESTION PERIOD

Question

You mentioned that French was of no use to you in your own college work. Last night Mr. Karenga put stress on teaching Swahili. Do you feel that something like this should be included?

Hare

Well, Ron Karenga's a linguist, among other things, and he would stress language more than I would. If it's a language that's going to be used as a basis for building identity and *esprit de corps* of a group, then I would say, 100 percent yes. But if it's going to be used as some sham standard or criterion which a person has to master in order to get an education, I say, no.

Question

As I look in the classroom the students I have tried to appeal to are people with whom I empathize, who already have a sense of identity, a sense of purpose and direction which are *essentially* Anglo-American, but which we now all agree must be modified to reflect Afro-Americanism. How can we affect this so that we begin to see changes *now?*

Hare

Well, this is all the kind of thing that we were talking about—we just set about doing it: organizing, somebody mentioned a black scholars journal, all kinds of efforts to propagandize people in the other direction. Now, on the college level many persons are a bit far gone, but I know many persons who have been altered on the college level: after they graduated they used to write back and say that they had realized what was going on—and these persons can go out and help to change the younger children, students at the lower levels. And it's understandable, it's not going to be done all at once. And of course, teachers and professors are going to probably increasingly find themselves sort of shut out by the black students. I know at one college the black students have a rule of thumb that if things don't go their way, things don't function, it's as simple as that. So, when the guy's talking a lot of jive about Greek and so forth, they just close him out or they start asking a lot of questions just to disrupt things and make him uncomfortable, and in one case they had to just go in and break up the class. This is not, possibly, the way in which we want things to happen, but that's the way things are happening—and will happen increasingly in the future if things don't change.

So, I don't have any magic formula for making it happen to-morrow. I just say we have to work for it in all the ways we know how, using social science and any other kind of science and our own reasons to try to devise ways and means to bring about in this kind of thinking and an awareness on the part of people. First, I think people have to become aware of some of the irrationalities of the society in which they live, which is just *now*, before they can set about trying to develop a new and positive replacement, just as the surgeon has to eradicate the sore or the cancer before he can nurse the body back to health. But I don't have a magic formula for doing it just now, except the one which I was talking about briefly involving the college student. But that's where you have enough college students—you don't have enough around here—but where there *are* a number of college students.

For example, at San Francisco State College we have got them to waive the entrance exam for 250 extra black students, and next year it will be more than that, the next year more than that, and the next more than that, until we have a body of persons there to be used—not to be exploited, because they will gain something in return—as manpower to help bring about the sort of aggressiveness and pro-blackness of the students at the lower levels in the school system of the black community. We're envisioning a five-year kind of plan, and that's putting it sort of fast. I think that after five years we'll see tremendous effects if it's instituted, but it's probably going to take ten years to really get the thing going, and twenty years before we wouldn't need it anymore in the way in which it is envisioned now. I don't know anything which can do it overnight. I think that's the only kind of thing which can do it ever, so to speak.

Question

I wonder whether you would care to comment on the possibility of immigration from the United States as one of the possible alternatives to what I understand you to believe will be a continued life—for black people and for white—of strife and crisis after crisis?

Hare

I don't know. I know that the United States was spawned by persons who immigrated to another land in a separatist movement—they didn't want to pay taxes—and chopped up the tea and blamed it on the Indians, same as the blacks might chop up something in Georgia and blame it on the Cuban refugees, if they were that ruthless. But I don't think much of separatism in that sense. There's no place really to go because this country, by its own admission, owns three-fifths of all the wealth in the whole world, even though it's about six percent or so of the population. And certainly, if we go to Africa, they've got control of that: Firestone owns both banks in Liberia and the rubber industry's owned by some of these companies. I understand that United Fruit owned most of Cuba before Castro kicked them out.

For example, I've been studying the separatist movement during the slavery era and the black radicals then, free blacks proposing to separate off, and what they were doing then is leaving the slave blacks here unattended. Moreover, most of the separatist groups in the slavery era never *went* anywhere. It's the same thing today: they talk about going somewhere but they never go anywhere. In fact, they set about being busier and getting themselves anchored here, going into business and so forth. The separatism merely becomes a sort of symbol, a sort of expressive behavior, a way of getting a sense of psychological independence from the white oppressors. I don't believe in any kind of absolutism—I think integrationism and separatism are both means for possible elevation of a people, but when the thing becomes the end in itself, then it loses its effectiveness.

It's the same as the separatist movement where you can't have any association with any white persons. Now, I have that problem because some of my best friends are white—and if you can't associate with the whites, you can't join the FBI. That's all regarded as undesirable, so what the FBI does is have a one-way spy system: they get black fellows to grow Afros, grow their hair out, give them Arabic names and teach them how to quote Frantz Fanon and Mao Tse-tung—which was probably good in their day and that particular society, but this is more industrialized, wealthier and all that, and maybe their things won't work here exactly as they did there; they certainly have to be altered to fit this particular demography, social and industrial system, and everything—but they give us these things (with Jean-Paul Sartre, a white man, having written the Introduction to *The Wretched of the Earth*), they give us these things, give us Mao, and then we spout them. They send these black fellows in spouting them, and they rise up to be high in our organization: we're planning a demolition job and they're sitting on the planning board, the FBI. So what we need to do is infiltrate the FBI. When the FBI infiltrated the KKK, the KKK infiltrated the FBI: surely we're as sophisticated as the Klan—so we need to have a two-way thing going: we need to have a black person in there knowing what the white folks are doing. I wrote an article for *Negro Digest* back in November which (because they've had special issues, as you know who have read the magazine for the past few months) won't be out until June, but it's called "New Roles for Uncle Toms," where I'm going into the way in which we can choose our own Uncle Toms and use this to get pragmatic and strategic, and stop being just expressive—and stop making everything we do a religion.

AFRICAN INFLUENCE ON THE ART OF
THE UNITED STATES

Robert Farris Thompson

African-influenced art in the United States attests the cultural vitality of the Afro-American. Recent research has discovered a wealth of
continuities in the Deep South, from wood sculpture and basketry
to ceramic sculptured forms in which Western types become the
basis for patterns of iconic intensity possibly derived from the
Congo-Angola section of Africa. The assumption has been that
slavery in the United States destroyed the creative memories of
newly arrived Africans, so that today no African influence can be
discerned in this country, apart from fragments in the verbal arts,
music, and the dance. The more extreme view holds that no form of
African influence whatsoever remains. The literature on African-
influenced art in the United States is consequently sparse (few are
likely to study a field believed not to exist) and is embedded in
larger controversy about the relative strength of African-influenced
custom in this country.

James A. Porter (1943: 13-28) described the contribution of African slave artisans to American folk art. Later, he rethought their
achievement in terms of subsaharan retentions. Porter detected,
without going into detail, "unmistakable signs of African recollection in peculiarities of surface design" characterizing effigy vessels
made in stoneware by men of African descent in South Carolina

NOTE: This lecture at the symposium was illustrated by about 125 lantern
slides, a thirty-minute film on the use of sculpture in dance context in West
African art, and demonstrations of praise drumming. It has not proved practical to reproduce any of these illustrations here, and I have revised my lecture
accordingly. The reader who is interested will find the entire thesis intact in a
forthcoming volume entitled *African and Afro-American Art: The Trans-
atlantic Tradition,* to be published by New York Graphic.

(1966: 6). More typical is the view of Cedric Dover (1960: 18), who found that:

> Africanism is rare even in American Negro woodcraft, though the material itself facilitates the continuity of decorative treatment from one generation to another—the walking stick carved in 1863 by Henry Gudgell, a slave in Missouri, is the only example we have been able to find from the continental United States. The interesting pottery to which Mr. Porter refers is no more than the descriptive phrase "slave pottery" implies. Its purposes, inspiration, and making are wholly American.

Dover is not convincing because he does not reason the function, sources, or meaning of the Afro-Carolinian vessels, nor does he juxtapose examples in order to prove, on the comparative basis, the process by which Anglo-American forms in Afro-American hands remain Anglo-American. He takes the self-limiting term, "slave pottery," assuredly invented by Anglo-Americans and not the makers of the objects, to serve an argument about nonexistence of African influence. Art will not be judged, however, in terms of racist verbalisms. Unfortunately, the writings of men who make up their minds before they initiate research into African continuities in this country influence our thinking about Afro-American art to this day.

There is another kind of scholarship that has a bearing on the problem. Here one studies the differences between the condition of slavery in North and South America, whose relevance to the formation of United States Afro-American art can be well imagined. To begin with, circumstances favoring self-assertion in terms of ideology and leadership were perhaps stronger in Brazil and the Caribbean than in the United States, for, as Eugene Genovese (1966) tells us, the cultivation of sugar in Latin American plantations led to the formation of work forces averaging two hundred slaves, directed by a relatively small population of Ibero-Americans. Thus there was less pressure against the sustaining of much of African culture and the tendency to lose identity was not severe. In the United States half of the slaves lived in units of twenty or less and most others in groups of fifty or less. The slaves were lost in a hostile white sea. Death awaited outside the plantation where the "cracker" (rural racist) farmers without slaves were plentiful, armed, and in complete sympathy with the policies of the great landholders.

The capacity to form independent states within states, composed of escape slaves, existed only where the state apparatus was weak and the proximity of empty tropical forest assured a haven under familiar African-like conditions of climate and ecology. An environment of total hostility in North America meant that development of the arts comparable to those of separate African-influenced states, founded by runaway slaves, such as the great carving styles of the Saramacca, Djuka, and Boni peoples in Dutch Surinam on the north coast of South America was well-nigh impossible.

The social organizations under the Catholic Church to which the Afro-Cuban slave might belong, for another example of a difference between slave experiences, simply did not exist in Protestant Virginia, so that there were no fraternal brotherhoods, no special holidays save Christmas, and no great street processionals brightened by displays of African-derived costume, sculpture, and the dance (cf. Klein, 1967: 120) Early St. Louis under the Spaniards might have been an exception to the point, for at least we know that Africans and other American-born slaves there were painting their bodies and adorning themselves with feathers in highly visible dancing. But even here the Spanish Lt.-Governor saw fit, on August 15, 1781, to forbid "all savages, whether free or slave, and all Negroes of this said post to clothe themselves in any other manner than according to our own usage and custom" (Houck, 1909, I: 245).

The most important enemy of African cultural tradition was racism. Artistic autonomy implies social autonomy. The suppression of all customs which did not confirm the dominance of the Westerner were more vigorously prosecuted in the British colonies than elsewhere in the New World, according to Roger Abrahams. Here the rationale was the notion of inherent superiority over "dark peoples," a conviction perhaps dating from the contact of the Anglo-Saxon with the Celt (Abrahams, 1967: 459).

Distinctions between North and South American experiences of slavery do not exhaust the nature of the problem. A given set of known cultural factors does not imply the whole. Nevertheless, many writers, modern or otherwise, guided by these facts or for reasons of their own, have asserted by fiat zero continuity of African traditions in the United States. Silberman (1964: 109) is typical: "In contrast to European immigrants who brought rich cultures and long histories with them, the Negro has been completely stripped of his past and severed from any culture save that of the United States." More serious is the theoretical account of Stanley Elkins, who in his influential *Slavery: a Problem in American Institutional and Intellectual Life* (1963: 101) describes "what happens" to the African culture of the arriving slave in the United States:

> Much of his past had been annihilated; nearly every prior connection had been severed. Not that he had really "forgotten" all these things—his family and kinship arrangements, his language, the tribal religion, the taboos, the name he had once borne, and so on—but none of it any longer carried much meaning . . . Where then was he to look for new standards, new cues—who would furnish them now? He could now look to none but his master.

Certainly it is true, probably, that North American slavery obliterated African patterns of political structure, economy, and familial institutions, but it is altogether wrong to extrapolate from known vicissitudes a total erasure of the past.

Research without prejudicing the case presents a more positive assessment. Musicology seems a more reliable index to the developments within the social life of the slaves, where they asserted their common humanity, than the deliberations of Elkins and kindred spirits. Here one learns that the basic structural traits which define West Africa as a province in World music (dominance of a percussive concept of music, off-beat phrasing of melodic accents, overlapping of vocal and instrumental patterns of call-and-response, and so forth) reappear in United States Afro-American musical forms such as the work song and the ring shout (Waterman, 1952: 211-18). These musical continuities are so visible and massive that they cannot by any stretch of the imagination be characterized as esoteric or circumstantial, and they demolish by virtue of existence the new myth of the disappearance of the Afro-American's past in the United States. Indeed, from the further development of the work song and the ring shout have arisen the basic café musics of the world in the twentieth century. The triumph of jazz and the blues indicates that something is wrong somewhere with the theory of slaves rejecting their meaningless past for the cultural standards of their master. This does not mean that there was no borrowing from Western music and other cultural forms, but jazz and the blues do not sound like weakened European folk music precisely because their innovators respected African traditions of timing, timbre, and so forth, which had not in the least been forgotten or jettisoned.

Then, too, it must be said that fresh research into the nature of differential slave status in the Americas tends to indicate that the experience of the Afro-American, whether in North or South America or the Caribbean, was not all that different in terms of debasement. Mintz (1961: 581) contests the notion of Latin American slavery as a single historical phenomenon. And Sio (1968: 327), in his interesting criticism of prior assumptions, cites Mintz' point that Cuban slavery "dehumanized the slave as viciously as had Jamaican or Northern America slavery" and Boxer's assertion that the widely accepted "belief that the Brazilian was an exceptionally kind master is applicable only to nineteenth-century slavery under the Empire, and not to the colonial period." Sio concludes that many more similarities existed between United States and Latin American slavery than were previously suspected.

If this is so, then the facile assumption of total disappearance of African custom in the United States might well be rethought. The notion that only generic continuities are possible in the necessarily more vicious social climate of North America has to be seriously modified, too, for if both North and South America were a kind of living hell for Afro-Americans, and Afro-Cubans and Afro-Brazilians managed to assert ethnicity, then it has to be considered whether specific or nearly specific continuities were not possible in the United States as well.

Art provides a possible avenue for the testing of these theories. The suppression of the more public African influences, such as religious ritual and the use of subsaharan costume, did not still the voice of more intimate expressions. Present to this day are African-influenced verbal arts (Aunt Nancy tales), healing (conjuring), cuisine (hog maws and collard greens), singing (field hollers and work songs), and dance forms in considerable quantity. And present, too, are parallel visual continuities: amazing stoneware vessels shaped in the form of anguished human faces made by Afro-Americans in South Carolina in the last century, multiple wood carving modes in tidewater Georgia, basketry modes of astonishing purity near Charleston, the deliberate decoration of graves in the African manner with surface deposits of broken earthenware and possessions in many parts of the Deep South, and isolated instances of Afro-American wood carving in Livingston County, Missouri, and Onondaga County, New York. If these visual traditions are less blatant than the programs of costuming, sculpture, and the dance with which Afro-Cubans used to bring their street fiestas to proper aesthetic pitch, they are no less valid for this difference. By the hand of individual Afro-American masters were fashioned works of art whose blending of remembered ancestral and encountered alien modes may now be estimated and explored.

Livingston County, Missouri

A striking example of what may be designated Afro-Missourian art is a walking stick carved by the Afro-American blacksmith, Henry Gudgell, in Livingston County some fifty miles northeast of Kansas City.

Henry Gudgell was born a slave in 1826 in Kentucky. Census records of 1880 at the Missouri State Historical Society at Columbia indicate that the father of Gudgell was born in Tennessee and his mother in Kentucky. His father was an Anglo-American and his mother a slave. The mother trekked on foot with her child, it is said, from Kentucky to Missouri with some of the slaves of what was to become the Spence Gudgell farm when the Anglo-American Gudgells came to the area at some point before 27 December 1867, when the name of Spence Gudgell appears for the first time in the records of the Livingston County Recorder's Office. Thus Henry Gudgell and his mother were from Kentucky, a state which in 1793 had absorbed large numbers of slaves from coastal America (Jordan, 1969: 320).

Accessible information does not permit the reconstitution of the world of the sculptor's childhood in Kentucky, nor the kinds of coastally derived aspects of African-influenced culture he may have experienced.

It is remembered that Gudgell was "fair"—i.e. a mulatto—and that not only was he a blacksmith and wheelwright of note but also a master of coppersmithing and silversmithing. Henry Gudgell made rings out of melted-down coins, a method not unlike that of the Navajo of New Mexico. He embellished these rings with minute geometric chasing and taught the craft to his son, Edmund. A surviving daughter of a slave who belonged to the Gudgells told the writer in November 1968 that she owned a plain silver ring adorned with the single figure of a heart, made from a dime piece by either Henry or Edmund Gudgell. Local testimony makes clear that Henry Gudgell was skilled in many crafts.

The magnificently embellished walking stick, first illustrated by James Porter in 1943, is still the only example of his wood sculpture known to survive. The making of the object intersects with an early battle of the Civil War. On August 10, 1861, a native of Livingston County who knew the Spence Gudgells, John Bryan, was wounded in the knee at the Battle of Wilson's Creek while serving in the First Missouri Cavalry of General Sterling Price's Confederate Army. Bryan sustained a limp for the rest of his life as a result of the wound. After the return of Bryan to Livingston County, Henry Gudgell carved the walking stick to compensate the infirmity of the friend of his master. The grandson of Bryan recalled in 1940 for the Index of American Design that the cane was carved in 1863, but the writer thinks it is more likely that the work was completed after the establishment of the Gudgell farm in 1867. John Bryan was proud of the cane and used it until his death in March 1899. The object then became the property of his son, Alfonso Albury Bryan, then of his grandson, John Albury Bryan, an architect in St. Louis, who sold the cane to the Yale University Art Gallery in March 1968.

This single piece of Henry Gudgell's wood sculpture exhibits skilled craftsmanship in the combination of abstract and figural motifs and seems imbued with the aesthetic precision characteristic of a silversmith. The handle is powerfully grooved with serpentine fluting. Immediately below follow a band of plain surface, a band of truncated fluting, more flat surface, two encircling rings, a circle of diamond-form pattern, and two final circular bands. Diminishment of motif artfully registers the tapering of the staff.

The decorative order then changes, from the circular geometric to the naturalistic representation of spaced, small figures. At the top appear a lizard and a tortoise, both carved as if seen from above. The figure of a man appears below. He is dressed in shirt, trousers, and shoes. His knees are bent and the arms are extended as if the figure were embracing the shaft of the cane. On the opposite side of the cane below the hands of the human figure is a bent branch from which sprouts a single veined leaf. The fork of the branch mirrors the bending of the knees of the human figure. The lower register of the cane is embellished with an entwined serpent, an echo of the serpentine coil of the handle. The entire staff was once entirely blackened but the color of the unfinished wood has broken through at the edges of the lizard and the tortoise, and the fluted handle has been rubbed bare by use.

Comparison of the cane with a chiefly staff from Woyo territory in the Bakongo cluster of people in West Africa elicits interesting similarities: human figure with bent legs, reptiles carved as if seen from above, entwined serpent motif. Functionally, the Woyo staff is a light scepter whereas the Missourian object is a working cane with marks of heavy use at the tip. Motifs are similar but their placement differs. Function guided the distinction, the ruler gripping the scepter at the entwined serpent, the Missourian at the entwined handle.

Each motif on the Gudgell cane shines with virtual metallic smoothness. The tortoise, for example, is like a fugitive from some forms of West African jewelry. And there may be an extension of the craft of the decoration of rings in the form of the fluting and diamond-shaped patterning which encircle the upper part of the cane, for both the making of rings and the carving of cane handles consider the problem of enlivening a continuously curved surface.

On July 16, 1870, Spence Gudgell, the former master of the sculptor, sold him twenty-two acres of land, carved out of the original one hundred and sixty acres which the Anglo-American had purchased in 1867 (Book 28, Livingston County Recorder: 188; Book

33: 145). Thus for the last twenty-five years of his life the craftsman was a landholder. He died in 1895 and is buried in the Utica, Missouri, cemetery.

In a sense, Afro-Missourian sculpture at Livingston County died with him. Afro-American canes have been recently found in this portion of Missouri—three attributed to the twentieth-century craftsman George Ballinger of Carlo, Missouri, have motifs vaguely reminiscent of West Africa—but none show the strength or the authority of the master. More research needs to be done on the origins of the style of Henry Gudgell, so that the links between the coastal work of Afro-Georgian sculptors, whose canes, embellished with reptile and human figures, are similar to the Missouri work, and the inland carver may be determined and analyzed together with elements of Western influence, the canon of proportion characterizing the human figure on the side of the cane, his dress, and the shape and conception of the veined leaf.

South Carolina

This state preserves a tradition of ash-glazed stoneware vessels shaped in the form of a tormented human face. These works are attributed to Afro-American craftsmen. A single example introduces the field, where formal quality is largely determined by the degree of imaginative transformation of gross ceramic structure into human expression.

The object at hand is glazed olive-grey. The eyes and bared teeth are rendered in another medium—kaolin (porcelain clay)—so that the image presents a startling contrast in color and texture. The vessel is small, about four inches high. The structural elements are quickly told: the spout is set centrally at the top and is grooved twice; a short oval section handle rises out of the bottom of the spout, at the back of the object, and curves down to end at the widest portion of the vessel.

The eyes project intensity. They are fashioned separately, as balls of kaolin, then set in rounded sockets, surrounded by oval rims overlaid with glaze, then fired together with the vessel. Their stare is striking because they have been placed slightly to each side of the face and have not been frontally sited. The eyebrows form high curves. The inner point of each eyebrow joins the line of the nose. The nose itself is narrow and has pinched nostrils. The nose is set high above the mouth. The open mouth reveals the clenched kaolin teeth. Lower teeth are larger than upper, suggesting bestial ferocity. Part of the upper lip seems taut and part of the upper lip seems relaxed. There is no chin, and the head seems cut off at the neck. The sculpture is a marvel of coherent expression: protrusion by protrusion, white against olive, smoothness against grain.

There are two further known examples by the same hand, one in the Smithsonian Institution, the other in the John Gordon Collection in New York City. These show virtually identical concentration of power within diminutive mass and shaping of the human face as a terrible force, like a skull partially revealed. The artist has taken spectacular advantage of the fact that kaolin remains white when it burns.

Shortly before the Second World War, William Raiford Eve of Augusta, Georgia, put together a collection of related jugs and cups, the fruit of several field trips to the Afro-American settlements between Aiken and Langley, South Carolina. On the basis of this collection and other pieces, such as the example I have described, which have been independently attributed to what is now Aiken County in South Carolina, it is possible to suggest a regional tradition based on the use of mixed sand and pine ash glaze, most frequently olive green or brown, ball-like eyes rendered in kaolin, with or without dotted pupil, and sometimes movable within their sockets; bared teeth in kaolin, occasionally indicated with diagonal strokes; and long noses with flaring nostrils, drooping at the tip, and slightly hooked in profile.

These vessels have been attributed in local traditions to the pottery of the plantation of Colonel Thomas Jones Davies (1830-1902) at Bath, in the western portion of the county of Aiken. Colonel Davies founded the Palmetto Firebrick Works in 1862 during the Civil War. On a field trip in January 1969 the writer found the ledger of Colonel Davies, kept by a surviving daughter of a second marriage, at Augusta, Georgia, and the first entry appears to be February 22, 1862.

The important fact is that the men who made the pottery at Bath

were mostly Afro-American. It is documented that in 1863 a mounting wartime demand for crockery caused Davies to direct his Afro-
American potters to fashion earthen jars, pitchers, cups, and saucers,
using the simple kickwheel, which has a treadle with a crank. When
the historian of American ceramics, Barber, viewed their work about
forty years later he found the vessels "crude and of primitive shape"
(in reaction to non-Western notions of approximate, as opposed to
absolute, measurement?) but he did admire their strength. Barber,
furthermore, found that the body of the pottery was composed of
three-fourths to five-sixths of kaolin and alluvial earth from the
Savannah River, which is six miles distant from Bath. This composition created a hard body which partially vitrified with a mixture of
sand and pine ashes to obtain an excellent glaze.

The story goes that by 1863 the slaves suddenly were fashioning
on their own initiative small vessels with human faces on them and
bringing these works to the Davies pottery to be fired. All operations
were suspended by the end of the Confederacy and the pottery
never reopened. One source maintains that the men of the army of
General Tecumseh Sherman set fire to the enterprise in 1865. In
effect, we are told by local tradition that the slaves dreamed up
these striking sculptures within two years, then disappeared.

To accept this uncritically is impossible. Important artistic events
do not emerge without historical basis. Kaolin deposits had been
known to exist in the hills between Augusta and Aiken since at least
the beginning of the nineteenth century, and when the Afro-American craftsmen took this substance and fashioned with it eyes and
teeth and set them into the firebrick-like body of their sculptures to
be fired they had, as far as can be determined, created an artistic
concept for which there is no precedent in the history of Western
ceramics. The importance of their contribution forces a rethinking
of the history of United States pottery.

The argument for the use of Afro-American artisans in South
Carolina was originally scarcity of labor. The entire province in 1731
had only one potter (Stavisky, 1948-9: 317). As potteries opened in
South Carolina during the next hundred and fifty years, the use of
Afro-American labor had become common. In 1796 a certain Mr.
Landrum established a pottery industry near Edgefield, some fifteen

miles north of what is now Aiken County, itself carved out of a larger geographic entity about 1872. There was also an active and important pottery at Lewis Miles Mill, between Trenton and Vaucluse, near Aiken, from about 1837 to 1894 (Webb, 1968: personal communications). Thus there was continuous pottery-making industry in the kaolin-rich Aiken area during most of the last century.

The most important fact remains that many of the potters of the region were of African descent. It must be made clear that at least three different hands can be detected in the corpus of face vessels attributed to Afro-Americans—"The Master of the Davies Pottery," "The Master of the Diagonal Teeth," "The Master of the Louis Miles Pottery"—and that a number of Afro-American potters, who gained recognition for their work and whose names are known, may soon be linked to these modes.

The most interesting of the documented Afro-American potters was a man known only as "Dave." He worked at the Miles Mill pottery and is said to have died about 1860 at the estimated age of eighty-three. Four extant works are attributed to Dave. Three are in the Charleston Museum, one in the South Caroliniana Library at Columbia. Dave is noted for having his work inscribed with rhymed couplets. One such inscription, on a glazed crock (Charleston Museum 29.255.1), establishes a cryptic sense of humour and the slave status of the maker:

> Dave belongs to Mr. Miles
> Where the oven bakes and the pot biles

Also inscribed is the date: July 31, 1840. On an impressive olive-glazed salt meat or lard jar which he made and which is now at Charleston we find the date May 13, 1859, and the inscription, "Dave & Baddler/ Great and Noble Jar/ Hold Sheep, Goat, or Bear." An identical vessel, also at the Charleston Museum, has the same date but a different couplet about the making of the object at Stoney Bluff, "for making [illegible] enuff." Archival material at the South Caroliniana Library indicates that, on a now missing jar, Dave repeats the verse about the "great and noble jar," and another document of a vanished pot seems to shed light on the effaced

Charleston inscription: "Made at Stoney Bluff/ For Making [Lard] Enuff." Like the stanza-shifting Afro-American singers of the nine-teenth-century South Carolinian spiritual, who sang stanzas of one song in another (Davis, 1914: 250), Dave chose for reasons of his own to place the same rhyme on more than one vessel. The short rhymed statements attest his wit and recall the sparing style of the three-line blues. Here is an Afro-American potter who distinguished himself during a career of more than nineteen years and who was active until very shortly before his death.

A second Afro-Carolinian ceramist was Jack Thurman, who also belonged to Louis Miles. Thurman allegedly died about 1908 at the age of eighty-four. A certain George Flesher, who worked at the Miles Mill pottery during the last years of its operation and who consequently was in a position to provide firsthand information about the wares of the pottery and the men who made them, re-called for a Charleston Museum archivist in the summer of 1930 the dignity of Jack Thurman, his impressive physique, and his gift as a raconteur. Flesher attributed two vessels in the Charleston Museum (29.271.21; 29.255.3) to the hand of Thurman. Most interesting is the recollection that Thurman not only worked at Miles Mill but also at one of the two Landrum potteries in the Aiken area, suggesting a measure of exchange in Afro-American labor and furnishing a clue to the unity of the Aiken County style range.

A third Carolina potter of African descent was a slave named Jim Lee. Lee worked at the pottery of Roundtree and Bodie, near Ninety-Six, in what is now Greenwood County (Charleston Museum *Bulletin,* October-November 1920: 52). One of his works, in the Charleston Museum, is known: a remarkable olive-glazed figure of an Anglo-American with pear-shaped head. The figure wears a jacket with front facing turned back to reveal the elegant buttons of his shirt. The hair, moustache, and jacket-facing of the figure are char-coal black. The back facing of the figure's garment is turned up at the right shoulder, giving a mildly dishevelled appearance. It is said that the image was a satiric likeness (but the writer thinks that the features seem generic) of a certain Reverend Pickett. The version fits the fact of the anomalous flapping up of part of the garment of the subject. It is said that Jim Lee made this sculpture "before 1860."

Thus four nineteenth-century Afro-Carolinian potters are known, assuming that "Baddler" was also of African descent, for it does not seem likely that an Anglo-American potter would have taken second billing to a slave.

The face vessels made at the Miles Mill pottery were Afro-American works, as attested by Charleston Museum documentation (6448; 18029). The finest of these holdings is a superbly glazed brown face vessel with elegant features and a haunting luminosity. Another is contrastingly crude and is dated to 1880, some fourteen years before the closing of the Louis Miles pottery.

The diffusion of the genre through Anglo-Saxon mimesis and Afro-American migration assured a certain continuity. The Smithsonian Institution has an interesting work by the Anglo-American potter Cheaver Meaders, who worked in the northeast corner of the state of Georgia, at Cleveland, until his death in 1967 at the age of eighty. Meaders made dark brown ash-glazed stoneware face jugs, among other ceramic types (Watkins, 1969: personal communication). He made eyes and teeth by inserting broken pieces of yellow glazed earthenware into the body of the stoneware, in evident imitation of the kaolin of the South Carolinian mode. He substituted the sharper glitter of fragmented crockery (Smithsonian 65. 192). He seems to mistake the artistic distortions of Afro-Carolinian for license, in the manner of rock-and-roll mistranslations of the blues. Finally, Herbert Hemphill, of the Museum of American Folk Arts, reports that an Afro-American living near Mobile was making stoneware sculpture in the Afro-Carolinian manner as late as the decade preceding World War II.

Thus the traditional account of a sudden burst of Afro-American creativity at the Davies Plantation is subsumed under a larger and more important history of individual Afro-American achievement. The broader reality of the Aiken County ceramic history also reveals the inadequacy of traditional forms of nomenclature applied to these face vessels. They are often called "monkey jugs," after an old designation for water cooler (Stow, 1932). Afro-Carolinians used to refer to the heat of the day in phrases like "monkey almost got me today," and Albert E. Sanders, curator of natural sciences at the Charleston Museum, recalls having heard similar expressions during his childhood at Columbia, South Carolina, used in the sense of heat prostration. But we have seen that the most visually intense of the face vessels are not more than four inches high and would not have been practical as containers of water for thirsty field hands. At some point, the writer suspects, a term for larger utilitarian stoneware water jugs was loosely applied to all face vessels and the imprecise designation acquired an inertia of its own.

An improper title can contribute to a lack of critical thought about artistic form. Afro-Carolinian face vessels are called "water jugs," "grotesque jugs," "slave jugs," "plantation jugs," and even, in one isolated instance, "voodoo pots." None of these terms suggest artistic viability. In addition, while many vessels are true jugs, many face cups and face jars are not, hence as a general designation the notion of the jug is not applicable. It might be useful to jettison, once and for all, all forms of past terminology and introduce the fresh term, Afro-Carolinian face vessels, first of all to honor the African descent of the makers, secondly to single out the province where the finest works were made, thirdly to allude to the inventive fusion of physiognomy and ceramic structure which characterizes the genre, and fourthly to suggest the extension of the tradition across a universe of ceramic forms, of which the jug is but one type.

However we title them, these sculptures are still considered craft curiosities, not works of art. The indifferent quality of many examples, many of these made by Anglo-American imitators, seem to have colored the impression of an entire field. One authority on "material culture," struck by the use of Western glaze and what he thinks is an obvious citation of the Toby Jug tradition of England, has written off altogether the possibility of African influence at the same time that he consigns the works to the nether regions of folk art limbo. But one does not judge Memling on the basis of Flemish daubers. The finest of the Afro-Carolinian ceramics are complex solutions of problems of form, quality, and meaning, and when the culture of the men who made them is remembered, it becomes dangerous to ignore the possibility of African cultural impulses reinstated in these works.

The main problem of analysis is the separation of the Western from the African elements. First of all, the Afro-American potters were working within a Western technical tradition of ash-glazed stoneware, which was common in Anglo-American potteries from the Carolinas to Florida. Stoneware vitrifies at the temperature of about 2200° to 2300° fahrenheit, and the ash glaze is a high-temperature glaze especially suited to the medium. The glaze, C. Malcolm Watkins (personal communication) has kindly informed the writer, is not colored when it is applied nor does it achieve its usual olive-green color by itself. Under normal firing conditions it combines chemically with the clay to produce the characteristic olive color. This color is recurrent on utilitarian stoneware from any number of potteries in the South. The same clay and the same glaze, with only slightly changed degrees of firing conditions, may produce a brown or some other color. It is therefore impossible to base an attribution upon color alone, nor can one impute intention to shifts in chromatic effect. A brown pot and a green pot, Watkins explains, both of the same clay and glaze and made by the same potter, could come out of the same kiln in the same firing. Hard-to-control wood-fired kilns prevailed in the South in the nineteenth century, and a change in the wind or the weather could literally create a variety of colors.

Secondly, the basic pottery shapes and the use of the wheel as means of production were imposed upon the Afro-American potters and show no sign of African influence; hand-modeling and the molding of hemispherical bowls upon upturned pot-bottoms are techniques employed along the Guinea Coast (Drost, 1967: 256). The dominant Western influences are therefore the use of the glaze, the wheel, and the basic structure, the jug, jar, or cup, all with oval-section handle.

The notion of embellishing such vessels with a human face might have come from Europe, but African precedents, especially at the mouth of the Congo can also be cited. Some sixteenth- and seventeenth-century German Bellarmine jugs have a rectangle framing a face, shaped in a mold and applied to the vessel. But the Afro-Carolinian faces are hand modeled, especially the eyes and teeth, and the concept of the face as an isolated framed unit of decoration is foreign to the Carolinian spontaneous humanizing of the entire frontal mass of the vessel. We may therefore safely ignore a Bellarmine excavated on the Bull Plantation near Sheldon as having noth-ing in common with the indigenous aesthetic. Bellarmines probably did not, after all, occur in sight of the slave potters.

Much more serious as a possible source is the English Toby Jug, essentially a hollow china figure seated on a low seat. The first examples are attributed to Ralph Wood (1716-72) of Burslem. The Toby Jug traditionally represents a short, corpulent, grinning man who wears a deep-pocketed coat with large buttons and wide cuffs, as well as a tricorn hat (Hansen, ed. 1968: 64). The description recalls somewhat the "satirized minister" by Jim Lee and suggests that a modicum of English influence may have guided the hand of this particular potter. But Lee was outside the circle of Aiken County potters. Even closer, at first sight, to the Aiken County face vessels was a variant on the Toby mode, a face occupying the entire front of a jug. Pottery was one of the free-thinking areas of late eighteenth-century English art and there were many interesting face pitchers made at this time (McNab, 1969: personal communication). However, the face jugs and face pitchers of the English have a char-acteristic buttery sheen and naturalistic detail, which are alien to the iconic intensity of the best of the Afro-Carolinian.

We must remember that there are at least three men working in the Aiken County tradition and that each man doubtless resolves the conflict between the wheel-turned technique which he was given and his own plastic sources of inspiration in different ways. Jim Lee, working north of the county, seems to have moved in a direction perceptively closer to Western propriety, but it is difficult to say, so paltry is relevant information about him. But the Aiken County masters created a face from which the eyes protrude and the teeth flash in a manner light years removed from the courtly Toby Jug.

The white clay eyes and teeth, set against the glaze, make the finest Afro-Carolinian face vessels appear to roar where works three times their size merely whisper. There is nothing in Europe remotely like them, for the use of kaolin inserts into the body of the pottery seems peculiar to the Afro-Carolinian and his imitators. One may object: but are there glazed kaolin eyes and teeth in African pot-tery? The answer is no, but this is not the point. The point is that kaolin has been used here in a manner which strongly recalls the insertion of white cowrie shells, white glittering pieces of mirror, or white strips of tin, or glass backed with white, to represent the eyes against the darker medium of wood in a wide variety of West African societies. The use of multiple media in figural sculpture—brass on wood, mirror insets in the eyes, cowrie shell insets to denote the eyes and mouth, buttons to denote the eyes, application of brass studs or iron nails to denote the pupil of the eye, the use of beads to mark the eyes within a face carved of wood; the recital of usages is potentially endless—is one of the important traits of West African sculpture as a cultural entity. Until evidence of similar mixing of the white medium of kaolin with darker glazed pottery can be proved in pre-Civil War pottery from Europe, it is surely more logical to suggest the influence of this basic West African tendency. The glaze and the gross shape of the Afro-Carolinian vessels have distracted the lay observer from the expressionist nuances of their modeling. The modeling of the faces finds much in common with Bakongo figural sculpture in wood.

Compare, as illustrations, examples of a variety of wood figures from this area of West Africa. The same pinpoint pupils within white eyes (white behind glass in lieu of kaolin), the same long hooked nose, the same siting of the nose at a point relatively high above the lips, the same open mouth with bared teeth, and the same widening of the mouth so that it extends across the width of the jaw, are highly suggestive similarities. It would be unwise in the absence of data about the ancestors of the Afro-Carolinian potters to press this comparison too far, but it is certainly true that no Western jar or pitcher known to the writer shows such striking kinship.

South Carolina is a state where artistic transmission from tropical Africa has been firmly established. The woven baskets and trays fashioned by Afro-Carolinian women between Mt. Pleasant and Sullivan's Island, across the harbor from Charleston, and elsewhere in the state, are made with the coiling technique of West Africa and the method of decoration, albeit achieved with available American materials—viz. marsh grass for the body of the basket, palmetto leaves for the binding, and the long-leafed pine for a decorative band of brown —seems decidedly African (Sturtevant, 1959; Chase, n.d.: 2) Some of these baskets have been convincingly related to virtually identical

140 Black Studies in the University

Senegambian wares by Judith Wragg Chase in an exhibit mounted at Charleston and visually cited by the Afro-American installation of the Hall of Africa exhibition, which opened in June 1968, at the American Museum of Natural History. It is strange that no one has criticized the cultural legitimacy of the "Gullah baskets" on account of the use of the needles of the American long-leafed pine as an element of decoration, while the use of glaze and the wheel seems to suffice to discredit any possibility of African influence upon South Carolinian stoneware.

The stylistic closeness of the Afro-Carolinian baskets to Senegambia makes sense in the light of slaving history, for the third largest quantity of Africans brought to South Carolina during the period 1752-1808 (12,441 out of a total of 65,466 African slaves) were from "Gambia to Sierra Leone" (Donnan, 1935: Vol. IV, pp. 278ff.). The overwhelming incursion was Congo-Angolan, however, for when the figures from these two adjacent areas of Africa are added together, it is clear that the sum—22,409—is almost double the Senegambian.

The fact that men and women of African descent in tidewater South Carolina are called Gullahs, and this word is supposed to derive from Angola, and the fact that the most convincing of the Africanisms detected in Gullah dialect by Lorenzo Dow Turner (1949) are, in the opinion of the writer, those of Congo and Angolan origin, make one rethink the notion that Anglo-Saxon America was normally correlated with an incursion of Ashanti slaves and hence Ashanti survivals.

Comparison of the Afro-Carolinian ceramic with the hushed, dignified heads of rulers in the funerary terracotta tradition of the Akan is more in the nature of a confrontation, for the harsh tenor of the American genre is far removed from the composure which the Akan noble heads evince. On the other hand, the moment the vessels are compared to the open-mouthed, bared-teeth, glassy-eyed figures of the Bakongo visual tradition, correspondences leap to life before the eyes of the observer. It is worth noting, in addition, that not only does the Ki-Kongo word for smoking pipe survive in South Carolina (Turner: 199) but Judith Wragg Chase has documented a clay smoking pipe with raised design that was found under a slave

cabin in South Carolina bearing comparison with the clay smoking
pipes of the Congo-Angolan region and their apparent descendants
among the Congo-Angola miners of the Minas Gerais province in
eighteenth-century Brazil.

The writer suggests that a connection between Congo-Angola arts
and South Carolina pottery made by Afro-Americans is a distinct
possibility and would seem likely in view of the particular slaving
history of the area. This correspondence, if proved, would make
definite the links between the Bakongo and Aiken County pottery.
Indeed, because there are complex compromises made with Western
technique, the phenomenon is more dynamic, historically, and consequently more interesting as a subject for study than a mechanical
carry-over.

Finally, what is the meaning of the stylized anguish which
contorts the face of the vessels, and for whom were the vessels
made? Taking the last question first, the writer would guess that
the Anglo-Americans who bought face vessels considered them
amusing craft curiosities, a kind of visual minstrelsy, and even
today the writer has heard an Anglo-American Georgian describe
these works as "their idea of art." A patronizing patronage does
not make much sense as a sustaining force for the autonomous wit
and invention and care which went into the making of the finest
of these vessels. Their excellence goes against the grain of what we
know about the low productivity of slaves in the ante-bellum
South. Bondage, Eugene Genovese (1965: 43) tells us, forced the
Afro-American to give his labor grudgingly and badly. The low
productivity resulted from inadequate care, training, and incentives. One can hardly suggest that the artistic excellence of the
Aiken County artisanate was the testament of a rare circle of con-
tented slaves. In the presence of the ferocity and energy expressed
by the best of these Afro-Carolinian vessels, one senses a shift in
attitude, a craft based on the self-generated incentive of a vital
culture, standing apart from the nature of most pre-Civil War
Southern Afro-American industry. The distinction, the writer
would guess, stems from the fact that the Afro-American craftsmen made these vessels for themselves and their people for traditional reasons of their own. Under the noses of their masters they

succeeded in carving out a world of aesthetic autonomy.

C. Malcolm Watkins has informed the writer of a notice of Afro-Carolinian vessels having been found in Afro-Carolinian burial grounds, and the William Raiford Eve Collection includes pieces in which holes have been very carefully chipped out of the bottom, as if to break the objects without spoiling them, to prepare them as items of broken crockery, which traditionally covered the graves of Carolinians of African descent (Davis: 248). It is worth mentioning that broken household objects are placed on top of the tombs of the dead among the Bwende (Manker, 1932), who are part of the Kongo cluster of peoples from whom so many Afro-Carolinians seem to derive.

In a mortuary context these striking vessels may have served as protective devices and simultaneously as elements of prestige, excellent works by Afro-Americans for Afro-Americans, imperishable forces which make their manful aggression very plain. They may have also been used as containers of magical substances, although there is no evidence to this effect, and such a practice would have been conspicuous and would have attracted unfavorable attention. Yet one sees precisely what one is prepared to see, and in their ignorance of the vitality of African and African-influenced religions (cf. Jordan: 20ff) the Anglo-Saxons were certainly capable of having missed an entire dimension of New World creativity. The smug assignment of the works to Anglo-American folk art in later years compounded the possibility of ignorance.

Possibly Afro-Carolinian potters also created these vessels as a deliberate gallery of tormented faces in order to vent response to a slave environment. If we have learned anything about the nature of the traditional arts of Africa in recent years, it is that it is dangerous to assume monofunctionality for works of art and, indeed, these vessels, as in African instances, may have served a variety of functions, separately or concurrently. The artists of imperial Benin worked images of long-nosed Portuguese soldiers into the coiffure of an ivory representation of their ruler as a suggestion of the power of their state to incorporate the power of the foreigner. So the potters of South Carolina may have alluded to their oppressor the better to absorb his power.

The pottery burlesque attributed to Jim Lee has more in common with Anglo-American potters' jests than with the parallel sculpture of social allusion in the African vein where sculptors shape noses with deliberate crookedness to poke fun at the pompous, the foreign, or the corrupt, or, at a different analytic level, massively exaggerate the eyes of an image to suggest the moral wrath of the ancestors in contexts of tribal jurisprudence.

Afro-Carolinian face vessels, at their best, represent a related deliberate shaping of generalized principles of visual disorder; they are not portraits of named buffoons. To this extent they seem palpably influenced by African notions of generic mimesis.

The possibility that these images were stylized assertions of Afro-American resistance in the face of the exploitative aggression of the Anglo-Saxon is suggested by the combination of sharp teeth, bulging eyes, and contorted lips. The suggestion dovetails with a documented instance of assertive satire in choreography, recounted by a South Carolina "strut gal" (accomplished dancer) who received special privileges at Beaufort in the 1840s because of her talent:

> Us slaves watched the white folks' parties where the guests danced a minuet and then paraded in a grand march. Then we'd do it too, but we used to mock 'em, every step. Sometimes the white folks noticed it but they seemed to like it. I guess they thought we couldn't dance any better [Stearns and Stearns, 1968: 22].

Afro-Carolinian potters could equally assume that their deliberate distortions, for whatever multiple purposes, would be misapprehended as lack of skill and therefore would be considered harmless and amusing. Is it possible that the small Afro-Carolinian vessels were provocatory devices, trapping the visually sensitive into a consideration of aggression in the Western world, the monkey on the back of the Afro-American and the conscience of a nation? Could this distillation of visual anguish have been simultaneously antidotal, on the theory that the best way to defeat an antagonistic force is to absorb its power? It is to be hoped that future research may bring to light evidence which will enable us to test such hypotheses.

Tidewater Georgia

Here an important source of Afro-American art in the United States was identified during a search for survivals organized in the late 1930s by Miss Mary Granger for the Georgia Writers' Project of the Works Project Administration. The amazing sculptures of the Afro-Americans of tidewater Georgia are correlated with a significant density of Afro-American population—70 percent black in 1790—and the fact that slaves were being brought to this area direct from Africa, illegally, as late as 1854. In older colonies like Virginia, Miss Granger points out, plantations were already sufficiently supplied with American-born slaves and the long period of contact with the West had blurred or complicated African customs.

Artistic consequences of this fact are immediate and very clear. Clay sculpture, for one instance, was fashioned on Wilmington Island in the last century:

> The African men used to all the time make little clay images. Sometimes they like men and sometimes they like animals. Once they made a big one. They put a spear in his hand and walk around him and say he was the chief [*Drums and Shadows*, Georgia Writers' Project: 106].

In an Afro-American quarter of Savannah, for another instance, Lonnon Denerson, himself African-born, cicatrized his daughter with an irregular circle one and one-eighth inch in diameter. She was perhaps one of the few citizens of the United States living in the present century with the mark of a West African form of cicatrization.

There was even a fleeting existence of African architecture, on St. Simons Island, when an African-born man named Okra suddenly built a habitation in the manner of his ancestors. The building is said to have measured approximately twelve by fourteen feet in plan, had a dirt floor, daub-and-wattle walls ("the side like basket weave with clay plaster on it"), and a flat brush and palmetto roof. In perfect evocation of the windowlessness of much subsaharan traditional architecture, the only source of light was the single door. But, "Massa make him pull it down. He say he ain't want no African hut on he place" (*Drums and Shadows:* 179).

Thus clay sculpture, cicatrization, and architecture briefly existed in isolated fragments. The main continuity, however, lasting well into this century and perhaps still alive in a few settlements, was wood sculpture. The forms of expression, such as canes and small animal figures, were familiar to Westerners and not blatantly African, as were a mark on the chest or a habitation made of earth, hence not so likely to challenge Anglo-Saxon propriety. There are three main types of Afro-Georgian sculpture: (1) walking sticks embellished with figural relief; (2) small statuary in the round; (3) virtuoso openwork abstraction carved out of single pieces of wood. The second type consists of full-length frontal human figures, small busts of human figures, armless frontal standing figures, and dolls. Reptiles seem the emphasized members of the animal kingdom (snakes, lizards, frogs, alligators), but small carvings of dogs and rabbits have also been documented. The implied interaction of man and the reptile world also characterizes much of the relief decoration of walking sticks. Some virtuoso abstractions are chains carved from single pieces of wood, recalling Surinam.

The work of the men following this tradition is qualitatively very uneven. This variability may be correlated with the vitality of consciously African-inspired artistic criticism within particular settlements, on the theory that distraction by Western materialism creates a weakening of visual inheritance. It seems that some of these men probably did not, despite the African flavor of their themes, identify themselves with Africa. Conscious separation from the cultures of Africa extends back several generations, as suggested by the comment of William Quarterman, of Darien, who remembered having heard African speech but added, "You can't understand much what these people say. They go 'quack, quack, quack' just as fast as a horse can run, and my pa say aint no good to listen to them."

But there were some Afro-Georgians who did hear the voices of the past. One was James Cooper of Port Wentworth, a suburb of Savannah. Inspiration came from his grandfather, Pharoah Cooper, who also carved objects in wood. James Cooper was a true *bricoleur* and earned his living not only selling lunches to the workers of the Savannah Sugar Refinery but also cobbling shoes and repairing as discrete a collection of objects as chinaware and rollerskates. Yet his real gift lay in the field of sculpture, a point which was not lost upon the Afro-American community, wherein he was widely known by the affectionate nickname of "Stick Daddy," in praise of his ingeniously embellished walking sticks. (A West African precedent may be cited: attributive names lauding artistic skills, names which may themselves become works of art, as in the instance of the master of Ilaro, Nigeria, whose praise name meant literally "possessed-of-a-knife-like-a-whip.")

Stick Daddy's sense of design was firm. Motifs (mostly snakes, tortoises, and alligators, to judge from a published sampling of his work) were carved on the side of the staff in low relief and stained; reptile relief was further outlined with a "nimbus" of unfinished wood against an even ground of stained area. Stick Daddy decorated his representations of reptiles with geometric incised designs of characteristic width and depth revealing the white of the unstained wood. In his style a tortoise shell becomes a kind of shield, bearing opposed half-circles flanking the long axis, smaller crescents the short. His representations of alligators are, like the tortoises, carved as if seen from above, except that in this case areas delimited by half-circles are sometimes bisected by two parallel short lines or are carved out as a shallow void. Subsequent research will identify the sources and continuities of this highly arbitrary method of linear embellishment.

Accessible data indicate that the master of the south coast of Georgia was William Rogers (1865-1952) of Darien, the county seat of McIntosh. Rogers was born when African languages were still being spoken in Georgia and he perhaps had the opportunity in his youth to observe subsaharan-influenced sculptural activity. On the other hand, he followed a Western career of cabinet-making. In 1938, at the age of seventy-two, he spent such time as failing hands allowed him making figural sculpture and canes of partial African flavor in addition to scrollwork and other Western crafts. The latter work is important to remember when assessing his creativity.

At some point before 1938 William Rogers carved at Darien a wooden frog which has a raised triangular head and beaded eyes focusing upward, as if in search of an insect. The mouth is seamless.

Powerful shoulders lift the brilliantly rounded body of the frog. Articulation of the solid mass is achieved in such a way that the shoulders and hind quarters are carved as matching accents of some elegance over the curve of the body. To a certain extent they recall the equally rhythmic repetitions of the limbs of a Dahomean frog, except that the legs of the latter reptile were flattened and bracket-like.

The eyes of the Georgian frog come from blooded African stock. They are glass beads secured by minute brass nails which mark the pupil. The discussion of their African qualitites will come later, but it might be pointed out that the eyes of the Dahomean frog in the collection of Charles Ratton make similar use of brass nails. By contrast, the three concentric rectangles forming the base, the inner-most of which suggests a natural surface upon which the reptile rests, seem to reflect, in the heightened realism of the effect and the arbitrary framing of the subject matter, considerable Western influence.

Another sculpture by William Rogers of Darien is known. He carved in 1938 a figurated walking stick for Miss Mary Granger of Savannah. At the top of the staff is the head and bust of a human figure, whose parted seamless lips, extending the breadth of the face, recall the stylized mouth of the frog. The eyes of the human are blue beads secured with minute steel pins which indicate the pupil. The smooth, square skull and high-set ears are striking qualities of the human figure, painted blueish-black to identify the subject as an Afro-American, according to the owner of the staff. Diminutive arms are carved in relief on either side of the block of the body and each hand ends with four fingers. Carved immediately below the front of the human figure is the form of an alligator, positioned vertically and superbly dominating the upper register of the staff. The taste of the artist intervenes most visibly where the shoulders of the reptile are stylized with the same rounded muscle convention of the frog. The alligator rests upon an abstract plane, cut into the cylinder of the staff. The back of the beast has textural pattern suggesting the horny, plate-like scales of the species. The eyes of the alligator are blue beads secured with pins. There are six enigmatic ovals carved in low relief, parallel to the alligator; perhaps they represent riverain stones. The contrast of black human figure against red cedar wood creates an aesthetic of handsome simplicity.

African influence is suggested by the choice of motifs (man and reptile), the simultaneous usage of two vantage points within a single composition (human seen from the front, alligator from above) and the implied conviction that beads are so valuable that their addition enhances the value of the object as a work of art. The African love of artistic bead-working is well known. More especially, the taste for mixing the main medium of the sculpture (wood, bone, brass) with a minor medium of beads, brass, or iron is very African and embraces such discrete traditions as the brass- or aluminum-plated figural sculpture of the Songye of Congo-Kinshasa, the iron-studded "konde" of the Bakongo, and even the beaded wood statuary of the Cameroon, where expressive roles are reversed and beads become the primary visual element. A Nigerian reference is very illuminating as to this tradition of mixing media and is in point with the Afro-Georgian sculpture:

> The Bini artist's values are different from those of any Western artist: to produce such skilled work as the ivory ornamental mask and then to put two nail-heads in the eyes as pupils . . . [is] quite alien to values which [Westerners] put on what materials match or are appropriate to certain aesthetic situations [Dark, 1960: 25] .

The point is richly illustrated by the wood twin figures of the Yoruba. In this tradition pupils are often indicated by nailheads of iron. But it is important to distinguish African bead or nail eyes from American. Two examples of Luba sculpture from Congo-Kinshasa (Fagg, 1968: 264-5) have blue beads to enhance the regard of the human visage. The beads are positioned, however, upon a protruding eye which reflects a complex tradition of sculptural intensification. The bead is the pupil. Oyo Yoruba twin figures also have eyes which often have nailheads indicating the pupil within a powerful curve of wood.

The face of the Afro-Georgian image by contrast is flat and the projection of the eye is formed by the bead and nail. The bead is the eye. The distinction vitiates any diffusionist attempt to establish a particular African influence and seems to determine a generic continuity from subsaharan plastic traditions. It is this interesting cultivation of a foreign sensibility that unifies observations of animal and human existence in the work of William Rogers. When he died on July 14, 1952, a chapter of United States Afro-American art history came to an end.

Sunbury

We turn now to art for the dead. Broken earthenware adorns the surface of the graves of some Afro-Americans in remote areas of Mississippi, Georgia, and South Carolina, and carved wooden grave-markers have been found in association with these remarkable deposits at Pine Harbor and Sunbury in Georgia.

The peoples of West Africa have placed earthenware and other possessions on the top of graves for hundreds of years. Bosman (1708: 273) noted at Axim, a site on the coast of modern Ghana, that earthenware images were placed on the top of graves after what he termed "the purification of the interred" (the formal funeral?). Sieber (1965) finds that among the Kwahu of Ghana, terracotta images are made after the death and burial of an important person and are exhibited under a palm leaf shelter next to a specially constructed hearth where food for the dead is prepared. On the last day of the funeral, after dark, the hearth, shelter, wooden utensils, including a wooden pestle spoon, earthenware, and the terracotta images are taken to the cemetery of the rulers and placed over the grave. Nassau (1904: 218), speaking of the Benga, Mpongwe, and the Fang in the area between Cameroon and Congo-Brazzaville, shows that "the dead man's goods, cloth, hardware, crockery, and so forth [are] laid by the body . . . on the top of the ground."

Similar burial customs are found in the Congo-Angola area, which, as has been said, was an important source of the slaves of tidewater South Carolina. Verly (1955) and others have described Bakongo graves in northern Angola as marked by granite boulders, heaps of pottery, including fragments of Delft and Swansea ware, wood sculpture, and human statuary carved in steatite. The burial ceremony of the Bwende, part of the Kongo cluster of peoples, has been described in some detail by E. Manker (1932: 159-172), from which is excerpted the fact that, after the interment, broken household objects are placed on top of the tomb, and the house of the dead kinsman is burned. The apparent symbolism is most interesting— body destroyed by death: broken possessions and burned house. The most important fact about the West African funeral use of earthenware fragments is that the pieces are not actually interred but are carefully placed on the surface of the grave.

The main outlines of this West African tradition reappear in parts of Mississippi, Georgia, and South Carolina as an almost classic demonstration of the nature of a generic survival. The fusion of slaves from the Gold Coast, the Congo-Angola area, and other parts of the Guinea Coast in Southern slavery could mean the reinforcement of the African notion that the funeral is the climax of life and that the dead should be honored by having their possessions placed upon the top of their graves. "Whatever else has been lost of aboriginal custom," wrote Herskovits (1958: 63), "the attitudes towards the dead, as manifested in meticulous rituals cast in the mold of West African patterns, have survived."

The deposit of chinaware and other objects on the Afro-American grave is in contrast with the stark plots of grass which cover the graves of Americans of European descent. Puckett (105) enumerates the sorts of memorial items found over the graves of Afro-South Carolinians: bleached sea shells, broken glassware, broken pitchers, soap dishes, lamp chimneys, tureens, coffee cups, syrup jugs, ornamental vases, cigar boxes, gun locks, tomato containers, teapots, fragments of stucco, plaster images, fragments of carved stonework, glass lamps, and tumblers. A touching variant identifies the grave of a child: diminutive china objects, the heads of dolls, and toys.

Two early twentieth-century graves in Mississippi (Puckett: 106) glitter with surface china, suggesting the rumpled vitality of a vanished life. The use of the fragments seems deliberate: pieces are aligned to show the length of the grave in a simple axial statement. Around another grave in the same state five poles have been placed, and these lean inward as if sheltering the spirit within the earth.

The associations in the mind of the Afro-Americans who practice this custom are extremely interesting. Consider the allegations of five Afro-Georgians, whose testimony, collected circa 1939, is preceded by the name of the particular settlement of the informant, from *Drums and Shadows.* Darien: "Them dishes and bottles what put on the grave is for the spirit and ain't for nobody to touch them. That's for the spirit to feel at home." Harris Neck: "At a funeral the bottles and dishes and other possessions belonging to the departed person were left on the grave. 'The spirit needs these—just like when they's alive.' " Harris Neck (another informant): "You put dishes and bottles and all the pretty pieces what they like on the grave. You always break these things before you put 'em down. You break [them] so that the chain will be broke. You see, the one person is dead and if you don't break the things, then the others in the family will die, too." Brownville: "They used to put the things a person used last on the grave. This was supposed to satisfy the spirit and keep it from following you back to the house." Pinpoint: "Everybody there threw a handful of dirt on the grave and when the gravediggers fixed the mound we put some of Catherine's things on the top. There was a little flower vase with the bottom knocked out, and the pitcher she made ice water in."

The last detail is impressive. An intimate act characteristic of the deceased is recalled forever on the surface of the grave by means of the particular object selected. What appears to be a random accumulation is in fact the distillation of a life.

The burial ground of the Bowens family at Sunbury, as landscaped and embellished by Cyrus Bowens, is a dramatic furthering of some of these themes. The small plot, fenced off as a unit, is found in the Sunbury Baptist Church Cemetery in the Trade Hill section of Liberty County, Georgia (Cate: 217). First, Cyrus Bowens created graves essentially as concrete slabs laid in the earth, with headstone at one end, smaller stone at the other, suggesting an eternal bed. Secondly, iron poles slung over a few of these graves serve as supports for pots occasionally overflowing with flowers, an evident extension of the desire to soften the nature of the site with deliberate domesticity. Thirdly, Bowens assembled some of the traditional means of Afro-American grave embellishment and set them in concrete while the substance was still wet, as permanently embedded parts of the headstone and grave. Thus, the grave of Aaron Bowens is

surmounted by a headstone in which is set the headlight of an auto-
mobile, gleaming like a glass eye, while the grave of Rachel Bowens
is decorated with a marker bearing an inscription over which presides
the mark of a human hand. A piece of mirror is embedded in the
palm of the hand. A neighboring grave has an enameled pitcher set in
the horizontal concrete slab covering the earth and might be compared to similar graves in concrete in modern Nigeria where the
teapots used by Muslim Yoruba for ablutions are added to their
graves as permanently installed decorations. Lastly, Bowens carved
wood sculpture as the focus of the burial ground.

Bowens creates real figural sculpture in space, not an ornamental
outline on the slate of a gravemarker. He seems to have mastered
two plastic traditions, the one static and rectilinear, the other
dynamic and free-soaring, to judge from a program of three sculptures he carved in wood. These sculptures were photographed in situ
in the early spring of 1940 by Muriel and Malcolm Bell, Jr., of
Savannah, for the Georgia Writers' Project.

The center sculpture is essentially a sphere on a cylinder. Ovals are
cut into the cylinder to represent human eyes and a slight curved
line below indicates the mouth. A few inches below the simplified
head are carved the letters spelling Bowens. The flanking sculptures
no longer exist, and when the writer studied the surviving central
sculpture in December 1968 he found that it had weathered considerably and that members of the Bowen family had whitewashed the
image in order to prevent further deterioration.

To the left of the human figure stood a work composed of two
elements, a base, and the representation of a serpent. The base was
an everted fork, the handle of which supports the whole. The serpent was carved from a single curved branch of a tree and was nailed
to the support. The serpent formed a single dramatic curve and the
neck was arched, as if the viper were about to strike. Although the
form of the base suggests striding legs, comparison with a replacement sculpture documented by Margaret Davis Cate confirms the
representation of a serpent, for in this version there is a distinct
separation between stand and reptile, and the modulation of the
curve occurs at the head, as in a serpent, and not at the body, as in a
bird. Flanking the other side of the human figure was an incredible

sculpture soaring more than twelve feet into the air. The sculpture was described by Mary Granger as the representation of a bird, but a visual check reveals that the powerful curve which forms the defining gesture of the work also recalls a serpent.

Sustained fieldwork is needed before a convincing exegesis of this construction can be written. Near the summit of the work a horizontal bar has been nailed against the vertical shaft and two short vertical strips of wood intersect the horizontal bar on either side of the shaft. The shaft descends from this point as a continuous line, dropping into a shallow curve before sweeping into a horseshoe arc. Within the curve of this portion of the sculpture is placed a horizontal bar, attached at one end to the widest point of the curve and, at the other, to a vertical bar which closes the curve and connects the base of the work to the shaft above. A short vertical strip of wood has been nailed to the center of this horizontal bar, a partial echo of the summit ornament. In sum, the long branch of a tree has been selected and set at the vertical by the sculptor to give rise to a memorable sculpture.

The uncompromising simplicity of the work recalls modern Western sculpture, especially Constantin Brancusi. The Rumanian and the Afro-Georgian share a common approach to fundamentals in the use of simplified masses, harnessed exponential curves, and reduction to geometric essences. Their convergence may well reflect distant and independent absorption of African influence (cf. Goldwater, 1967: 233). The possibility of a relationship between the use of natural tree branches as the given of sculpture in the work of Bowens and the famous bent-branch sculpture traditions of the Congo-Angola area remains to be tested. Both Bowens and Congo-Angola sculptors exploit the accidental features of branches to make a work of art in human form.

The death of Bowens on February 19, 1966, marks the end of the Afro-American artistic heritage of his village. The writer visited the ruins of his house on December 22, 1968. The house is overwhelmed, today, by a sea of wild grass and the roof is open to the sky, the blue of heaven reflected brilliantly in the mirror of the dressing table of the dead sculptor, which his friends and survivors have not touched but allowed to fall to pieces slowly in the Georgia sun. Before the vanished steps of the front of the house, scratched in a kind of concrete stepping stone, is still visible a date and the impress of the sole of the shoe of the artist. It seems certain that Cyrus Bowens realized that historians would be interested in the story of his life.

Fayetteville, New York

An important sculpture, evidently Afro-American, was carved in wood in this village ten miles east of Syracuse, possibly during the period 1836-65. The work represents a male figure seated upon a block. He is frontally positioned and encircles with both arms a large vessel which rests upon his knees. The pose recalls some forms of African sculpture, as for example the frontally disposed figures with vessel characterizing the cult statuary for the riverain king Eyinle in southwest Yoruba country.

The face of the figure is like a mask. The small eyes are in low relief and the nose is broad but projecting slightly, so that the strongest trait is the mouth. The form of the nose and the lips suggest an Afro-American subject. The pursed lips create an impression of dignity and collectedness of mind. On the other hand, the pressing of the knees together, the gesture of the hands (right fingers closed, left open), and the slight turning of the head to the left suggest the lack of tension is only apparent. As to the neutral details of the sculpture, the shirt of the figure is high-collared and has long sleeves, the trousers are cuffed, and the shoes (or feet) are unfinished. The image may have been once completely painted a dark indigo blue, but traces of red pigment are now visible.

The sobriety of palette, equilibrated pose, frozen face, pursed lips, and the holding of a vessel forward are mixed formal and iconographic traits which suggest a degree of African influence. But the Western elements are very strong—the "proper" relation of head to body, the phrasing of the fingers (African hands in wood sculpture are often simplified and calm) and, of course, the style of dress. Most especially, the facial traits are rendered according to Western canons of dimension and siting, with the eyes carefully centered and small instead of having been sited on the sides of the face for expressionist flavor, or glittering with added available metal or beads or shells. The blending of Western and possibly African elements seems to favor the former source, and one might consider the sculpture a visual parallel to contemporary spirituals marked by considerable Western influence. Yet the interweaving of aspects tense and decorous, although achieved with many non-African means, distinguishes a masterpiece in the Afro-American vein.

The attribution is based on the fact that no trace of caricature or social distance, between maker and subject, can be detected. This is extremely rare for a century when the Afro-American as grotesque was all the rage in the lithographs of Currier and Ives and black-faced performers in minstrelsy parodied a world they never understood. The manly dignity of the image at hand is removed from the half-apologetic, half-ingratiating smiles of this other world. If the piece was carved by an Anglo-American, his sympathy for his subject and the cultural accuracy of his stylistic means were amazing for his century and would almost make him qualify as a kind of honorary Afro-American in the manner of John Brown.

A prominent Anglo-American miller at Fayetteville, Hiram Wood, first owned the image and told his daughter, Martha Louise (born in 1842), when he gave the image to her, that a hired man working in one of his mills had carved the piece in his leisure time. The son of Martha Wood, Harry Wood Andrews, sold the work via two antique dealers to the Abby Aldrich Rockefeller Museum in Colonial Williamsburg.

The career of Hiram Wood provides a key to the dating of the sculpture. Wood entered the milling business in 1836 and maintained two grist and flouring mills until 1840. He resumed trade in 1849. In October 1865 he sold what was by then one of the largest milling operations in Onondaga County and retired (Rivette, 1968: 5; personal communication). One infers, consequently, that the object was carved during the period 1836-65.

Fayetteville is one mile from the Erie Canal and was witness to considerable migration in the last century, including a heavy traffic in fugitive slaves, which may explain why an Afro-American work of art appears in Onondaga County. In 1845 the Reverend Samuel Joseph May, an abolitionist and a follower of William Lloyd Garrison, moved to Syracuse, where Afro-American fugitives from several

Southern states came to him. The fact that an ex-slave from Tennessee, the Reverend Jermain W. Loguen, founded the African Methodist Church in Syracuse at the same time implies a considerable number of free Afro-Americans in Onondaga County.

The anonymous sculptor might have been a free Afro-American of the Fayetteville area. There were ten persons of African descent living about Fayetteville in 1830, fourteen in 1840, five in 1850, and six in 1855. Half of the ten families in 1865 were of Southern origin (Rivette, 1969: personal communication). Insufficient evidence makes impossible at present the identification of a millworker in this group. Federal and state census documents do not record the names of the men who worked for Hiram Wood. All that can be established is that there was a pool of Afro-American labor from which the talented carver might have come.

The assumption of Afro-American authorship turns on the visual evidence alone. Data furnish no absolute proof. Whoever he was, the artist seems no stranger to the idealist qualities which characterize many of the aristocratic arts of the Guinea Coast. This mid-nineteenth-century work transcends with subtle dignity the complicated and acrid savor of Afro-American existence.

Conclusions

Contrary to general opinion, important Afro-American and African-influenced art exists in the United States. The tradition lacks the richness of the Afro-Caribbean and Afro-Brazilian aesthetic, but there are a number of sculptures of comparable merit. The fact that wood sculpture is the predominant medium suggests the depth of the tradition, for while painting is the classic art of the West, sculpture in wood plays a comparably central role south of the Sahara.

There are seven traits common to most United States Afro-American sculpture that suggest African influence.

1. *Monochromy or bichromy.* The deep red and blueish-black painted wood at Fayetteville, the reddish cedar complicated by blueish-black painted wood at Darien, the single black tone used by Henry Gudgell in Livingston County, and the monochromy of the work of Cyrus Bowens recall the West African economy of palette. Olbrechts (1934) went too far when he characterized the use of

polychromy in traditional African sculpture as a mark of decadence, but the fact remains that, in the main, the African sculptor—or his patron—paints the carved image in black or red monochrome (Wingert, 1950: 4). In many instances these are the very colors combined in Afro-American bichromy. The Afro-Carolinian ceramic presents a new but equally restricted usage: kaolin against glaze.

2. *Smooth, luminous surfaces.* The relative glitter of carefully smoothed surfaces defines the method of finishing in much tropical African and Afro-American sculpture. The troubling of the surface of a representation of a human being with the signs and furrows of emotion or old age is rare in tropical Africa (but satire and moral vengeance are important exceptions) and does not appear in the United States at all with the exception of the gritty sand glaze surface of some Afro-Carolinian ceramics.

3. *Equilibrated gestures.* Statuary made by men of African-derived culture stands or is seated upright, in frontal position, with arms symmetrically disposed. This calm and ordered appearance mirrors the equilibrated compositions of most of West Africa (with the exception of Bakongo torsion and the forceful diagonals of the art of the Fon people of Dahomey). The Nigerian potter Abatan of Oke-Odan and the anonymous sculptor of Fayetteville achieve a mood of repose by similar structural means.

4. *Frozen faces.* This quality extends the calm of much West African figural sculpture. Available evidence suggests that many West African dancers and sculptures alike present to the world a "mask" uncompromised by signs of specific emotion. Identically "cool" faces characterize most Afro-United States statuary, with the exception of the Afro-Carolinian ceramic.

The calm face seems an aspect of ideal human conduct, pursed-lip dignity. Consider the experience of a Works Project Administration fieldworker at an Afro-American settlement on the margin of Savannah in the late 1930s. Here she encountered a man named George Boddison, one of the two rulers of the barrio called "Tin City." Boddison met her with a copper wire wound about his head, to which were attached two broken pieces of mirror, reflecting side up, so that they flashed and glittered whenever he moved his head. Boddison presented a spectacular instance of the continuity of the

use of African-derived charms in modern Georgia, his headdress
recalling, to cite but one precedent, the circlets of ornamented talis-
mans which protect the head of some of the traditional rulers of the
Ashanti today in Ghana (Kyerematen, 1964: 31). But what really
haunted the interviewer was the frozen face of George Boddison:
"When we thanked him he did not smile but only bowed his head.
To the end of the interview he kept his dignified and serious de-
meanor" (*Drums and Shadows:* 21). Afro-American sculpture is
striking for a similar expression of concentrated hauteur.

5. *Beaded, shell, or metal eyes.* The use of available metal or
beads to mark the eyes in West African sculpture creates a visual
experience distinct from that conjured by works of art in the Western world. The taste reflects a larger pattern in West African cultures
of mixed media compositions; an image can not only be adorned
with nail-head eyes, driven into the wood, but also brass studs,
feathers, tin, or sheet brass in such a way as to sometimes disguise
the wood basis of the figure altogether.

The distinction between Yoruba and Luba usages of beaded eyes
and the cognate stylistic device of William Rogers of Darien has been
noted. The possible West African sources of this trait are in fact
almost limitless, for bead as well as nail or cowrie shell eyes are
found in a variety of societies. As early as 1926 Guillaume and
Munro had noted that the West African is "especially fond of giving
a flashing regard to the eyes by inserting beads, shells, stones, or bits
of metal." It is just possible, furthermore, that the Afro-Carolinian
ceramic represents a transformation of this tradition as the natural
consequence of Western craft adoption, transposing glaze for the
surface of the wood, setting spheres of white clay into the pottery
for the white of cowrie shell eyes, or setting tin into wood.

6. *Synoptic vision.* The term has been used by William Fagg
(1963) to designate in the court art of Benin in Nigeria the simultaneous use of two or more vantage points within the same frame of
visual reference. The same remark might be made apropos of the
men-seen-from-the-front in juxtaposition with reptiles-seen-from-
above in Afro-Georgian modes of walking stick relief, as well as the
variant mode at Livingston County, Missouri (man viewed from
behind, reptiles viewed from above). A reasonable objection might

be that a sculptor would have no recourse but to depict men and reptiles in this manner within the compass of a restricted composition. But, in fact, examination of the grotesque walking sticks peculiar to the folk traditions of the Netherlands province of North Brabant, which involve a certain amount of mixed human and reptilian imagery, demonstrates that this is not necessarily the case and that the normal rules of Western one-point perspective can still apply (cf. Hansen: 226). One of these Netherlandish walking sticks shows a snake in full relief that surges off the plane of the cane and into the hand of a human figure which surmounts the cane. At the point where this contact occurs, both serpent and man are viewed from one point. In other words, the Netherlandish folk carvers could not resist carving the heads of their reptiles so that they break the plane of the cane realistically at the same time that they are viewed in tightly organized perspectival schemes. Afro-American and African depictions of reptiles are by contrast iconic and frozen parallel to the plane of the cane, identical in this regard to the flattened lizards and crocodiles which figure in much of the relief sculpture seen on doors in a variety of West African architectural sculpture.

7. *The repertory of motifs.* Reptiles (frogs, lizards, tortoises, alligators, serpents) and human figures are the pervasive themes of the African-influenced sculpture of the American South. Stick Daddy carved a walking stick ending with an improvised metal finial in which was inserted the photograph of an Afro-American female. The staff itself was decorated with relief representations, consisting of, from top to bottom, a tortoise, an alligator, and a serpent. The design is like a permutation of the composition used by Henry Gudgell, where similar motifs were arranged in slightly different order. These compositions may, in turn, be compared to a Woyo chiefly staff from Congo-Kinshasa, reflecting in its lighter weight usage as a baton or scepter. The African staff is surmounted by a human figure over a shaft decorated with a serpent and a lizard.

The carved frog from Darien relates to the carved representations of the same reptile in the sculpture of the barrios of Afro-American Savannah (*Drums and Shadows:* 70). The abstract figure of a man set beside a reptile in the Bowens burial ground at Sunbury is analogous to the man over the reptile in the walking stick carved at

Darien.

Anthropologists have long noted the dangers of lifting cultural facts out of context in comparison with other facts lifted out of context. However, the historic ties between coastal Georgia and West Africa have been documented; hence the comparison of the repertory of iconic themes in Afro-American sculpture from Georgia with African art is conducted within a known historical framework. Reptiles are often metaphors of human achievement in West African art. Are they so interpreted by Afro-Americans in Georgia? One would reason that at least fragments of the original communicative function reappear in the United States, but the fact is that we do not know.

A single motif in the absence of further African-seeming details, such as the use of beads to mark the eyes, is insufficient evidence of continuity. There is a Civil War cane which has an entwined serpent, but its maker was an officer of the Confederate Army (Burtscher, 1945: 50). Only where humans and reptiles appear in the same composition and are carved, as in Africa, with a clarity and iconic strength suggesting the incarnation of special power may one hazard the guess that the themes transcend the realm of independent invention or derivation from Europe.

The careful spacing of the depiction of tortoises, lizards, and so forth in Afro-Georgian modes is distinct from Netherlandish walking sticks, which are embellished with human couples surprised in the act of coitus, groups of reptiles, and other grotesqueries, recalling to a certain extent some of the paintings of Brueghel. In this European tradition, reptiles are crowded together, in contrast to the careful separation of motifs, one from the other, in Afro-American sculpture. If grotesque walking sticks from Europe influenced the Afro-Georgian aesthetic (and the writer does not think it is very likely), stronger ancestral impulses transformed these naturalistic whimsies into a sober iconic art of deeper purpose. Were the motifs determined by the ecology of tidewater Georgia, this would not explain why they recur in Missouri or why other tidewater fauna are not included in the thematic vocabulary of the Afro-American carvers. And why is there an evident absence of a corresponding Anglo-American form of sculpture in this province?

It is more reasonable to suppose, in the opinion of the writer, that reptiles are privileged forms of the African-derived visual tradition of coastal Georgia, and some other parts of the South, as a direct reflection of their great importance in the arcana of the native Afro-American medicine of the area. In former times Afro-Americans in tidewater Georgia ascribed illness to witches in the form of reptile familiars. Consider these four allegations, again listed by settlement followed by source in *Drums and Shadows* Springfield: "There's a human round you what can make a hand to put any kind of insect in your body. She can kill an insect and grind it to powder and rub it on the skin of a person or give it to him to drink. When it enter the body it turn back into insect, sometimes a lizard, or a frog, or a snake." Brownfield: "Conjure is being practiced all the time. Frogs and lizards and such things is injected into peoples' bodies and the people fall ill and sometimes die." Pine Barren: "Folks what is con-jured have snakes in 'em and sometimes frogs." Springfield: "I could feel the snake running all through me. If I had killed that snake, it sure would have been Flossie Hopkins."

Puckett (1926: 249ff) shows how these beliefs were once preva-lent throughout the Afro-American quarters of the South. He cites an instance where a woman was conjured but went immediately to a "hoodoo doctor," who took a frog and a lizard out of her. And he describes how these exorcisms were done:

> A woman thought she had lizards running up and down under her skin. A Negro hoodoo woman was called in . . . this woman had a lizard hidden in her sleeve, and, waiting for the frenzy to come upon the patient, she gently massaged her arm, pretending to work the lizard down the patient's arm to the fingertips. Then she gave a sudden fling and [slung the lizard out of her sleeve and onto the floor]. Curious onlookers cried and fled. The woman was from that moment cured [p. 303-04].

It is a traditional belief in some parts of West Africa that witches travel in the form of animals—owls, bats, black cats, and so on—to visit death or disease upon their victims (Parrinder, 1961: 168).

Compare in this regard the testimony of George Boddison of Tin City, Georgia: "A person can take such a thing as a cat or a dog or a lizard. They can kill this animal and they have some way to cause its spirit to be evil. But these [charms] that I wears keeps all these things from hurting me." On the opposite side of Savannah, in another Afro-American quarter, a woman testified: "Witches is like folks. Some get a grudge against you and starts to ride you. No matter what you do, they can get in your house. Sometimes they come like a mouse, sometimes a rabbit, and sometimes even a roach." But the main forms in the South seem to be reptiles.

Information from the Congo-Angola sector of West Africa (Biebuyck, 1969: personal communication) suggests an origin for these beliefs. Whereas the Yoruba and related peoples ascribe illness to witches in the form of birds, some of the traditional societies of the lower reaches of the Congo River believe that all kinds of enemies present themselves in the form of crocodiles and certain species of snakes.

Southern Afro-Americans in coastal Georgia, having relatively little access to Anglo-American medicine, used the "parallel science of magic" (cf. Lévi-Strauss, 1962) to provide a theater where conventionalized notions of pathological causation could be isolated and controlled. Traditional Afro-American healers cured their patients by presenting them with the cause of their illness and their fears in tangible reptilian form. And it is a fact that in economically insecure societies psychosomatic disorders are common and respond often dramatically to psychotherapy (cf. Lévi-Strauss, 1967: 174).

The existence of a carved walking stick embellished with an entwined serpent has been reported in the Charleston, South Carolina, area, and the name of the object was given as a "conjure stick." (Chase, 1969: personal communication). It is also interesting to note that the career of Allen Parker, of the quarter of Tatemville in Savannah, embraced both sculpture and conjuring, so that perhaps by no accident the sorts of animals he carved—snakes, lizards, frogs, dogs, alligators, and rabbits—are almost without exception the traditional zoomorphic metaphors of human pathology in the folklore of the Afro-Georgian. In addition, one Afro-American traditional doctor in the South was famed for a crooked stick which, it is said, when thrown down and picked up, admonished and thrown down again, writhed like a serpent, becoming still when picked up by its master (*Southern Workman,* 1895, Vol. 24: 118). This interesting legend may have been inspired by the presence of an entwined serpent, carved in wood, on an actual conjuring cane.

Since the world of witches and enemies is very real in the minds of traditional West Africans and some of their descendants in the South of the United States, both culture areas believe that it is imperative to have someone—in Africa the ruler or the diviner, in Georgia the healer—who can operate within this world on behalf of mankind, and such a person must of necessity incarnate powers of witchcraft himself. Can it be that the frequent opposition of reptilian and human themes in the relief sculpture adorning walking sticks and a documented "conjuring stick" constitutes a coded visual declaration of the power of the healer, and perhaps others, to discover those enemies who come in the form of snakes and lizards and to neutralize them? We do not have the data to test this theory. The writer would suggest, however, that close comparative study of the iconology of the chiefly staffs found along the lower reaches of the Congo and the walking sticks and conjuring sticks of tidewater Georgia and South Carolina might yield provocative information which would considerably deepen our knowledge of African artistic continuity in the United States.

The traditional art of the Afro-American in the United States represents a fusion and simplification of some of the themes of the sculpture of West Africa. The American mosaic by and large defies assignment to exact West African civilizations, although the Congo-Angola area seems a most plausible source for some of the aspects we have noted. The situation reflects a traumatic slave experience. Artistic continuities are consequently generic, simple, and restricted to areas of dense and recent contact with tropical Africa, with occasional isolated instances such as Fayetteville and Livingston County. Here are treasures from a sensibility which could not be policed out of existence.

It must not be assumed that the subject is limited to the areas briefly remarked in the preceding pages. Louisiana awaits an intensive search for possible Afro-American visual continuities, and a related possible field of research is the coast of Alabama, where it is reported (Charters, 1967: 148) that fragments of the West African religion of the Fon of Dahomey (*vodun*) exist as an element of contemporary folk culture. The slight possibility that fragments of a visual tradition might be recoverable among groups of Afro-Alabamians living along the Tombigbee River and in the Taladega National Forest, who reportedly use some African phrases in their speech, merits investigation. And a wrought-iron standing figure, found on the site of slave quarters in Virginia, attributed to the eighteenth century (University of St. Thomas Art Department, 1966: 107), needs study against the history of Afro-American black-smithing and the history of wrought-iron sculpture in tropical Africa.

Finally, the Smithsonian Institution recently acquired an interesting "bible quilt," said to have been made by an elderly Afro-American farm woman, thus far known only as Harriett, about 1886 on the outskirts of Athens, Georgia. The work is divided into rectangular panels, each devoted to a particular biblical scene. The panels are filled with appliquéd silhouettes of human figures and animals, human figures with geometric motifs (rosettes and circles), and other design combinations. Stylistically, the sharply outlined figures recall, somewhat, the chiefly textiles of Dahomey in West Africa, as does the technique of appliqué itself, but this Afro-Georgian textile shows considerable Western influence in the attempt to tell an entire story in each panel and, of course, in the nature of the iconography. An artistic biography of the maker, if possible, would clarify her influences at the same time that the nature of her individuality would be established. The Smithsonian acquisition is mentioned as an indication of the fact that undoubtedly further treasures of Afro-United States art await discovery by students of the field.

In time the contours of an entire tradition will emerge, sufficient to discredit the apriorists, who believe that the traditional Afro-American art of the United States is "devoid of tribal and religious associations" and is merely the work of isolated folk craftsmen, hence not on the level of legitimate art historical concern (cf. Canaday, 1968: 37). The old assumptions, which elevate ignorance to definition, will disappear before the truth.

If there are few specific ties to West African civilizations, generic resemblances are certainly present and shared ideas about certain reptiles as emblems of power may have informed the rise of some of the preferred motifs of coastal Georgian relief sculpture. Moreover, in Georgia, at least, the artists were not isolated. Many of them lived and worked in the city of Savannah, and the relationships between their art and the art of Sunbury and Darien suggests a shared intellectual history. Afro-United States art is also multifacetted: dignified and cool at Fayetteville, discordant and hot at Aiken, reduced to essences at Sunbury, voiced elegantly in Livingston County.

To point out with surprise that the tradition does not mirror the heroic nature of the aristocratic arts of Ghana, Nigeria, or Congo-Kinshasa is to suffer from historical amnesia. This was an art of slaves and the descendants of slaves. Their creative vision persisted in the face of a system designed to make children forever of men. Slavery and crypto-slavery might have destroyed those realities by which the Afro-American experienced self-awareness had it not been for his profound and intractable sense of beauty. Mankind must applaud Afro-American art in the United States for its sheer existence, a triumph of creative will over forces of destruction.

Acknowledgments

This work profits from the cooperation of a variety of people whose aid it is a pleasure to specify. First and foremost, I am grateful to the Afro-American students at Yale, most especially Armstead Robinson, '68, for the thoughtfulness with which they brought to fruition the conference of which this publication is the document. I am, in addition, grateful to Armstead Robinson for his patience as I tried to finish a work which, in a fundamental sense, will never be finished.

Secondly, Richard Neal Henderson, a colleague at Yale, was kind enough to spare long hours in the night in the careful criticisms of several drafts of the essay, and the clarity of the writing has been immeasurably improved by his suggestions. Sidney Mintz kindly checked a portion of the essay and the last sentence reflects, in part, a conversation in January 1969 during which he remarked that "that it exists at all is what is important about Afro-American art."

The response of scholars and librarians asked to check certain details is very warmly recorded. I am especially in the debt of Mrs. Edward Webb and Mr. Albert Sanders, of the Charleston Museum, for their efforts to elucidate the nature of the Afro-Carolinian artisanate in pottery and for their copying of precious data about Afro-Carolinian creativity in the archives of the Charleston Museum. Thanks to their labors it is possible to talk about four named Afro-Carolinian ceramists. Mrs. Barbara Rivette, Manlius Town Historian, labored valiantly to furnish census records on Afro-Americans in Onondaga County during the time when the Fayetteville image was believed to have been carved. The story of Henry Gudgell of Livingston County, Missouri, has been clarified by the researches of Elizabeth Coffman and Earle S. Teegarden, of Chillicothe. The latter interviewed the daughter of a slave who worked for Gudgell's master in order to clarify certain points. Patrick Pleskunas made a field trip to Chillicothe where he discovered the fact that Gudgell had been a silversmith in addition to his known talent as woodcarver. Pleskunas also brought to my attention Houck's interesting notice of apparent African-influenced body painting in eighteenth-century St. Louis. Roy Sieber found time from his tasks as chairman of the Indiana University Department of Fine Arts to share many insights on the art history of Ghana and considerably enriched the section on Afro-American funerary art.

C. Malcolm Watkins, of the Smithsonian Institution, was especially generous with his incomparable knowledge of American ceramics. The technical statement about the firing of Afro-Carolinian sculpture is borrowed from his expertise and that of his wife, who is an accomplished potter. Jessie McNab, of the Metropolitan Museum, considerably sharpened my knowledge of the possibilities of English influences on the South Carolinian ceramic. Finally, Jules David Prown was kind enough to bring the Fayetteville sculpture to my attention, negotiate the gift of study photographs of Afro-Carolinian stoneware for students at Yale (including the author), and for many useful comments about the mode of presentation of the present

work. And my wife will know who has most safeguarded my enthusiasm for the glory of the Afro-American artistic heritage.

R.F.T.

New Haven, April 1969

References

Abrahams, Roger D.
  1967   The Shaping of Folklore Traditions in the British
           West Indies, *Journal of Inter-American Studies, 3,*
           456-80.

Biebuyck, Daniel
  1969   Communication, April 24.

Bosman, William
  1705   *Description of the Coast of Guinea,* London.

Burtscher, William J.
  1945   *The Romance Behind Walking Canes,* Philadelphia.

Canaday, John
  1968   Perhaps I Never Got It Clear, *New York Times,* p.
           37, October 13.

Cate, Margaret Davis
  1955   *Early Days of Coastal Georgia,* St. Simons Island.

Charleston. The Charleston Museum
  1920   *Bulletin* (October-November).

Charters, Samuel
  1967   *The Bluesman,* New York.

Chase, Judith Wragg
  n.d.   Sea Island Baskets (leaflet), Charleston.
  1969   Communication, January 30.

Dark, Philip
  1960   *Benin Art,* London.

Davis, Henry C.
  1914   Negro Folklore in South Carolina, *Journal of Ameri-*
           can Folklore, 27 (July-September), 241-54.

Donnan, Elizabeth
    1935   Documents Illustrative of the Slave Trade to America, Carnegie Institution Publication No. 409, Vols. I-IV.

Dover, Cedric
    1960   *American Negro Art,* New York.

Drost, Dietrich
    1967   *Topferie in Afrika,* Berlin.

Elkins, Stanley
    1963   *Slavery: A Problem in American Institutional and Intellectual Life,* Universal Library Edition, New York.

Fagg, William
    1963   *Nigerian Images,* New York.
    1968   African Tribal Images (exhibition catalogue), Cleveland.

Genovese, Eugene
    1965   *The Political Economy of Slavery,* New York.
    1966   The Legacy of Slavery and the Roots of Black Nationalism, *Studies on the Left,* Vol. 6, No. 6.
    1968   On Stanley M. Elkins' Slavery. *In: American Negro Slavery,* A. Weinstein and F. O. Gatell (eds.), New York.

Georgia Writers' Project
    1940   *Drums and Shadows,* Athens.

Goldwater, Robert
    1967   *Primitivism in Modern Art,* Revised Edition, New York.

Guillaume, Paul and Munroe, Thomas
    1926   *Primitive Negro Sculpture,* New York.

Hansen, H. J. (ed.)
    1968   *European Folk Art in Europe and the Americas,* New York.

Herskovits, Melville J.
    1958   *The Myth of the Negro Past,* Beacon Press Edition, Boston.

Houck, Louis
    1909   *The Spanish Regime in Missouri,* Vol. I, Chicago.

Jordan, Winthrop
    1969   *White over Black: American Attitudes towards the Negro, 1550-1812,* Penguin Edition, Baltimore.

Klein, Herbert S.
1967   *Slavery in the Americas: A Comparative Study of Virginia and Cuba,* Chicago.

Köbben, A. J. F.
1968   Continuity in Change: Cottica Djuka Society as a Changing System, *Bijdragen, 124,* 56-90.

Kyerematen, A. A. Y.
1964   *Panoply of Ghana,* New York.

Lévi-Strauss, Claude
1962   *La Pensée Sauvage,* Paris.
1967   *Structural Anthropology,* Garden City.

Livingston County Recorder
1867-70   Books 28 and 33. Chillicothe, Missouri.

McNab, Jessie
1969   Communication, January 31.

Manker, Ernst
1932   Niombo: Die Totenbestattung der Babwende, *Zeitschrift für Ethnologie, 64* (2), 159-72.

Mintz, Sidney W.
1961   Review of *Slavery* by Stanley Elkins, *American Anthropologist, 63,* 579-87.

Nassau, Rev. Robert Hamill
1904   *Fetichism in West Africa,* New York.

Olbrechts, Frans M.
1943   Contribution to the Study of the Chronology of African Plastic Art, *Africa, 14,* No. 4, 183-93.

Parrinder, Geoffrey
1961   *West African Religion,* Second Edition, London.

Porter, James A.
1943   *Modern Negro Art,* New York.
1966   One Hundred and Fifty Years of Afro-American Art. *In: The Negro in American Art* (exhibition catalogue), UCLA Art Galleries, Los Angeles, pp. 5-12.

Puckett, Newbell N.
1926   *Folk Beliefs of the Southern Negro,* Chapel Hill.

Rivette, Barbara S.
1968   Footnote to History: "Practical Miller" Was an Early Village Developer, *Eagle-Bulletin, DeWitt News-Time* (March 14), p. 5, Fayetteville.
1969   Communication, March 3.

Sieber, Roy
    1965   Kwahu Funerary Terracottas, Paper read at Columbia University Symposium on Art and Leadership in Africa, May 15.

Silberman, Charles E.
    1964   *Crisis in Black and White,* Vintage Book Edition, New York.

Sio, Arnold A.
    1968   Interpretations of Slavery: The Slave Status in the Americas. *In: American Negro Slavery,* A. Weinstein and F. O. Gatell (eds.), New York, pp. 310-32.

Southern Workman
    1895   No. 24, p. 118.

Stavisky, Leonard Price
    1948-49   Negro Craftsmanship in Early America, *American Historical Review, 54,* 315-25.

Stearns, Marshall and Jean
    1968   *Jazz Dance: The Story of American Vernacular Dance,* New York.

Stow, Millicent D.
    1932   Monkey Jugs, New York *Sun* (Antiques Section) (May 7).

Sturtevant, William C.
    1959   Gullah Negro Basketry (unpublished ethnographic note).

Turner, Lorenzo Dow
    1949   *Africanisms in the Gullah Dialect,* Chicago.

University of St. Thomas Art Department
    1966   *Made of Iron* (exhibition catalogue), Houston.

Verly, Robert
    1955   Les Mintadi; la statuaire de pierre du Bas-Congo, *Zaire,* May 5, pp. 451-528.

Waterman, Richard Alan
    1952   African Influence on the Music of the Americas. *In: Acculturation in the Americas,* Sol Tax (ed.), Chicago.

Watkins, C. Malcolm
    1969   Communication, February 26.

Webb, Mrs. Edward K.
    1968   Communication, July 30.

Wingert, Paul
    1950   *The Sculpture of Negro Africa,* New York.

SOME THOUGHTS ON AFRO-AMERICAN STUDIES

McGeorge Bundy

It's been a great white experience for me to be here for the last twenty-four hours and to have a chance to learn so many different things, and to observe the unequaled skill with which Yale College invites large groups to discuss matters which the authorities of Yale College have already decided! That's the way it was when I was here, and it was particularly agreeable to have the preliminary brain-washing conducted in the ugliest room in the College, one which I remember as the scene of a series of examinations in German, French, and other low, white topics.

However, the discussion has been helpful to me, certainly, and the decision, equally certainly—as I hope the Course of Study Committee and the Yale College Faculty will agree—is a good one: good, timely, corresponding to both the reality of what a university is in academic and intellectual terms, and the reality of what an American institution ought to be in 1968. So, in one sense all I have come to do is to say that I am grateful to those who have organized this meeting, that for all of us who are concerned with the question of the role and place of the black man in the society of the United States it cannot but be educational to be exposed to this kind of continuous discussion, both formal and informal; and also, as one graduate, to express my strong agreement with the direction in which Professor Robert Dahl and his committee propose to move.

As I listened to the discussion in the last twenty-four hours, it seemed to me that we were moving back and forth, sometimes explicitly and sometimes not quite, between a number of different points of view and purposes. I have the impression that underneath the reasonably thick ice of agreement, there is a set of currents and concerns and there are rips and eddies which we may learn more about as studies in the black experience become more and more the rule and not the exception in major American academic institutions.

The easiest part of the discussion was that which was concerned explicitly with learning. It is really self-evident that an experience as extended through time and through space, engaging as it has the lives and the fortunes and misfortunes of hundreds of millions of people over hundreds of years, deserves attention; that it is a proper part of the concern of an institution which takes, within a measure and to the limit of its resources, all learning for its province (and that is certainly the role of the American university as a whole, if of no specific university as an individual case, because no one place can do everything); that this subject has that size and scope really is self-evident—and that it has color and quality and extraordinary and unexpected meaning and value was demonstrated, with unusual skill, I thought, in Dr. Thompson's lecture. And what is true, I am sure, in that field, where I proceed, myself, with the complete ignorance and the semi-superstitious suspicion of one who has been misled by many art historians over a long period of time—because if there is any one part of the guild of scholars which regards the administrators as innocents to be diddled, it is the art historians—in spite of that suspicion, I found myself entirely captured this morning, and I took courage from the fact that wiser and more sensitive men were obviously equally impressed, at least.

So, the first part of the problem, Is there a subject here? really was settled before we came, and it is doubly settled now. We could go on, then, to look at some of the other parts of it, and I'm not sure we've done that as carefully or as searchingly as we might. When you agree that there is a topic, there still follows the question of what you want it for, and how you will pursue it—and it was evident, I thought, that different speakers had different views of that question. Now, that in itself is not wrong, but the differences are interesting. It was made very clear by Maulana Karenga that his interest in these matters is a *political* interest, and that his purpose is to establish a balance of power. That seems to me a first-class purpose and a proper target. It also seems to me *not* to be the way to define the interesting topics in black history. The people that he named and the people that he left out in his description of the black experience historically are people that a man of *one* position and *one* strongly held view might properly name and people that such a man might well omit. But no professor teaching in a university could treat the history of the black man in the United States in those terms without a fundamental failure in his obligations as a member of an academic community. So, there is a difference, to put it no more sharply, between the *political* view of a set of historical events and the *historical* view of those events. I myself believe that with all the difficulties that may occur at the margin between one's political sense and one's historical sense—and they are very great; I would like to come back to them in a moment—it remains not only serviceable but *essential* to make the distinction between what one has as an explicit point of view for the purpose of achieving a given political result, and the way one goes about the assessment and analysis of evidence.

Another dividing line which seemed to me to be present but not sharply delineated is the dividing line between the importance of these studies because they are there, because they are a great part of the experience of mankind and a valid part, as valid, as relevant as any other, and perhaps especially valid, and there's no harm in this, to people who have a particular concern because of their own situation and their own experience and their own interests—between *that* kind of picture of the subject in its own right and the picture of the subject as a *means* for providing a sense of purpose, identity, and direction for young black men and women, black students in the university. Now, as I say, there is nothing *wrong* with providing a sense of direction, identity, and purpose; but it is a very dangerous thing to start pushing the subject around for that purpose. It has to be taken on its own terms—and I took it that both with respect to the politics at the edge of the subject *and* with respect to the quest for personal identity at another edge of the subject, we were being warned by one or two of the speakers, with whom I found myself in agreement, that it was important to distinguish. When Professor Kilson told us that he smelled a rat, he was speaking of the political worry, and once or twice in other parts of the discussion it seemed to me that other speakers were saying, Look, these topics will help you whether you're black or white—and I had great sympathy with the point that the white man has at least as much to learn as the black man here.

But what I thought I detected at the edge was, Be careful if this is something you study only because it makes *you* feel better about yourself. People do this all the time. The quest for identity is, as far as I know, a phenomenon of the contemporary academic world which draws no color line, and courses whose justification is how you help yourself to grow up along the way—some of them were introduced at Harvard when I was still a responsible administrator there—can be enormously effective. But they are also things to be taken with care. Why? Because in the end, in a university the therapy that comes from a subject that is *only* therapeutic will not last. If you undertake to study a subject because of the *subject's* importance, then at least you are doing something real. If you undertake to study a subject because of the importance of that act to *you,* then in the long run what you are doing is unreal. Therefore, it is of no value, in the long pull, to erect a construct, to create a subject which is not there, or to study it simply because the *act* defines *you*—in the end you have to respect *it,* as well as its meaning to you.

Now, that question is, in a sense, a more subjective than an objective one: we have already decided that the subject exists. On the other hand, the question does arise, and was pressed very sharply by Professor McWorter, whether the subject is fit yet for effective teaching in our colleges and universities—not because it lacks size or meaning, but because the instruments of teaching, the bibliographic and library tools and above all the properly trained and qualified instructors, do not yet exist. Now, that's true on a national scale; there is a shocking shortage of persons with proper qualifications, whether they be white or black and whether the subject be the study of the black experience within the boundaries of the United States or the study of that experience in other continents, and there is certainly more than one. There *is* a shortage, but I myself don't find that very serious, certainly not here—not in *any* college or university where there is sufficient flexibility both in the rules of the faculty and in the faculty itself to permit the processes of individual study, for which the American undergraduate is now so substantially equipped.

And I myself would say about this difficulty at the edge between the maturity of the subject in formal academic terms and the interest of the student ("This is what grabs me and I have to do it") that the solution is precisely in the areas of individual endeavor, in branching out from the regular disciplines in studies supervised by men who do not claim to be themselves the great expert on the subject but who do at least know something about method—I would believe that there is plenty of room here and that this is *not* a problem, provided, always provided, that the rules of serious study, the rules of evidence, and the processes of the academy in that honorable sense are respected. And I was a little troubled, not because Professor Hare told us that it was possible to get a quick A—that's an ancient and rather vulgar skill in which, again, there is no color line—but I think there is a sense in which *these* subjects, precisely because of their novelty, precisely because they are making their way in the institutions, deserve the honor of unusually careful and unusually honorable study—unusually *free,* and this is hard, from the belief that merely to have made this choice is to have carried the point.

And yet, to make the choice *is* to make a point, to have persuaded distinguished scholars on the initiative of a relatively small group in a relatively short time that a move as significant as the one which we are discussing today is to be made is to have done *more* in terms of the politics of the academy than most undergraduates accomplish in much longer time. There will be more acts like this, and it is certain, I think, that in *this* sense the politics of this question is at a beginning and not at an end; that these studies begun here will be imitated or matched elsewhere; that a kind of honorable race will occur; and that therefore there will be an accentuation and intensification of the differences which were mostly latent and only occasionally exposed but which do exist, between the attitude of the scholar who believes that somehow the word "politics" and the word "learning" are wholly separate, and those who have had to learn, as administrators have had to learn, that the word "politics" and the word "learning" live in an uneasy symbiosis.

So I would offer just this comment, as an ex-administrator: there *is* "politics" in this—but in a quite different sense from the politics of a particular external position. There is the politics of the concern to see that the university itself becomes the mirror not simply of the society as it *is* but of the society that we hope is coming, a society which we would all *expect* to be responsive not only to the history and the art and the economics, and the politics too, and the current sociology of a group as large and important as the black element in our society, but a society that somehow takes it *for granted* that *all* of these things *do* turn up in the life of the university. That isn't so easy. The university is not as political as radical critics suggest. The university is not, for example, in its teachings about the nature of the economic system, the instrument of large-scale corporate organizations: their complaints about the way *their* part of things are taught are noisy and continuous and a reasonable test of the health of any economics department. The university *should* give offense, at regular, carefully chosen, reasonably paced intervals, to every element in society—including itself, which is something it does less often; *certainly* including foundations, which it does regularly; and specifically, including blacks. (And here is where there will be some blood before the battle is over.) Because if you are going to study the black experience, you must expect the university to study parts of it that you don't like. To close it off to the parts that serve immediate political purpose is to do something else. You must also expect, if it is to be studied in a university, that it will be studied by men and women without regard to nationality or color or specific commitment to a particular political cause. Most of the people who study it will think of themselves as sympathetic to the subject, because sympathy to a subject is what draws men, by and large, in the social sciences and the humanities. But not all of them.

So, there is a box here which is being opened which contains not only pain and trouble for those who in a kind of nervous way have refused or feared the importance of the subject, but trouble and nervousness for those who think that all it tells will be to their advantage in the wide political purpose—which they are right to have, and which I think the majority of us in this room would try to share, the purpose of the *full* equality of opportunity and of identity and of meaning and of role for the black man, the black woman, the black family in the United States. It is when *these* realities come to the surface that the quality and the integrity of the individual, and still more perhaps, the quality and integrity of the institution, will be tested. And that is why, for myself, having lived and worked here when I was an undergraduate, it seems to me extremely fortunate that one of the places which intends to be at the front in these matters is Yale. Because, with all her manifold weaknesses and deficiencies, and with all her historic limitations, she has had a *habit* of effective communication across differences of judgment and a capacity to reconcile the requirements of learning with the inevitability of that kind of exchange which is political, which is bred into the atmosphere of this place. That this is so has been demonstrated in these discussions in no small way—I think in a quite significant way—by the degree to which those pressing their point have pressed it not only with intelligence and force, but also with great political skill. All that I am saying is that it seems to me dead right to have come this far—and dead wrong to suppose that there is no rough country ahead.

QUESTION PERIOD

Question

[McWorter:] I wonder if Mr. Bundy could tell me about the suggestion that I made last night in terms of the financial role of foundations?

Bundy

I realized as I sat down that I had skillfully omitted to answer that question, but I am glad to have it recalled to me. The Foundation is now making its budget for next year, and we do expect to have several categories which will be relevant to academic studies of the black experience. And we have had for years. I was proud as I listened and learned this morning to the art history lecture that we have just made a substantial grant in the area of the oral history of Africa. We have been a principal supporter of the scholarly association concerned with African studies, and we will continue in the support of African studies—rather against our will, but out of necessity, because we had hoped that in this whole field of overseas area studies the International Education Act of 1966 would not remain an empty basket. It's an excellent enactment totally without appropriations. And while I think universities have greedy appetites, *zero* is a small amount of money with which to run an important program.

But coming to your particular point, should there be a major center for general black studies on a research level, we have been up and down that question with a number of scholars, black and white, and have not found any consensus (we're not waiting for consensus). We've found a wide variety of views as to whether it can be done, where it should be done, and under what auspices. You yourself, I thought, rightly said that such a center ought to have not only scholars deeply committed to the black experience as the center of their being, presumably black scholars, but also others—"Negro scholars, colored scholars, and white scholars," I thought you said. I can't do all the gradations of color that are appropriate to one black man judging another, but I thought you were saying that people of quite different political and cultural points of view would be needed in such a center—I would agree with that, and I also think that will be easier to say than to do.

Now, what we have done as an interim measure is to pick a limited number of people who seem to us to have unusual qualifications in particular sectors of the area, and to give them or the institutions to which they are responsible substantial support. We've done that for Kenneth Clark, at Metropolitan Applied Research Corporation, not, of course, for a study of the black experience in the deeper historical dimension, but for a highly relevant series of studies of the current urban experience—which is increasingly and centrally, I think, myself, a question of the black man in the metropolis. We have also done the same thing—or are in the process of doing it (and if there is a newspaper man here I would like him to suppress this, because I'm not sure it's announced)—for some work under the direction of Bayard Rustin in the A. Phillip Randolph Institute. And I would be glad to have a private argument with any angry young black nationalists who think that these are backward and elderly characters, because there is a compelling set of evidence, in my judgment, to the contrary.

We are hospitable to proposals from institutions predominantly white and predominantly black, but we are going to have a brutal problem of choice simply because what is happening here is happening elsewhere, and there is going to be the kind of problem of allocation of *human* resources, as distinct from dollar resources, which was apparent in the difference of emphasis between what Mr. McWorter said last night and what Mr. Ogilvie said the first thing this morning. I resist that kind of choice myself. I think this subject is going to have to grow both ways—I think there will have to be serious research centers, and there will have to be a finding and a using of teaching resources up and down the colleges and universities of the country. It's growing *that* fast, and it *won't wait*. My own experience of subjects of this kind in the past is that when you get that kind of contest, when, for example, in the years just after the Second World War, you had an explosive expansion of concern for Slavic studies—coming in part from the new political posture of the United States and the Soviet Union up against each other, and in part from a genuine interest, largely divorced from politics, of under-graduates and graduate students in Slavic studies—when you have that kind of explosion, you had at one and the same time, or at least at a very short interval in time one from each other, the expansion of research centers in a number of institutions *and* a frantic search by all kinds of places—large and small, East and West, North and South—for professors of Slavic studies. Well, the law of supply and demand has not lost all its effect, and it was stimulating to graduate students in Slavic studies to know that they could get an assistant-professorship without passing their generals. It leads to a certain amount of nodding of heads among the greybeards, but over time it strengthens the subject.

Now, I know I've said something that's unpopular with at least one or two of my old friends, but this subject is going to grow at forced draft. And I think if a foundation made an absolutely hard-boiled choice as between starting a center and giving appropriate smaller-level support to promising experiments here or there, it would be pre-judging the priorities in a way that one would have to be a lot smarter than I am, at least, to do. My guess is that we will find ourselves in a running dialogue with a lot of different people over the next year or so, and that out of that dialogue a variety of actions—not only on our part, but I am happy to say by other foundations—are likely to emerge.

So, I've given you a non-answer to your question—but I honestly believe that to give it a sharp and clear-cut answer *today* would be not only intellectually inaccurate but, as I think of what my mail would be like on Monday morning, politically crazy.

ON TEACHING AND LEARNING BLACK HISTORY

Edwin S. Redkey

The call for black studies usually begins with a demand for a course in black history. There is a strong desire on the part of black students to discover the truth about their past, to find what they trust will be honorable and brave ancestors, to document the centuries of oppression by whites. Other students, white students, also want to discover how things got the way they are now, to search for origins in the past of the problems of the present in hopes of bringing justice and peace in the future. Whether or not history can live up to these expectations, there is intrinsic value in studying and teaching the history of Afro-Americans, because it forms an integral part of American history; there can be no true understanding of the American past without consideration of the black experience.

The call for black history has implications for both school teachers and historians. For historians, it means new research, new methods, and new understandings of the past. But let me first address those school teachers and administrators who may be troubled or puzzled about whether or how to meet the demands for black history.

That people want to learn and that there is a body of material to be taught is sufficient reason to teach black history. This is a period of crisis and turmoil in American life, and the demand for Afro-American history is part of that crisis. Perhaps what we teach and the way we teach it may change in generations to come, when this particular crisis is past, but let us deal now with the questions that are being asked in our own time.

There has been considerable debate about how to get black children to learn, how to get them acculturated, how to bring them into American life. Black history is one subject in which they are interested: let us use this vehicle to teach. Whatever else may be involved, this is a topic which black youth in particular desires to study; let us use it to teach not only history itself, but as a vehicle to teach language arts and social studies as well.

If we can spend millions of dollars on trying to improve the ghetto, we can invest intellectual effort, money, and organization to understand what its origins are. McGeorge Bundy has observed that politics and learning are in a very uneasy symbiosis—yet crash programs have been launched when Americans became truly worried. In 1957, when the Russians sent up Sputnik, the nation began a crash program to teach mathematics, physics, and other sciences in a new and intensive way. We are in no less an intellectual and social emergency now than we were at that time. In order to meet this crisis, the effort and money should be expended to teach and understand the black experience in America not just to appease the demands of black militants but to help our children deal more adequately with our nation's social problems than we have done.

A number of people object to the idea of teaching the black experience in the schools. Perhaps the most common objection is that this is special treatment for one segment of the population. To some extent this is true, but blacks have usually received the negative side of special treatment. If our schools are to fulfill their mandate, they must teach material that is relevant to their students, including black students. At this point in American life, helping black youngsters understand and cope with their peculiar problems requires flexible, willing, and special treatment of history. Furthermore, there are unique factors in the American experience of black people which have a profound effect not only on the blacks but on the entire nation, factors which we continue to ignore at our children's peril. We can and must make a special endeavor to fulfill a missing element in our social education. Does this mean, then, that we must teach Irish-American, or Italian-American, or Jewish-American history? These subjects are academically valid, but they do little to help us understand the crisis the nation now faces. At this point in history there is a desire to learn about the black experience—let us meet that demand and worry about other ethnic histories when they become socially necessary.

Another objection raised to the teaching of black history in the schools and colleges is that this kind of special treatment for black people implies an endorsement of the two-nation theory, or black nationalism. This is not necessarily so; it does not necessarily reflect a man's social philosophy if he cares to learn about the black people in America. For example, integrationist college admissions officers have found that, in order to integrate their institutions, they must identify the blacks who apply for admission. The old application blanks which had a check-place for "race or color" had been eliminated. But then it was found that the officials could not tell who was applying. In order to carry out their plan to integrate, they had either to ask explicitly for race or subtly request a "recent photograph" of the would-be integrated student. The point is simply that explicit and specific attention must be paid to the racial problem whatever one's social philosophy. Those who advocate integration must learn why integration has been so difficult; they must learn who the people are who seek to be brought into American life on an equal basis. What is done with the identification that is made, what use is made of the history that is learned, is essentially the responsibility of those who learn it. If the teacher feels that the use being made of black history is not legitimate, that is a risk he must take. Race education is like sex education: If proper training is not given by responsible adults, bad training will be received on the street corners. It is our responsibility to provide sound education.

Another frequent objection to teaching black history is that in some way this is a kind of "special education" for black people, that in some way it takes us back to the 1900s, to the age of Booker T. Washington, who advocated industrial education to bring black people into financial responsibility and moral prosperity. Booker T. Washington's plans failed for a number of reasons, and we certainly do not want to retreat again to a type of second-class education for blacks. On the contrary, we need to do all in our power to improve the training of black youngsters, to make it equal to the best education available. Teaching black history, however, is not special education *for* blacks but special education *about* blacks. White people need this education today as much as blacks do. Whites need to understand all they can about the eleven percent of our nation whose presence worries so many. Blacks need to know their own history in order to grapple realistically with their future. As Nathan Hare has remarked, we all must "learn our collective past in order to design a collective destiny." To plan that destiny all of us need adequate education about the past, including the black past.

Much of the desire of black people to study their own history is based on their need to find a historical identity, or, as Ron Karenga has said, their "need to build a mythology." In 1940, Melville J. Herskovits wrote *The Myth of the Negro Past.* In that book he attacked the myth commonly believed by white Americans that the black American has no past worthy of mention, specifically in Africa, but also in the American experience. That kind of myth, hopefully, is disappearing. But the kind of mythology which Mr. Karenga called for could be defined as Herskovits himself defined it, as "historical sanction for the deep-seated belief that gives coherence to behavior." In other words, a mythology is an explanation of how we got where we are, giving an understanding of our present situation and providing a basis for future action. This kind of mythology is present in all healthy societies—certainly it is taught in American history courses as commonly presented in our schools. But black people cannot see themselves fitting into that kind of American myth. For them, the American dream has become a nightmare. The sacred terms "freedom," "liberty," and "equality" take on different meanings when flouted in black people's faces. American history omits them as it stresses the ideology of the American dream. That the healthy society needs its own myths for its psychological well-being and responsible political action has been discussed extensively by social scientists—Robert M. MacIver, Ernest Cassirer, John Marcus, and Georges Sorel. The teaching of black history will assist Afro-Americans to form a mythology which, hopefully, will be based on the accurate, skillful, and professional study of their past. Some blacks will be dismayed at what further study of the black past reveals. Most whites will be surprised by what such study presents. But in the open forum, certainly of the universities and hopefully of the American school system, the give-and-take, the shared responses to the teaching of black history, will provide a healthier mythology for all Americans.

One last objection to the teaching of black history in the schools runs something like this: "This kind of history is so different from what is normally taught in American history courses: it just does not fit." Beneath that rhetoric could be a number of hidden objections. One might be that the teacher simply does not want to teach black history. Such a reaction may be based on racism; local authorities must deal with that problem. Or that objection may be based on professional elitism; pressure from both blacks and whites is helping break down such inertia. More likely, that objection grows from the fact that the teachers do not know what to teach. Then let us educate the teachers. We found ways, money, and opportunity to educate teachers in the new math, the new physics, and so on; let us use the same in-service training programs, summer courses, and local workshops—whatever is needed—to teach social studies teachers about the black experience. It has been done before and it can be done again.

Another objection hidden in the "It doesn't fit" criticism comes even from teachers of good will, even from teachers who have a knowledge of the black past who feel that somehow the black cultural heroes—men like Frederick Douglass, who led the black abolitionists, or W. E. B. DuBois, the black intellectual spokesman, or Malcolm X, or others—somehow these men are not in the same categories as the generals and presidents and industrial leaders who are normally introduced in American history courses. Part of this problem lies in the fact that black history is indeed a different genre of history. Most American history courses are based on national politics and policy—and the complaint of black people is that their forebears appear in the history books only when their "troublesome presence" becomes a national political issue, only when they have made trouble.

Black history is a different kind of history: it is social history. Social history is usually assumed as the background for national political and policy history, rather than being explicitly analyzed. Political historians usually assume a basically homogeneous society with homogeneous institutions based on an individualistic view of American social mobility, without considering ethnic or other subgroups in American life. Social history, in contrast, focuses its attention on ethnic history, urban history, the history of fashions, labor movements, churches, and other institutions.

The teacher who is asked to teach black history must keep in mind that he is dealing with a different kind of history, a different category of study, a different kind of people. He must understand that black cultural heroes are not necessarily to be compared to presidents and generals and captains of industry, although the comparison may not be without profit, but essentially with the culture heroes of other social groups within the United States. This puts their individual achievements into the perspective of the social structure of the nation. Such study will show that black Americans have an honorable and vigorous past despite tremendous odds, a past which can form the core of a modern identity, a true mythology.

Let me now share some thoughts on the implications for the historian of the black consciousness which has been discussed here this weekend. Sociologist Milton Gordon, in his book *Assimilation in American Life,* discusses the three basic patterns in which American acculturation takes place. The first is "Anglo-assimilation," the second is "the melting pot," and the third is "cultural pluralism." "Anglo-assimilation" assumes that to become a proper American, one must adopt the prevailing Anglo-American forms and standards of life. "The melting pot" idea holds that each ethnic group, each group of migrants, people from each section of the country, contribute their own unique qualities to the standard American culture, and that in the end we are a homogeneous American blend. "Cultural pluralism" assumes that there are subcultures within American society which have their own values, their own aesthetics, and their own traditions. The work done recently by political scientists in voting behavior, and by the pollsters who predict election results, have taken serious account of the ethnic, religious, and cultural background of American voters. It is in this category of cultural pluralism that black nationalism or black consciousness must be placed.

Let the historian assume cultural pluralism. What are the implications of this basic social outlook for historical research and writing? It assumes, inherently, that the black community within the United States has its own existence, its own social structure, its own culture, its own internal organization. The questions raised by this assumption for the study of black history are many. How does this black community *organize* itself? And how has this organization changed through the years, from slavery to emancipation through the dark ages at the turn of the century to the civil rights revolution to the present? Why have these changes taken place? How does collective self-consciousness occur, what forms has it taken, and how does it grow? How are the actions of the dominant society received and interpreted within this black community? As Harold Cruse inquired, why is social mobility in the black community truncated? Why has the formation of a black middle class been curtailed? And how does mobility within this black community work? How has it worked in the past? What is the subculture of the black community? Or are there several black subcultures? How did they develop? What are the historical changes which brought us to the social situation that we find ourselves in today? What elements compose this subculture? Within this black community what is the style of life of its inhabitants? How has that style changed over the years?

Two recent books, neither of them by historians, make exciting new explorations into the life of the black ghettoes. Charles Keil, in his book *Urban Blues,* examined the culture which surrounds the bluesman, the cultural idol of many urban blacks. Elliot Liebow, in *Tally's Corner,* has intensively studied the lives of the black men who hung around a certain ghetto street corner. The kinds of assumptions and questions used by Keil and Liebow can be adapted to the historian's use. The features these two anthropologists found in ghetto life can be traced in their change and development. The history of a life style can reveal much about the black experience.

If we assume a coherent community we must also look more intensely at the institutions which black people created to make their society function. We know very little about the history of black education in this country. We know even less about the institution which for years held together the black community, gave its leaders a chance to rise, gave it a platform and a forum for its ideas—the black church.

We are learning more about the ideas which circulate within the black community. But we must study not just the articulate, the leaders, especially the "leaders" who are created by white people, but the whole community, the folk ideas within the black community.

Ron Karenga and others have used the analogy of colonialism to describe the situation of black people in this country. If we assume the existence of a coherent black community, we can pursue this analogy. Often colonialism has been used as an epithet, and justly so—but there is more to be said after condemning colonialism. Let us examine the colonial process, the colonial experience, on all of its levels, including decolonization, and compare that with the experience of the black community in the United States. There will be parallels and there will be contrasts, but I think that both the comparisons and the contrasts will teach us much about black history. Mr. Karenga also mentioned foregin aid, as it were, for the black community from the white community. The parallel here is with the developing, post-colonial nations. Again, it's an analogy. One should not make the analogy walk on all fours; but let us learn from the comparison—let us see where the analogy breaks down, let us see what we can learn about the American black community from that comparison.

The idea of the black community being its own nation also offers concepts for study—I'll just touch on one, that of foreign relations. In this case I am not referring to the separation of the black community from the white community, in a political sense. If we assume, as I have suggested, that the black community has a coherent existence of its own, let us see how representatives of that community have related to other countries outside the United States—their attitudes to Africa, their attitudes to other black societies (Latin America, the Caribbean). Let us examine the experiences of travelers, the attitudes and accounts of missionaries. Professor George Sheperson, of Edinburgh University, has blazed the trail in demonstrating that angry American black people around the turn of this century had an important role in stirring and nurturing the nationalism which blossomed in Africa later in the twentieth century. The national analogy leads us to ask new questions, in this case those of foreign relations.

A coherent black community as a working hypothesis for a historian can lead to other comparisons. We can compare this black community with the black communities of other countries, other countries where black people are in the minority—Brazil, for example, or contemporary Great Britain. Or compare and contrast it with the black majority cultures—South Africa, for example, or Nigeria, or Haiti, for three widely disparate examples.

Let us also compare this coherent community with the other American ethnic communities which exist beside it. Nathan Glazer and Daniel Patrick Moynihan, in their book *Beyond the Melting Pot,* have demonstrated that there are still many ethnic differences in the United States. The question has been bandied back and forth as to whether black Americans are just another immigrant group or not. This has been heatedly asserted and heatedly denied; unfortunately, it has not been heatedly explored and analyzed. Let us explore the parallels. Let us examine the contrasts. Let us compare the contemporary black community and its experience with, for example, the contemporary Italian-American community. Let us compare the development of black consciousness with the development and maintenance of Jewish consciousness within the American context.

For another example, Black Power advocates are now urging black people to take political power in the cities. A hundred years ago Irish-Americans were advocating a similar platform. Let us compare what black nationalists are now saying with what Irish nationalists and politicians did a century ago. Let us also explore, compare, and contrast local black communities within the larger black community. Look at the history of the ghettoes, for example. There are in New York City marked differences from the development of the ghetto in Chicago, or from that of Philadelphia, or Los Angeles. If we assume a coherent black community as a working hypothesis for historical study, we create uncounted new opportunities for comparison, contrast, and research.

There is a serious problem of methodology in the study of black history. For much of their American experience, black people have been nonliterate. The traditional sources from which historians work—manuscripts, documents, and so forth—are rarely available prior to the turn of this century for the black community. So, we have to explore and search, tentatively to be sure, but I hope persistently, for new historical methods to study the black experience. The social scientists, I believe, have some advice and experience to share with us. The cultural anthropologists in particular—as represented in the recent work of Charles Keil and Elliot Liebow—can give us methodology, categories, questions with which to explore aspects of the black experience.

Let us also look at the work of historians in other countries. Traditionally in this country we have assumed a classless society in which mobility based on individual effort is possible and, indeed, probable. In other countries the development of class structures has been more obvious and therefore better studied. Perhaps, since the advent of the Marxist historian, class structure within our own society has also become more obvious. For the study of this coherent black community which shares some class characteristics, let us utilize the work and experience of, say, the English historians who have studied the rise of the British working class—E. P. Thompson in his monumental *Making of the English Working Class,* E. P. Hobsbawm in his study of *Primitive Rebels,* George Rudé in his study *The Crowd in History.* These people are using archival sources that were hitherto untapped—police reports, church records, tax records, voting records, city directories, and so on, sources which have previously been unexploited in studying the black community.

To be sure, we must judiciously apply these new methods, questions, and research. We must cross-check with what we know, with our few manuscripts and documents and the legal-historical information which is available. But we must break out of the straitjacket of not having the usual manuscripts and materials to study black history.

Another potentially helpful methodology is that being explored by African historians, who also deal with an essentially nonliterate people, who are finding new ways to delve into the African past. Oral-tradition historiography, in particular, has been pioneered by Africanists—Jan Vansina in his *Oral Tradition* and *Kingdoms of the Savannah,* and by Daniel McCall in his *Africa in Time Perspective.* The oral tradition is a very tenuous tradition, to be sure, especially in the "post McLuhan age." Nevertheless, I have been constantly surprised in my own research, and frequently informed by others, that there are numerous black people in this country, especially in the older generation, who have vivid memories of things gone by—not only of events, but of processes, attitudes, and other cultural values. This is a tricky kind of historiography, a risky methodology, and it needs all the safeguards the skillful historian can bring to it. But we must break out of the shackles that have surrounded the study of black history in this country. We must take some risks, historically and methodologically, to find the true picture of the black past.

What is it going to take to do this kind of work in the study of Afro-American history? Essentially it will take skill and commitment. It demands the very best in technique and thought of the historian. It demands the very best ingenuity, imagination and writing, as well as dogged research and cumulative experience.

In addition to skill, commitment is required. In a note in the April 1968 issue of the *American Historical Association Newsletter,* August Meier observed that historians of the black experience have often "dipped in lightly," have written but one book on black history—usually in the area of race relations rather than the internal history of the black community—and then have moved on to other areas of study. This is not wrong: much of what we know about the black experience has been discovered by people writing their first book, their dissertation, or a seminar paper. But, if the status of the study of black history in this country is to advance to its needed caliber and quantity, commitment is demanded—commitment to long-term study, commitment to the kinds of questions that are being asked by black people themselves.

Can this be done satisfactorily by white scholars? I think it can, though I think there will be differences between white and black interpretations. Professor Boniface Obichere has mentioned the difficulties a black African faces in acculturating himself to the black milieu in this country. I believe that a white American, a white man of any nationality, just as the African, can make certain adjustments in understanding the black experience, in learning to be sympathetic to it. I suspect that eventually black people will do most of the front-line scholarship in this area—and I hope that day is not too far off—but the teaching and learning of Afro-American history must be the concern of all Americans, black and white alike.

The study of black history cannot save this nation, but a knowledge of our past can help us tolerate the present and better plan the future.

QUESTION PERIOD

Question

I should actually like to ask several questions. I teach a course in black history with a college enrollment of about 90 percent black young people, and there are three questions I would like to ask. First, is there any special problem of relevance concerned with what you teach and how you teach it with regard to white young people? Secondly, there is the question of the relationship between what has become known or characterized these days as white racism refracted by and related to black history, and what role this issue has to play. And thirdly, the question of some kind of overarching configurations aside from rather clerical but important studies of the social history of the black community—questions like Is the main line of the development of black history basically one of resistance or accommodation? I would like to get your reactions to these things.

Redkey

The type of question which you've asked is not one which lends itself to an easy answer—I'm sure you're aware of that. As to special problems in the teaching of the black experience to white students, yes, there are, in that certain cultural assumptions have to be dealt with explicitly. In my own course here at Yale of essentially half black and half white make-up, I find myself frequently after class discussing a particular point or a particular kind of assumption, or explaining a particular black student reaction to a topic to some of the white students. I think that there is no specific plan or pattern which one can adopt to deal with this—this has to be, at least in my experience, an *ad hoc* kind of treatment.

As to the question of white racism and black history, certainly much of the work that has been done which deals with the black experience in the United States has been done in the area of race relations. This is excellent and needed work; however, it is not history of the black community itself. In my teaching I try to focus on the history of the black community. But, the experience of that community has been such that the culture, the life, the economics, the striving of the black people has been so truncated by white racism that black people through the years have had to focus on that oppression. One cannot get away from the question of race relations in teaching black history—one can only change the focus of one's attention: it's a matter of emphasis, rather than of exclusiveness.

As to the main line of black reaction to the American situation as it now stands, whether it is one of resistance or accommodation, this is very difficult to tell when one is caught up in it. I think a historian can safely take refuge in saying, let's describe it as it was, rather than trying particularly to analyze it as it now is. It seems to me in my own work—forgive me for being personal on this, because my experience is limited—in my own research and study that there has been an underlying current of resistance *throughout* the black experience. It surfaces when conditions allow it to do so, or where conditions become so bad that it *has* to surface. At the current time, I think resistance has come to the surface because it is allowed to do so. Corollary to that is that, because it is allowed to come to the surface, the oppression which remains is seen to be that much more grievous. As to the historical trend, I will plead the historian's traditional plea and talk about the past rather than the future.

THE ROLE OF EDUCATION IN PROVIDING A BASIS FOR HONEST SELF-IDENTIFICATION

Dr. Alvin Poussaint

My title is a very large one and to meaningfully consider it I must address myself to racism and racial conflict. We've had racial conflict with us since mankind began—very severe conflict: there have been very few civilizations that have really resolved this problem. And there's some question whether we really *can* resolve it positively. People have murdered for racial reasons, and civilizations have fallen because of violent racial encounters. In fact, some people are quite pessimistic about solving racial problems. Even some psychiatrists believe that people *need* prejudices: they need some type of boogie-man in order to keep their personalities integrated and to stay intact. They need a mechanism to project onto other people some of their own unacceptable impulses and drives, and they need this defense because they have to remain civilized. Thus, a minority group, in this case black Americans, becomes a victim of this type of racist projection that says, *you're* the violent one, even though the white man commits most of the violence; or, *you're* the one who doesn't have control over your sexual impulses, even though it's the white man who has mainly exploited black people, particularly black women, sexually. We have these conflicts, in part, because racial groups represent vested interest groups and people protect their own interests, their own needs individually and their own group needs.

Some psychiatrists feel that there is some type of "universal unconscious," that things aren't completely determined psychologically by what happens in the environment—so that some psychiatrists say that one of the reasons why black people have a negative self-image, or have a lot of self-hatred, is because they unconsciously compare themselves to feces, which they see as negative, and this is true whether a black man lives in America or whether a black man lives in Africa.

But these theories are hard to really grasp and understand as relevant when you're dealing with societies that are racist. (Even feces is neither good nor bad, except as thinking makes it so.) Both white men's and black men's psyches are affected or controlled by racial types of thinking that is very profound. I learned myself how profound it is through psychiatry—how much interwoven with people's adjustment and adaptation is the whole issue of race. It comes up in therapy, not just with me but with other psychiatrists, in many, many different ways with white people and black people. It's very hard to change or eliminate racism with psychotherapy, it's so profound. That's why it has been so difficult—despite attempts, most of which have been superficial, to resolve this problem in the United States. Despite these attempts, there seems to be increasing racial polarization.

And I want to remind you that integration failed among the most idealistic, dedicated, and flexible people in this country: I'm talking about the white and black civil rights workers who went South, who were fighting together for freedom and equality for the black man— idealistic young people who really believed in integration. I recall all the many problems that they encountered—*not* just with the racist system, but among themselves. They couldn't overcome many of the psychological effects that white racism has had on both the white psyche and the black psyche. They struggled and fought and finally *resolved* these conflicts by eliminating white people from the movement. (At least many organizations did.) Many of their problems resulted mainly because of racism, most of it unconscious, in the white civil rights workers. Much of the conflict also resulted because of feelings and stigmata in black people that have developed as a result of living in a racist society.

Remember that this society doesn't just discriminate against the black man, or think that black is bad. This society is always teaching white superiority to their white children; this occurs intuitively, without people thinking about it very much. It begins, of course, in the mass media, in families, in schools, on television, because white people have all of the controlling status and power roles in this society. And this is the way reality is depicted to both black and white children on television, in the schools and churches. On TV almost all of the heroes, even in the cartoons, are *white* people. God is white. Santa Claus is white. Usually the white man learns how he should relate to black people mainly through institutions that, to one degree or the other, represent the Tarzan type of approach: white supremacy. This type of intuitive feeling of superiority in white people makes it very difficult for them to relate in noncondescending, nonpaternalistic ways to black people. Sometimes this is obvious, and sometimes it is much more subtle.

I think it affects our whole relationship to the world. It is not very hard to see, particularly from a psychiatric vantage point, how the racism in many white people in America affects their foreign policy, and how they treat other nations in the world—how they treat the Chinese, the Vietnamese, the Africans. It's hard for me to conceive that Senator Eastland or Stennis of Mississippi can weed out their racism when thinking of other foreign peoples, particularly black and colored peoples.

A previous speaker referred to Styron's novel. I read Styron's novel on Nat Turner very thoroughly, and I think that book represents, again, a form of intuitive type of racist thinking—in its constructs, in its values, the things that Styron selects out as being valid for black people. He ignores Nat Turner's relationship to black people. The book is conceived in terms of Nat Turner's relationship and development of contact with white people. Styron is an intelligent man. But I think even he cannot escape these unconscious feelings.

There are many psychological affects of racism that influence identity in black people. But we can't discuss identity in isolation, because when we say "identity" we generally mean something positive; so that we are also talking about self-image, and we are also talking about a sense of manhood. All of these factors are intimately connected, so that a black person can't develop a positive sense of identity just from learning black history. If one cannot function as a man in this society, if this society continues to politically and socially castrate the black man, all the black history and black arts in the world aren't going to bring him a positive sense of identity or self-esteem. It's true that black people *do* suffer from a negative self-image and low self-esteem (and I'm generalizing), and nearly every black person has to deal with this on some level and at some point. In addition to having a negative concept about being black, there is the all-pervading and profound corollary that "White is right." That expression is used very frequently, but that concept is very important for both white people and black people to fully grasp. "White is right" means that it's white people who give the confirmation and approbation to what's good, what's real, even what "reality" is. And I mean white in the broad sense, too; I mean Western civilization. You can speak of Columbus "discovering America," because he was white and Western—as if it didn't exist when Indians or other people were here. Again, we project such myths in a very intuitive manner. It seems natural that people in a majority, white people as a dominant historical group, would have this propensity.

There is a lot of conditioning that goes on continually in this society—that's passed on from generation to generation—that has made black people seek out white identification, that has made black people admire most things white, so that they're constantly plagued with an ambivalence or approach-avoidance to white people —one that even the black nationalists constantly struggle with. We are all acquainted with black nationalists who are trying to free themselves from whiteness, who become very militant but, on the other hand, cannot really give up white people—to the point that this has become for black nationalist organizations a very real problem. Some preach "Black is beautiful" and "Black is wonderful" but continue to date white girls, or the black girls continue to date white fellows. And that's all right. I'm just pointing this up to demonstrate some of the contradictions and some of the struggle that goes on internally, and also to remind you that black people are not just seeking equality, full rights, and freedom. What's going on now is also a search and fight for an *inner* emancipation from the effects of white racism—to become somehow internally *purged*. So it's not just a question of moving freely in white society. It's also a question of legitimizing blackness.

What has been the role of integration in helping black people and white people to more honestly face their identifications? How has it generally worked? Some people describe integration as it takes place in America as a subterfuge for white supremacy: that really, what integration accomplished frequently in the United States was to take a token number of Negroes and make white racists out of them. Such blacks were no longer of service, frequently, to the black community. Now, this may sound rash, but it takes place frequently in subtle and unconscious ways. For instance, if you take a black child or black student, and you "integrate" him, what this means is that you send him not to an integrated school, but you send him to a white school. Now, if we assume that the people at the institution, the white people, in one degree or another are infected with racism, that puts an awful psychological pressure on the child, and since all children want to belong and be accepted, they begin to conform. If the white people react negatively to black cultural and physical traits, then the child tends to play them down and adopt a negative attitude about them himself. So, black people frequently have to expend a great deal of time showing that they're "good human beings," expending a lot of energy making themselves "acceptable." And white people frequently *reward* this behavior, because as the black person changes his style, or conforms, the white community permits him more access. In its more gross form you would have instances where light-skinned Negroes "made it" much easier than black-skinned Negroes, because the light-skinned people look "more white." And this still occurs.

Then frequently white people will give compliments to blacks in integrated situations, and the blacks may feel very complimented by these statements. They'll say such things to the black person as, "You don't seem Negro to me," or, "You're different," or, "You don't act like all the other Negroes"—and this is the most flattering comment you can give sometimes to a member of a minority group if they are also infected, or have internalized, much of the racism. Thus, such an individual may more and more divorce himself from the black community. Now this historically has been what has *happened!*

In addition, it really doesn't change the attitudes of white people much for them to *individually* accept any black man, because they usually make an exception of that person. Their attitude toward the black community and black people as a whole does not really seem to change. The evidence, in part, for this is the fact that even though we have more token integration on many different levels, the attitudes of white Americans to the black people as a community has not significantly changed. They still don't want to live next to them, they still don't want them in their schools, etc. So, black people, even with integration, are still put in the position of begging for acceptance into the white man's institutions, even though they know frequently the white man doesn't want him. This in itself can be very degrading, or demeaning, particularly for the youth who have a new sense of consciousness.

Not long ago, I remember talking to a sixteen-year-old Negro girl. I asked about her plans to attend the newly integrated high school, and she said, "First of all, that's not an 'integrated' school, that's a white school, and I'm not going any place where I have to be 'accepted' by any old white Southern racists." I asked her, didn't she believe in integration? She said, yes, but not that kind of integration—"If the white folks want to integrate, they can come to *my* school." Now, this may appear a bit ludicrous, or impractical. Yet it has very important psychological meaning regarding what's going on today among black students: they would rather be separate than compromise their integrity; they would rather separate themselves on white campuses than put up with the day-to-day indignities and pressures they feel from white people; this becomes a burden that they no longer wish to bear. But maybe, with the nature of reality, or the white reality, much of this they are going to have to bear for a very long time to come.

I mentioned tokenism earlier because this was an important reason why blacks turned more earnestly to black-consciousness programs. I know what they are saying *now* about black consciousness, but back just four years ago most blacks, including those in the movement, were for integration, but they just didn't get it—and they saw that it wasn't coming soon. Even with "integration," we still have our all-black schools, and all-black communities, where people are being demoralized and where very little aid seems to be forthcoming. And this makes it even *more* urgent for universities both black and white to help and encourage black consciousness and black unity. For too long our society has pushed individualism—and I think they sold the black man a false bill of goods on how to achieve salvation in this society. The system kept saying that if you work hard, you study hard, you become educated, you could "make it." A lot of black people felt that by following such tenets they could become free. But it doesn't operate that way, because white America, by and large, has lumped black people into one collective image. It's a *delusion* to believe that you can "make it" individually in the face of the contradicting reality. The personal acceptability that a black person gains among any group of whites is not necessarily transferable to other groups of whites.

Almost every Negro in this country, whether he likes it or not, must bear the anguish and the pain of what racism remains. When the police gun down college students, some Negro middle-class, in Orangeburg, South Carolina, *all* black people have to feel that, though there are many who will deny that they have experienced any racial discrimination. Thus, it seems to me that since the white society seems to lump black people together in *one* image, it appears that the salvation—both psychological and social—of black people lies in a greater sense of community and group effort. The Negro lawyer's salvation is very much tied in with the salvation of a Mississippi sharecropper in the Delta. The whole idea of Individualism and the Protestant ethic has really tended to disunite black people, at least in this country. Therefore blacks have to adopt *new* styles and *new* methods—and I stress again, not only for *political* reasons, but also for *psychological* reasons.

Some people are worried that the black-consciousness people are really trying to withdraw from society, that they are afraid of white people, that they're afraid of integration, afraid of competition with white folks, and that Black Power is a *retreat*. This may be true for some, and there are certain social advantages in having Black Power and black-consciousness movements, particularly for the black female. But the black-consciousness movement, or the New Unity, has not been one that has been characterized by a retreat or a withdrawal: these groups have become launching pads for attacks on the system and on society; they've become launching pads for more effectively fighting for the rights of black Americans. You can see this around the country, not only in local communities but also on our campuses where it's the Afro-American societies that are showing a great deal of the leadership in changing the *status quo,* not only in terms of how it affects their condition, but also how it affects the condition of *all* students on the campus. Frequently black people—and this is where I think whites' salvation may also be tied up with black people—show more *acutely* how society affects them: they may be the barometers for something defective in the whole system and how it operates in an institution. Thus, in changing what affects black students negatively, perhaps better things are in store for white students.

It is important to teach and include African history, Chinese history, all these subjects, subjects outside the Western experience, in a curriculum at colleges. For black students—but perhaps more important, too, is that they make some of these courses required for white students. When you are living in a world in which black people vastly outnumber whites, and when the world is shrinking and all people have to learn how better to communicate with each other, it's very important that white students know and understand other cultures, other ways of thinking, so that they may be able to modify and undo some of their own biases and rigidity. It seems to me that if colleges can have courses required in Western civilization, they should also have courses required in the civilizations of other countries, and particularly those that have been omitted from the curriculum—the African and Asian peoples.

There is a growing black solidarity, as black people are more concerned, in a real way, with survival. There are many things valuable to the whole of society in black culture (even though some people don't believe there's a black culture, or a black subculture, including many Negro scholars). However, it's important to examine in black history or the black subculture what represents the stigmata of oppression—that is, what in black experience and behavior really represents adaptations to oppression; or the stigmata of incorporated feelings of self-hatred and negative self-image, and what represents the positive and valuable side of the black experience. It has to be examined in this way—unless we make the error of actually perpetuating many aspects of the culture that are really manifestations, transformed, of white racism.

SUMMARY AND COMMENTARY

Sidney W. Mintz

We were given a revealing glimpse today of the richness of Afro-American culture—one that surely confirms Dr. McWorter's assertion that even to ask the question of the "intellectual validity" of the study of the black experience is ludicrous. As we learn about these materials and hear men like Professors Redkey and Thompson tell us of the sources for their study, we might pause a moment to acknowledge an intellectual debt to those scholars who, though largely ignored, were studying and documenting Afro-American culture long before it became the vogue to do so. I am thinking of men like W. E. B. DuBois and E. Franklin Frazier, Carter G. Woodson, and St. Clair Drake—Negro scholars—and Melville J. and Frances S. Herskovits, Elizabeth Donnan, and Martha Beckwith—white scholars. And may I add, since it only rarely gets mentioned, that I am also thinking of those who were concerned with Afro-Americana and with the fate of the Negro people during the 1930s, when hardly anyone else in the United States seemed to notice what was matter-of-factly being done to black folk in this country—men like Herbert Aptheker and Philip S. Foner, socialist scholars.

DuBois and Frazier, among others, did most of their scholarly work in university settings. They sought the truth within the university walls as do, I am sure, Professors Hare and Cruse and McWorter and Obichere, and so many others among us. This merits stress, it seems to me, as does our presence and purpose here. I believe that the university is indeed an appanage of the power structure, as some of our speakers have contended. But it does need to be remembered that the university is not only an appanage of the power structure; it is also a place where truth can be sought, and one presumes that we are here in search of it.

Professor Dahl's announcement of an Afro-American studies curriculum makes clear that Yale intends to realize some of the intellectual potentialities of this theme. One hopes that serious students, trained to a scholarship that transcends rhetoric but never despises it, will be able to make a massive contribution to the understanding of our past, as well as of our present. Then, perhaps, the institution of slavery in the United States may begin to receive as much attention as Lee's last thoughts at Appomattox, and a historical tradition that tended to romanticize dead Indians while defaming or ignoring live Negroes will be endowed with a new perspective.

But the full meaning of the history of the Negro people in the United States will never be realized until that history is linked to the histories of all minority peoples everywhere—and particularly to the histories of colored peoples in Latin America and in Africa. As a Caribbeanist, I was gratified today by the stress Dr. Obichere and others put upon the experience of black folk outside the United States. For so many of us, black as well as white, the North American case stands alone, unmitigated and unilluminated by other histories. And yet the United States is but a sample of one, in a hemisphere where perhaps two score societies could cast needed light upon the black experience.

The Caribbean region illustrates this well. It needs to be recalled that Frantz Fanon was not an Algerian, but a Martiniquan; while George Padmore, a principal architect of African nationalism, was a Trinidadian. No North American, black or white, interested in Afro-Americana, should fail to know the name of Toussaint; but how many also know of Dessalines and Christophe, of Antonio Maceo and Rafael Serra of Cuba, or Paul Bogle and George William Gordon of Jamaica? The list of colored Caribbean patriots—and one properly includes here a good many colors, may I say—is a long one. But even those of us to whom such names of the past have little meaning would do well to notice that Marcus Garvey, Malcolm X, Stokely Carmichael, Lincoln Lynch, and Roy Innis—among others—are of Caribbean ancestry.

In fact, the histories of Antillean, North American, and African peoples have been entangled for nearly five centuries. We may forget the immensely profitable triangle trade that once linked British and New England ports, West African slave depots and the Antilles, then the world's richest colonies; but only at our peril may we forget the

204 Black Studies in the University

things that link Africa, the Antilles, and the Negro people of the United States today. The political, social, and cultural relationships within and among these massive regions need to be studied and understood—in part, at least, as an aspect of Afro-Americana. Beyond such studies, the relationship of color, of physical type, of so-called "race," to such ideological themes as pan-Africanism, the African tradition, and *négritude* will have to be plumbed, but with more coolness and perspective, though with no less passion, than is now possible.

One may fairly ask what the role of the white Afro-Americanist can be in the growth of such studies. Clearly, to the extent that black students are willing to accept what white scholars have to offer, the answer is an easy one. Moreover, the academic arrangements required to make this amplified pursuit of knowledge possible are, probably, quite matter-of-factly soluble. At Yale, for instance, we will develop an adequate curriculum, work out satisfactory dormitory solutions, clarify the role of Negro scholars on predominantly white faculties, and so on, I am sure. Is there anything of wider relevance, then, that one can say about what this symposium has revealed? I think there is; but my comments are purely personal in nature.

Black people organized this conference, doubtless on the presumption that they might be able to enlighten their white fellow-citizens. Black scholars have come to it from elsewhere; I think we whites are in their debt for their having tried to tell us what they believe to be the truth. As some of the speakers have pointed out, we whites are here because in some way we have felt that we had better be here. The speakers have made clear to us that we white scholars who really care about this country must seek to civilize ourselves by civilizing our fellow-whites—and I think this is correct. Trying to civilize oneself by civilizing one's white fellow-citizens may prove very frustrating, for one may so easily end up hating—rather than loving or educating—one's white fellow-Americans. But our speakers imply that our choices are few, and they are probably right. If those whites concerned to secure and to maintain civil liberties for all citizens cannot confront the majority community in order to bring this about, the society as we know it simply may not survive. American

Negroes who have discovered that the notion of liberty or death is as American as apple pie now hold out to us whites the challenge to educate our society to practice what it preaches. We, of course, are free to believe or not believe that the society is worth it and that the challenge is an urgent one.

There is a process of social selection at work in the black community in the United States. By this process, leaders, ideologies, and symbols are appearing with unusual rapidity; coalitions are being formed, broken, and re-formed, almost weekly. We do not know who the leaders of the Negro community will be in ten or twenty years, or what their ideological positions will be; but we can be sure that, over time, larger and more cohesive groupings will emerge, built up around particular men, particular credos, particular symbols. The precise ways in which this will happen—and around which leaders, symbols, and ideologies—no one is prepared to predict; it will depend, as Mr. Karenga suggested, on what actually happens politically and economically: whether the distribution of political and economic power actually changes and, if so, in what ways.

As this process continues, white people who believe in the promise of America should try to understand what, indeed, is going on, both among black folk and within the white majority. They should be particularly careful not to misinterpret the symbolic and ideological explorations of Negro leaders. Black men who do not choose to see themselves as an inversion of a white society are searching for new ways to express their unity and direction—symbols serve such purposes, be they amulets, bop beards, or daishiki. There is a democracy in symbolism of these kinds that must be noticed: what may seem bizarre when worn by six or sixty looks very different when worn by 60,000 or a million. We know that Swahili was the language of slavers, as "black" was their word for "Negro." But should a million North American Negroes learn Swahili and call themselves blacks, then in one important sense, history has been changed by fiat. White Americans need to come to terms with the awakening consciousness of black Americans as a people, and to recognize that the symbolic and ideological variety of that awakening symptomizes a need for fundamental political education and fundamental political change. Whites need very much to notice that social reality, so far as the

Negro people in the United States is concerned, is not what *is*, but what is *believed to be* so. Nor is this any less true for the white majority, too many of whom are still unpersuaded that the Bill of Rights was intended for black people, too. White people who care can still play a role, if they dare, in changing those realities.

A CONCLUDING STATEMENT

Armstead L. Robinson

The symposium is drawing to a close, and the unenviable task of saying its last words has fallen upon me. Fortunately, there are several things I want to say. A number of persons have approached me over the last two days with a variety of questions about black studies, black students, campus unrest, and the crisis in public education. I have been asked to express the feelings of black students and black people on these subjects. I do not feel that any one man can speak adequately for blacks at Yale or elsewhere. Instead, I will offer one student's impressions of the significance and importance of this symposium and the issues it has raised.

The major questions fall under two headings. First, administrators want to know what the ferment over black studies is all about; second, they want to know how to respond to these pressures.

Gerald McWorter put his finger squarely on an essential point when he said: "We all know why the educators are here." You are here because a lot of you are scared—scared about what might happen in your school districts and on your campuses. But black students and black parents all over the country are tired of an educational system which is fundamentally racist and which does not speak to their needs. More than being tired, however, they are refusing to accept passively the continuation of an educational policy which excludes their legitimate concerns from decisions which vitally affect them. As a result, colleges, universities, and school systems across the country are facing escalating black protests against curricular irrelevance, irresponsibility, and negligence.

American educators must face the reality that their educational system has failed in the most fundamental ways to provide learning experiences that are relevant to blacks. They must also realize that the root cause of this failure is racism—the type of racism, conscious and unconscious, which dictates not only the choice of materials to be presented and the way they are presented, but also the way black students' problems are perceived and dealt with by teachers and administrators. You ask what the ferment among black students is all about; I answer, it is about these fundamental problems and the urgent necessity for correcting them.

In this context, the symposium's basic issue is fairly simple. Black studies, or Afro-American studies, *must* be included in the general curriculum as a necessary first step in the process of reforming education in this country. But one thing must be made quite clear. You must not assume that by "giving in" to black students' demands and instituting a black studies curriculum, you will have "solved" the problems of black unrest on your campuses and in your school systems. The surest way to stimulate more "disturbances" is to promise black students a taste of real education and then try to renege later on—when the heat is off.

That black studies are important for blacks is, I would hope, beyond doubt by now. Of much greater importance to you, however, as purveyors of this country's cultural heritage, is the crying necessity for such studies because they are needed, literally, to remove the scales of ignorance from the eyes of black and white America. Professor Redkey put this point bluntly but well. If adequate and accurate education about the black experience is not provided in the classroom, then racial attitudes will be formed on the basis of misinformation gained from "other" sources. Racism feeds on ignorance. A commitment to social change in this society means a commitment to lift the appalling veil of ignorance about black people under which so many of America's youths, especially white youths, now operate.

The ferment created on campuses among black students and in schools by parents for the inclusion of black studies in the curriculum is real. Harold Cruse pointed out that many blacks do not have a completely clear understanding of the implications of the black cultural nationalism they are espousing. This, however, does not minimize the legitimacy of these demands. Black students are no longer playing games—and you can no longer afford to take the demands of black students or black parents lightly; you do so at your peril. Black studies is not a *gift* to black students or to black parents. The institution of black studies programs and the inclusion of black studies materials in public school curricula will not mollify or lessen the pressures blacks will continue to place upon the educational system and upon this society for the *total reforms* we feel are desperately needed. Frankly, you should not expect such results; you will be rudely disillusioned if you do.

How, then, should concerned educators respond to black people's demands? This question is of immense significance not only to the prospects for preserving peace on campuses and in schools but, more importantly, to the ability of this country's educational system to endure the revolutionary changes it must undergo. One of the great ironies of the present situation is the way so many *potentially* fruitful exchanges between blacks and white administrators turn into angry confrontations. While it is true that blacks often present their cases in strident language, it is equally true that most black demands raise fundamental questions about the nature and design of the educational process. Educators, oftentimes, are not prepared to answer these questions. Caught off guard and unable to explain coherently a system which—like Topsy—"just growed," educational administrators resort to indignant cries of outrage at attempts to drag their sacred schools into the "political thicket."

Brother Cruse and Maulana Karenga have already "smelled the rat" in this argument, dissected it, and exposed the speciousness of such contentions. Educational institutions in this society have necessary and inherent political and social obligations. As educators you represent financial power, community influence, and social prestige. If your function of equipping students to cope successfully with reality is to be fulfilled, then you must not only be responsible, in terms of your educational functions, but you must also be responsive to the legitimate needs of the communities you supposedly serve. Unless this country's educational system chooses to be properly responsive to the legitimate claim of parents and students that it live up to its functional goals, it will not survive. Blacks are tired of schools whose only function is that of serving as day care centers; black parents and students want their schools on *all* levels—primary, secondary, and collegiate—to provide information and training that are relevant to the realities with which we all must live.

Though the above imperatives seem self-explanatory, many educators continue to wonder whether they should respond favorably to demands from blacks for curriculum reform. Some even question the validity and rigor of any curriculum that would be developed in response to protest.

Such wrongheaded notions about the nature of an academic curriculum must be scuttled. A distinction should be made between validity and rigor as they relate to scholarly research and writing, and validity and rigor in terms of the way these materials are selected and presented to students. A *curriculum* is rigorous and valid if it communicates useful information to students in ways which enable them to perceive reality clearly and to deal with it successfully on an individual as well as a group level. If a curriculum fails to communicate effective and useful information to a group of students, then it is not a rigorous or valid curriculum for those particular students. Put another way, is it the fault of the children or of the educational system if a schoolful of high school students cannot read?

Is there a better way to discover how well or how badly an educational system works than to ask the students? What worse way to organize a curriculum than to arrange it according to some arbitrary conceptions of social relevance that are incomprehensible to the particular students involved? It is a sad commentary on the state of education in this society that educators hesitate to include a subject in the curriculum *because* students *want* to learn about it.

Many of the problems of educational institutions in this country stem from a tendency among educators toward what Mr. Cruse would call a type of "educational particularism." Many of you are afflicted with a peculiar sense of parochial *"ingrown-ness."* This tendency often hides beneath the rubric of "professionalism" and is best described as a feeling that there really isn't much that people in the community can tell you because after all, you're *professional* educators. You tend to get stuck in an endless internal dialogue about the nature of education, discussing over and over again the methodology of teaching and other vital topics. In and of themselves, these concerns are not inappropriate; in fact, they are essential to the proper functioning of any educational system. Unfortunately, while you are pursuing them, you tend *not* to consider what other equally concerned people have to say. This is a tragic mistake and its consequences can be seen all over the country. The politician who ignores his constituency is in trouble. First and foremost, the school is the servant of the people; students and parents are the educational system's constituents. You, as educators, are servants of the people, with an obligation to make the people's schools reflect the legitimate needs and demands of the communities you supposedly serve.

How often have we all heard the plaintive cry, "We can't seem to understand what *they* want"? One could infer from such comments that many of you actually expect black people to phrase their demands in the kind of programmatic language you find comfortable and easy to hear. Yet this is utter nonsense. If community people had the time and training needed to formulate coherent and consistent curriculum plans, what use would they have for you, the *professional* curriculum formulators?

Speaking historically, public schools did not develop because professional educators recognized a need for them. Public elementary, secondary, and collegiate schools came into being because many community people recognized the need for institutionalizing the effective transfer of socially useful information to the majority of young people and acted to satisfy this need. Thus, the professional educator came into existence as a *response* to the legitimate concerns of many communities about the need for well-structured and well-run schools. Black parents' and black students' expressions of dissatisfaction with the contemporary educational process are legitimate extensions of the historical trends which led to the development of public schools.

The ferment concerning black studies is only the first and most visible manifestation of a widespread and growing movement aimed at healing the malaise of education in this society; one need but refer to Columbia University's experience to realize that white students are also becoming increasingly restive. "Professional" educators will have to pay a heavy price for the degree to which they have been guilty of ignoring the proper concerns of their constituents. Mr. Bundy was right when he argued that black studies has opened a Pandora's box. The box is now open and America's educational system is on trial. Only time will tell how much "trouble" will ensue before the system is purged of its institutionalized pedantry and begins to deal fairly and honestly with reality. One thing is certain. Trouble in schools will continue and increase, both in the number of incidents and in their intensity.

Much has been made of the fact that a group of black students conceived, planned, and executed this symposium, with no more than financial assistance from Yale's administration. Our achievement is remarkable, among other reasons, because it proves that students can do this type of work. It would be foolish, however, for any of you to leave here thinking that you can sit back and wait for your students or parent groups to bring you an "acceptable" program for including the black experience in your curricular offerings. Yale has been extremely fortunate because, in effect, the Black Student Alliance here not only made clear that a problem existed but was able to go on to diagnose the causes of the illness and to prescribe workable improvements.

Such exertions are not the proper function of a black student or parent group. As the most intelligent, articulate, and free segment of the community, educators first have an obligation to *listen* carefully and sympathetically to complaints about their system; they must also *understand* black people's demands. After listening to and understanding local demands, you as educators have a further obligation to weigh them in terms of their broader implications, not simply to your own highly specific internal rhetoric but also in terms of their significance to the larger context in which the educational community operates.

Local people have a *right* to be listened to and heeded in decisions about what is to be taught in their schools; if you listen carefully, you will discover that there is much of value in what community people have to say. The fundamental imperative is a willingness to listen, understand, and empathize with what blacks have to say. Educational institutions in this society must respond in this way if they are to survive.

How, then, can black studies be implemented most effectively? The specific answers to this question are obviously beyond the scope of these brief remarks. In general, however, it is possible to see the trend toward black studies moving on three separate yet complementary levels. First, there must be a movement, to use the words of Professor Hare, to "darken" existing courses and curricula. Attempts *must* be made to correct the glaring inadequacies which already exist in the treatment of the black experience. At the same time a second step *must* be undertaken to design new courses and curricula that deal specifically with the black experience. Professor Obichere argued that, after so long a period of neglect, it is necessary to lean very far to one side in order to correct the balance, and I think he is right. The third step is that which Professor McWorter suggested— namely, that there should be a joint black studies institute whose mission is to design ideal black studies curricula and to train new scholars in the field, in order that research and writing efforts aimed at closing the gaping holes in our knowledge of the black experience may go forward as rapidly as possible. Taken together, these elements constitute a total black studies program; this is something which must be created.

There will obviously be a transitional period during which many false starts will be made in efforts to design black studies curricula and courses. It is also true that there simply are not enough good black and/or white instructors available to satisfy the demand for black studies personnel. Efforts must be and will be made to resolve these problems, but an uncomfortable period of escalating competition for available scholars and teachers has already begun; it can be expected to continue.

Does this mean that action for implementing black studies must be delayed until there are enough specially trained personnel to teach all the needed courses? I think not, primarily because most black students and parents will not wait that long; and they need not wait that long. Professor Redkey has already pointed out that this country has previously undertaken crash programs in education to train personnel and design curricula when the national interest was at stake. A similar situation exists today, and the country *must* do it again. In the interim, interested and dedicated teachers will have to be given relief from their other duties to enable them to gain sufficient information to offer desperately needed black studies-oriented courses *now*. Such a temporary burden is not too much to ask of those charged with preparing America's youth to resolve problems with which you have been unable to cope.

In conclusion, I would like to offer a few thoughts about the larger societal implications of the discussions we have been having these last two days. In February, Mr. Bundy issued a précis of his annual report for the Ford Foundation, in which he argued that racial problems were one of the country's two most pressing concerns; he also *assumed* that white men will succeed in ridding themselves of the cancer of racism. I tend to agree with Dr. Poussaint. I am much less optimistic about the ability of whites to rid themselves of their pathetic dependence on degrading blacks as a means of establishing their own identities and sense of self-worth.

Something has got to be done, *very soon,* to begin to resolve the social and intellectual problems that have grown out of the inherent racist assumptions—sometimes subtle and sometimes explicit—pervading our national consciousness and our system of education. If "responsible" professional educators fail to react swiftly and positively by recognizing and acting upon the necessity for honest re-evaluation, then there is little hope that the mass of Americans will ever recognize that necessity—and pessimism about America's future becomes a just and rational response to the unpleasant realities and potentialities of the present racial crisis.

REFLECTIONS

David Brion Davis

This has been a truly remarkable conference and an invaluable experience for the participating whites. Without doubt many of the whites arrived with unsettled minds concerning the questions posed by President Brewster: "Is race a proper organizing concept for a curriculum? Is the study of the black experience intellectually valid?" Yet the very fact that such questions could still be asked and debated is a cause of deep resentment among black students. The symposium, which was organized with great efficiency by the Yale Black Student Alliance, was not a forum for abstract debate on educational values. A group of some two hundred is too large for productive questioning and discussion; in effect, the blacks had arranged for a time and place to speak their minds to a national group of administrators and scholars. The audience was predominantly white, especially on the second day. In order to avoid the weak strategic position of appealing to a white majority, several of the black speakers used the opening gambit of looking over the assembly with some disgust and remarking that they had come on the assumption they would be speaking mainly to black brothers. There were expressions of defiance and mild insult—i.e. "I thought this would be an Afro-American gathering, but I see many here who are just Americans, or the kind of Afro-Americans who might have come from South Africa."

Yet despite these opening sallies, the addresses had all obviously been prepared for whites. The manner of most of the speakers was beautifully calculated to demonstrate pride and self-confidence and to let the distinguished gathering of university administrators and scholars know that the blacks were not begging or even trying to appeal to the moral sense or good nature of the white community. From the start, the symposium was designed to let the whites know that the blacks understood why they were there and that it was up to the whites to listen and try to understand. Moreover, the haughty attitude of some of the blacks easily dissolved into good-humored repartee; indeed, on several occasions the blacks showed themselves capable of making jibes at the more comic aspects of black separatism. Ron Karenga proved himself a master of the barbed joke, and no doubt astonished many whites when, after making fun of academic sociology, he noted the great number of Negroes who majored in the field and concluded that therefore it must be the easiest subject.

It would be a great mistake, however, to underestimate the seriousness and unity of the blacks. Even before they arrived, the white participants had clearly been shaken and were prepared to reconsider many of their basic values and premises regarding education and the place of the university in society. Of the whites who spoke from the floor, only one represented the noncomprehending generation and tried to explain and defend the old liberal, integrationist faith. But he seemed almost pathetic when he tried to persuade the blacks that the Jews had suffered far more in Europe than the Negroes in America, and that racial differences are of minor importance compared with the common experience of persecution and acculturation. Karenga had the quickness of mind to make him appear naive and totally insensitive to the realities of modern America. The comments from younger white participants showed the pervasive realization that the liberal premises of the social scientists of the 1940s and 50s have failed to prepare us for the present crisis, that the conventional wisdom of our academies is on the point of bankruptcy.

Despite the exaggerated rhetoric of the blacks, they have convinced many whites of the validity of their basic contention— namely, that the university, which has thought of itself as enlightened and objective, has in reality been a racist institution. We have assumed that we could admit increasing numbers of Negro students without modifying our traditional educational standards and our ideal of the educated man; we expected Negroes to assimilate our culture and to integrate on our terms. But as Professor Nathan Hare pointed out with respect to San Francisco State College, more blacks will be admitted in the freshman class next fall, still more the following year, and this will soon provide an impressive pool of manpower which will inevitably alter the character of the university. Even now, the black university students are mobilizing and propagandizing the black youth in the neighboring high schools and junior high schools. Once universities have committed themselves to admit more than a token number of blacks, they cannot evade the consequences. Black professors like Hare talk of a five-year and ten-year plan and envision the university as a key agent for forging racial solidarity and revitalizing the black community.

It was extremely fortunate that the most inspiring and informative lecture of the symposium was delivered by a white professor of art history who displayed an astonishing knowledge of West African culture. Professor Thompson's main message was to convey some sense of the rich and magnificent culture of the Yorubas and to suggest how it had been transplanted and adapted in various parts of the New World. Professor Thompson made it clear that one cannot get the study of African art off the ground without a knowledge of African music and dance. His film strips of ceremonial dances, supplemented by his own playing of musical instruments, succeeded in illustrating the themes of "coolness," balance, and control.

Above all, Professor Thompson convinced the audience that most of our images of "savage" Africa are based on ignorance. He pointed to the subtle intellectual formulations and resolutions in African architecture, sculpture, music, and calligraphy. Particularly fascinating were examples of Yoruba motifs in Cuba, Georgia, Brazil, and especially Surinam. The total effect of his talk was to reinforce the sense of complex difference in African and Afro-American cultures and to prove that many of our prevalent assumptions—such as the conviction that African artistic styles were static and underwent no formal development, and that a nonliterate society is incapable of a calligraphy expressing complex ideas—are based on prejudice. Professor Thompson's lecture represented Afro-American studies at their best and established the vital point that a sympathetic understanding can be achieved without sacrificing the highest standards of scholarship.

Professor Robert Thompson's ability to speak Yoruba, to decipher and explicate African calligraphy, to beat out intricate rhythms on a drum, and to analyze the symbolic meanings of dance steps underscored an essential point which even the militant blacks conceded: one does not have to be black in order to teach the black experience. One might conclude from the symposium that physical color is irrelevant to Afro-American studies, since the black nationalists accuse many American Negroes of being white in mind and attitude, and since Professor Thompson insisted that a white scholar must negritize himself to some extent if he is to study or teach the black experience. Even Professor Hare suggested that black nationalism need not imply physical separation of the races; in response to a question from a young black student about migration to another country, he said in all seriousness that some of his best friends were whites. While all of the blacks demonstrated their antipathy to covert white paternalism, their insistence on protecting the integrity of blackness seemed more connected with *attitude* than with color of skin.

Clearly the liberal academician is caught in the middle between militant blacks and a fearful white majority, between his commitment to truth and scholarship and an awakening feeling of social responsibility. While the reputable scholar strives for objectivity, he knows that knowledge represents power and often serves an ideological function. It would appear that our greatest danger is not from a black upsurge but from a potential tidal wave of white reaction which could extinguish all the values we live by. We cannot change the direction which the blacks have taken, even if they are on a collision course, but we might conceivably have some effect on the white community. One cannot deny either the importance or validity of black separatism, which has revealed our own unconscious paternalism and smug ethnocentrism and which is giving blacks a long-needed self-confidence and sense of manhood. Nor can we warn the blacks of the danger of backlash, since this is the very brickbat that has always been used to defeat their aspirations. Threats of what the "bad whites" will do will bring only renewed defiance and dedications to self-sacrifice.

Our most immediate educational challenge is to convey a sense of understanding among the white community. But we are also faced with the specific demands of the black nationalists. And here we face a great dilemma. One can appreciate the origin and character of black needs and desires. Yet the white scholar remains convinced that truth and objectivity are not white and are something more than a cultural preference. Indeed, the ability of self-transcendence and detachment, which is nourished by the university, is precisely what enables us to listen sympathetically to the blacks at this conference. If the university were as racist and as culturally biased as has been said, we would be teaching Carleton Putnam's theories of Negro inferiority. Even the most militant blacks sometimes acknowledge the humanizing function of the university, that is, its universality; otherwise, they would not be here addressing university scholars and administrators, nor would they choose the university as the most promising instrument for social change. To charge that universities are not living up to their ideals is not to say that they have no ideals.

It is true, of course, that blacks have long been excluded from our institutions of higher education. It is also true that our curriculum, administrative framework, and educational goals are reflections of white middle-class society, and as such, strike many blacks as foreign and hostile. It is understandable that for many blacks who are struggling for their own souls and for their own survival, the ideal of objective truth appears as an encumbrance or luxury they cannot afford. Too often, appeals to truth and objectivity have been used to undermine legitimate aspirations. We must remember that Parson Weems, George Bancroft, and other writers created an American mythology and nationalistic history to validate our own independence and sense of cultural mission. Yet we must insist on maintaining the distinction between political ideology and education. There is a serious danger of allowing our educational machinery to become an instrument for propaganda. On this issue we must hold firm and not retreat behind procedural and administrative evasions. It will be all too easy for whites who are burdened by fear and guilt to shrink from defending their essential beliefs and values and to offer lame excuses about the proper procedures for setting up courses or hiring professors. One must be absolutely clear about distinguishing free intellectual inquiry from a party line, no matter how justified the party line may be.

There is an added danger presented by the blacks' demand for practicality and utility. American universities have fought a long and arduous struggle to establish the worth of free inquiry in the face of native American practicalism and vocationalism. It would be a catastrophe if research and teaching in the social sciences were to become enslaved to the standard of contemporary "relevance." Obviously there is much about the university that is not sacrosanct. There is considerable room for experiment and innovation, especially in breaking with the traditional role as the upholder of the status quo. Yet it is essential that we retain a certain quality of ivory-towerism, in the sense that the university provides a place where man may transcend the immediate and the present. A certain degree of detachment is necessary for genuinely critical thought as well as for the adventure of intellectual discovery.

The university is a custodian as well as an innovator. Indeed, the two roles are mutually interdependent. These values will be increasingly difficult to maintain. Yet it will be a disaster if we lose our vantage point apart from the pressures of the moment—the very vantage point which has allowed us partially to rise above our heritage of racism. There will be inevitable friction between blacks who are just beginning to explore their own culture and history and the white scholars who have long worked in the same areas. Such tension can be creative. No doubt black scholars will open new questions for investigation and will present familiar materials from a new perspective. It is an untenable position, however, that only blacks can study or understand the black experience. Professor Kilson is surely right when he insists that oppression conveys no special intellectual or moral virtues. Ultimately we must convince black scholars that the whites do not form a monolithic culture, that "racism" is not all of a piece—any more than the blacks all occupy the same position.

Our great challenge is to recognize our past failings and our unconscious or institutional racism while feeling free to defend our basic beliefs and to criticize irresponsible argument. In practical terms, this means keeping a separation between any black studies program on the campus and the "black movement," except as the movement may be a subject for study or as such study may produce leaders of the movement. The university must resist, however, being appropriated as a training camp for black cadre.

The great question in one's mind at the symposium was where the white's concern and fear would lead. The papers and discussions revealed conflicts of the most serious and fundamental nature. One could not say whether the majority of white participants truly understood the black demands, or whether the white educators were prepared to stand firm in defending the values which lie at the core of free inquiry. And if the white educators are able to meet the mounting pressures from the black community without resorting to new forms of paternalism and condescension, can they convey any understanding of the issues at stake to the white community at large?

Since I was unable to stay through the end of the symposium, I was most gratified to be able to read transcripts of the portions I missed. The following reflections, then, round out my thoughts on the conference.

In spite of McGeorge Bundy's opening statement, I suspect that Yale has not yet decided the matters that had previously been discussed. The issues are far too momentous to be resolved by any administrative decision, however laudable the decision may have been. I would also qualify the point about the political character of Mr. Karenga's interests. As Alvin Poussaint's trenchant paper makes clear, we are dealing with conflicts that go far deeper than politics, at least in any traditional sense of the word. No doubt Mr. Bundy is right when he insists on the difference between a political view of events and a historical view of the same events. Yet the distinction can never be as clear as he intimates, especially if racist feelings and intuitions are as deep-rooted as Dr. Poussaint suggests. At the very least, the Yale symposium should have conveyed a sense of the profound psychological complexity of racism. Given Dr. Poussaint's remarks on unconscious racism, on the definition of basic standards in accordance with the conviction "White is right," and on the need for inner emancipation and a legitimizing of blackness, how are we to keep the conventional curriculum immaculate from "ideological purposes"? How are we to define the teacher's obligations as a member of the "academic community"?

I agree with Sidney Mintz—and Mr. Bundy made the same point—that the university is not only an "appanage of the power structure" but a place where truth can be sought. The really central question is how to free the values and procedures of free inquiry from the intolerable syndrome of blacks adjusting to white standards, white sanctions, and white rewards. White scholars are convinced that universities, for all their overt and implicit racism, still embody priceless and hard-won values of universal worth. Black students may agree in principle, but their perception is different; they are understandably suspicious of trite claims to universality which have demonstrably been used to justify slavery, enforced segregation, exploitation, and effacement of non-white, non-Western identities. The fundamental question is how these two quite valid and sincere perceptions can be brought into a working arrangement.

Edwin Redkey's excellent paper on black history gives one encouragement. Brief as it is, the statement points to possible ways of combining a kind of ideological relevance with the rigorous standards and procedures esteemed by the academic community. Surely no sensible person would defend the history now being taught in secondary schools as either nonideological or as "respectable" by current scholarly standards. It lacks even the saving grace of being interesting. A major national program to introduce black history in the high school curriculum would not only redress the effects of systematic and destructive omission, but might help reform the general teaching of the social sciences. I am particularly impressed by Mr. Redkey's points about social history, cultural pluralism, and the educational responsibility of lifting "race education" above the street-corner level. There is one danger, however, that needs to be emphasized. Some way must be found to keep black studies programs from being exploited by commercial interests. This sad process has already begun, as textbook publishers scramble to get on what appears to be a very profitable bandwagon. Both the quality and genuineness of black history will suffer unless some means is found to keep the subject from becoming a commercial fad.

Armstead Robinson's concluding remarks bring me back to the elemental questions. Obviously Mr. Robinson is correct when he warns that the surest way to stimulate more "disturbances" on cam-

pus is to promise black students a taste of real education and then
renege later on when the heat is off. Black studies programs cannot
be thought of as a gift. But neither can they be thought of as prizes
captured by the threat of violence. Indeed, I see little hope of creating a curriculum which will be relevant and truly rewarding for
both blacks and whites so long as the shaping of policy is conceived
fundamentally as a power confrontation between two antagonistic
and polarized groups. This is not to say that blacks and whites can
simply sit down as color-blind individuals and harmoniously resolve
issues over a table. We are both heirs of an accumulated tradition of
oppression, exclusion, and submission. We are both victims of an
extremely unhappy history, which no good will can undo. Yet this
means we are caught up, like it or not, in a common predicament. I
stress the word "common," since it is high time whites learned that
their definition of the predicament is not the only one and cannot
be imposed on blacks. But conversely, one must insist that there are
legitimate interests at stake on both sides.

Mr. Robinson, summing up the view of many of the speakers,
makes it clear that white educators must become aware of the institutional racism which they have long accepted as part of their un-
questioned environment. I would add that black students should be
careful not to confuse white-dominated and white-oriented curricula
with the protections accorded free expression and free inquiry both
in the classroom and outside. Surely it is not racism to say, as Mr.
Bundy has done, that universities should "give offense" to every
element in society, including itself. No matter how flexible or revo-
lutionizing the university may become—and there is vast room here
for improvement—it must continue to defend the traditional academic freedoms, including the rights of tenure, or cease to be a
university. And this means, to put it bluntly, that the university
must be prepared to stand firm against all forms of force or harass-
ment that threaten academic freedoms.

The most dangerous aspects of the present situation arise from the
common fact that recent confrontations have not been simply between blacks and whites but between outsiders and insiders, between
students in transit and the more permanent academic community.
Hopefully we will be able to see the racial elements more clearly and

be able to deal with them more effectively as significant numbers of blacks become a permanent part of university faculties and administrations. Even if black deans and black professors consider themselves a separate community in many respects, they will presumably share the nonracial, situational concerns of deans and professors. But that day is still far in the future, and in the meantime we have a formidable job of careful listening and imaginative understanding.

APPENDIX: AFRO-AMERICAN STUDIES MAJOR AT YALE

Reactions to the symposium, both at Yale and elsewhere, were very enthusiastic. One professor called it one of the most exciting experiences in his twenty years at Yale. Others remarked that they entered the symposium with serious doubts about the worth of Afro-American studies as an academic discipline and left completely convinced not only of its worth but also of the urgent necessity of its implementation.

The momentum generated by the symposium was maintained. Working over the summer, student members of the joint student-faculty study group that planned the symposium completed preliminary drafts of a proposal to establish an interdisciplinary program in Afro-American studies in Yale College. On December 12, 1968, these efforts resulted in unanimous approval by the Yale College faculty of the first degree-granting Afro-American studies program at a major university in the United States.

The final draft of that program is included here as an aftermath to the symposium. In large measure, swift passage of this program was a direct result of the widespread enthusiasm for and acceptance of the concept of Afro-American studies that the symposium produced. This document was written in complete awareness of the enormous implications of its pioneering attempt to establish an intellectually defensible and educationally desirable program of studies of the black experience. It is offered as one model of how to establish an Afro-American studies program that is both relevant and valid and that allows students the maximum latitude to explore the great scope of the story of Afro-Americans while at the same time avoiding the pitfalls of institutionalized intellectual dilettantism.

A Proposal for a Major in Afro-American Studies, submitted by the African-American Study Group

We propose that Yale College provide an interdisciplinary major in Afro-American Studies in which a student will have an opportunity to study, in a systematic way, the experiences, conditions and origins of people of African ancestry in the United States, called here Afro-Americans. The major will focus, then, on a large and important cultural group in the United States comprised of people who, despite great diversity, share a history and a culture different in a number of important respects from the rest of the population.

Although the major will focus on Afro-Americans, it will provide the student with an opportunity to deepen his understanding of these people and their experiences by studying their earlier history in Africa and their transition to the New World as slaves; and by examining the relevant experiences outside the United States of other groups of African origin, particularly elsewhere in the Americas, as in the Caribbean or in Brazil.

The study of Africa per se is outside the purview of this program. Nonetheless, in special cases a student who wishes to concentrate his attention primarily on Africa will be allowed such a concentration within his major, after consultation with members of the Council on African Studies.

The major can be inaugurated, we believe, by September, 1969.

The experience of Afro-Americans and the relevant historical and comparative experiences of black peoples elsewhere furnish an important and relevant body of experience to be investigated by scholars and understood by interested students. This body of experience is of such great variety that no existing arrangement for undergraduate concentration, whether in a department, an area studies program, or a divisional major, can adequately comprehend it. Of course no major could acquaint a student with every important aspect of the experiences of black people. The Afro-American major we propose does not claim to do so. It is intended instead as a framework within which a student can study some important aspects of that experience and acquire competence in the findings and methods of a relevant discipline.

To achieve this goal, the Major in Afro-American Studies will take advantage of those characteristics of Afro-American experience that make it uniquely valuable for serious academic study and teaching: its essentially interdisciplinary and often international nature. The major is intended to acquaint its student with:

1. The diversity of peoples of African ancestry and their living conditions in the perspective of time.
2. The diversity as well as the unity of the African-American cultural experience, and the similarities and differences among the cultures of people of African origin in the Americas and Africa.
3. The various modes of artistic expression in the literature, art, and music characteristic of black cultures.
4. The philosophies and values of these cultures, with major emphasis on continuity and change among the geographic areas.
5. The interrelationships among these factors.

We propose to do this by establishing a program of interdisciplinary and intercontinental studies using courses and personnel from the following departments and special studies programs: Anthropology, Economics, English, History, History of Art, History of Music, Political Science, Psychology and Sociology in addition to African Studies, Latin American Studies, and Urban Studies.

The Major in Afro-American Studies would be organized as follows: A Committee, drawn from the faculty of Yale College and representing the various departments and special studies programs, would be appointed and charged with administration of the program. The Committee would be responsible for:

1. Direction of the program to conform to the academic standards of Yale College.
2. Design of the requirements for the Major and recommendations for degrees.
3. Selection of courses relevant to the major.
4. Selection and advice of students.
5. Conduct of the Seminars and Colloquium.
6. Liaison with the departments which contribute courses and students to the program.
7. Identification of areas of study not covered by existing courses.

Personnel recruited to teach courses for the Afro-American Studies major should have appointments in one of the formal disciplines contributing to the major.

The Major would be organized as follows:

A. Each student would concentrate in one of the disciplines relevant to Afro-American Studies (e.g. History).

    1. The definition and extent of concentration would be determined jointly by the divisional faculty committee and the departments concerned.

    2. Concentration would assure competence in the basic methods and content of the discipline.

B. In the Junior year each student would participate in a Seminar designed to broaden his perspectives by acquainting him with the relevant problems, methods and bibliography of Afro-American Studies.

C. In conjunction with a Colloquium, each student would prepare a major paper during his senior year. This paper would be written under the guidance of a faculty member.

D. In addition to the Seminar and Colloquium, each student would select courses from a list prepared by the faculty committee. Some of these courses may also meet the requirement for departmental concentration, but at least six semester courses would have to be selected from disciplines other than the student's department of concentration.

E. A portion of each student's work would normally involve geographical areas other than the area of his main concentration.

F. A student's program would also be expected normally to reflect a primary emphasis either on the social sciences or on the humanities.

Students in the program would be selected by the Faculty Committee. Selection would depend on the presentation of a satisfactory prospectus for study in the junior and senior years. Applicants would prepare these plans in consultation with a member of the faculty committee. Selection would also depend on satisfactory completion of any preliminary courses the faculty committee might prescribe.

The following is a list of relevant courses currently offered in Yale College:

Anthropology—Anthro. 20 Man and Culture; Anthro. 25b Prehistory—the Non-Western World; Anthro. 27 Human Evolution; Anthro. 34 Peoples and Cultures of Africa; Anthro. 41a The Arts of Africa.

Economics—Econ. 45a Urban Economics; Econ. 74b Economics of Underdeveloped Areas.

History—Hist. 22 The American Nation; Hist. 30 Colonial History; Hist. 31b Problems in Afro-American History; Hist. 34 Latin American History; Hist. 35 Politics and Culture in the Twentieth Century; Hist. 36b The Ante-Bellum South; Hist. 37 The West in the Development of the U.S.; Hist. 65b Latin American Political Cultures; Hist. 70 African History; Hist. 73 The British Empire and Commonwealth; Hist. 91 Seminars.

History of Art—Hist. of Art 73b Arts of Africa.

History of Music—Hist. of Music 13a African Music; Hist. of Music 14b Afro-American Music.

Political Science—Pol. Sci. 47b Government, Politics, and the Urban Environment; Pol. Sci. 59a Violence and Politics; Pol. Sci. 59b Revolutions and Revolutionary Thought; Pol. Sci. 68 Government and Politics in Latin America; Pol. Sci. 69b Government and Politics in Africa; Pol. Sci. 89b Urban Government.

Psychology—Psych. 58a Psychology in Community Settings; Psych. 63a The Psychology of Prejudice; Psych. 75a Psychology of Conflict; Psych. 68b Clinical Psychology in the Community; Psych. 36a Psych. of Communications; Psych. 92 Individual Research.

Sociology—Soc. 11a American Society and Culture; Soc. 16b American Racial and Ethnic Groups; Soc. 23 Problems of Race in the Modern World; Soc. 37b Education and Society; Soc. 51a American Communities; Soc. 59a Social Change; Soc. 61a

Social Structure in Latin American Countries; Soc. 54a Political Sociology; Soc. 35b Afro-American Literature.

American Studies—Am. Stu. 31 History of Religion in American Life and Thought; Am. Stu. 59 Twentieth Century American Literature; Am. Stu. 60a Black Literature; Am. Stu. 92-3 Negro History; Am. Stu. 92-5 Civil War and Reconstruction.

In addition to these undergraduate courses, there are a number of courses directly related to Afro-American Studies currently offered in the Graduate School. The development of the Urban Studies Program will also be of particular importance to Afro-American Studies because it promises to provide an additional number of useful courses. The number and variety of courses already offered at Yale indicates strongly that a sufficient basis exists for initiating an intellectually rigorous and academically challenging interdisciplinary major in Afro-American Studies.

There are gaps. For example, there are at present no courses specifically devoted to the economics of the impact of slaves, the politics of poverty, the history of slavery on a comparative basis, African literature, or the sociology of the ghetto. To develop a large number of additional courses in Yale College is probably impractical, but covering certain areas now inadequately provided for would enrich the total program of the College significantly. Moreover, one means of meeting the need for particular courses would be the judicious use of tutorials and in special courses. This would greatly expand the areas of interest that could be dealt with in the major, and would allow greater flexibility and freedom to students in setting up programs of study tailored to their needs. Several hypothetical programs for students concentration in different disciplines are attached.

To be sure, much of the necessary research and writing about the Black Experience remains to be done. However, enough knowledge already exists to provide a good beginning. Although gaps in our knowledge already exist, it can be expected that the attempt to close these gaps—which are critical deficits in our contemporary knowledge and understanding—will now go forward in many universities. Consequently, it seems wholly reasonable to think that from now on each year will see a rapid increase in the amount of worthwhile scholarship available to students.

> The African-American Study Group:
> Craig Foster, '69
> Ray Nunn, '69
> Donald H. Ogilvie,* '68
> Armstead L. Robinson, '68
> Howard Lamar†
> Robert A. Dahl
> William Kessen
> Edwin S. Redkey*
> Charles H. Taylor, Jr.

*Until September, 1968.
†From September, 1968.

Work on the Afro-American studies program continued at an accelerated pace after it was approved. Dr. Sidney Mintz, Professor of Anthropology and a life-long specialist in studies of Afro-American peoples in the Caribbean, agreed to serve as Chairman of the faculty Committee on Afro-American Studies described in the proposal. Subsequently, Dr. Roy-Simon Bryce-Laporte was appointed Director of the Afro-American Studies Program.

Far from being over, the fight for Afro-American studies has just begun. This proposal is not an end but only the beginning. Much more work will have to be done before the black experience assumes its rightful place as an absolutely essential part of the story of mankind. It is toward the promotion of that end that this volume is dedicated.

A. L. R.